BEHOLD THE SPIRIT

ALAN WATTS

BEHOLD
THE SPIRIT

A STUDY IN THE NECESSITY
OF MYSTICAL RELIGION

VINTAGE BOOKS
A Division of Random House, New York

123456789C
Vintage Books Edition, March 1972

TO MY FATHER AND MOTHER

CONTENTS

ACKNOWLEDGEMENTS

I am greatly indebted to the following publishing houses for their kind permission to make some substantial quotations from certain authors: to Messrs. Charles Scribner's Sons, of New York, and Geoffrey Bles, of London, publishers of the works of Nicolas Berdyaev; to Messrs. Sheed and Ward, publishers of Mr. E. I. Watkin's *Catholic Art and Culture;* and to Messrs. Harper and Brothers, publishers of Mr. Raymond Blakney's *Meister Eckhart.*

PREFACE
TO THE NEW EDITION

This book was written twenty-five years ago, during the experiment of trying to immerse myself in Christianity —to the extent of being a priest of the Anglican Communion, Episcopal Chaplain at Northwestern University, and an examining chaplain for candidates for holy orders in the Diocese of Chicago. Prior to this experiment, indeed since the age of fifteen, my outlook had been Buddhist rather than Christian even though I had been schooled in the heart of the Church of England and had learned a version of Christianity which was not that of this book. In adolescence I had rejected it, but as time went on the study of comparative religion and Christian mysticism suggested a way in which I might operate through the forms and in the terms of the official religion of Western culture. I did not want to be an eccentric outsider, and felt that Catholic Christianity might be taught and practised as a form of that perennial philosophy which is the gold within the sectarian dross of every great religion.

I still believe that this experiment had validity, and I have consented to the republication of *Behold the Spirit* with the thought that it may prove useful to the many Catholic and Protestant theologians who are now revolutionary enough to understand it. For it speaks to their condition in their own language—more so, perhaps, than my later theological essays, *The Supreme Identity* (1950), *Myth and Ritual in Christianity* (1953), and *Beyond Theology* (1964), which last represents my present way of thinking within this context.

Even twenty-five years ago this experiment had some success. I did not pursue it for the purely personal reason that my bohemian style of life did not fit well with the clerical stereotype, and because even then I was ill at ease with the commitment to spiritual imperialism which most Christians feel to be the *sine qua non* of being Christian, as if one could not be a true Christian without being a militant missionary. But then, and more than ever today, there were both clergy and laity who hungered for a mystical approach to Christianity, concerned with the non-verbal spiritual experience of the divine rather than mere doctrine and precept. Yet now, as then, the Church is still overwhelmingly didactic and verbose, both as it faces God and as it faces the world. Its liturgies consist almost entirely of telling God what to do and the people how to behave. By rationalizing the Mass and celebrating it in the vernacular instead of Latin, even the Roman Church has made the liturgy an occasion for filling one's head with thoughts, aspirations, considerations and resolutions, so that it is almost impossible to use the Mass as a support for pure contemplation, free from discursive chatter in the skull.

Today, the idea of the mystical finds greater acceptance, both within and outside the Church, than in 1946. A vast and well-informed literature on the subject has made it clear that "mysticism" is not a collective term for such spookeries as levitation, astrology, telekinesis, and projection of the astral body. Theologians can no longer dismiss or distort the mystical teachings of either East or West without revealing plain lack of scholarship. Scientists—now familiar with field theory, ecological dynamics and the transactional nature of perception—can no longer see man as the independent observer of an alien and rigidly mechanical world of separate objects. The clearly mystical sensation of self-and-universe, or organism-and-environment, as a unified field or process seems to fit the facts. The sensation of man as an island-ego in a hostile, stupid or indifferent universe seems more of a dangerous hallucination.

At the same time it is less and less plausible to conceive God in the thought-graven image of a transcendental monarch modelled on the Pharaohs and Cyruses. But the dissolution of this idol need not leave us with no other alternative than the insipid humanism suggested by "death of God" and "religionless Christianity" theologians. The God of mystical experience may not be the ethically obstreperous and precisely defined autocrat beloved of religious authoritarians; but as an experience, not concept, as vividly real as indefinable, this God does not violate the intellectual conscience, the aesthetic imagination, or the religious intuition. A Christianity which is not basically mystical must become either a political ideology or a mindless fundamentalism. This is, indeed, already happening, and it is curious to note that, for lack of the mystical element, both trends fall back on the Bible as their basic inspiration—and it has always struck me that Biblical idolatry is one of the most depressing and sterile fixations of the religious mind.

We now know beyond doubt that large and widely scattered numbers of otherwise sane and sober people have had experiences of "cosmic consciousness" in which the sense of life becomes perfectly clear. The antagonisms of good and evil, life and death, being and nothing, self and other are felt as the poles or undulations of a single, eternal and harmonious energy—exuding a sense of joy and love. The feeling may be purely subjective and without reference to "external reality" (as if "external" could be independent of "internal"), but it comes upon us with the same startling independence of wishing and willing as a flash of lightning. Debates as to whether this vision is or is not "true" seem as pointless as asking whether my sensation of green is just the same as yours. But the vision is not pointless because, when seen, it is obviously the whole point of life and, often enough, it transforms one's way of living.

In our inevitably clumsy attempts to describe this vision it often seems necessary to say that everything is God, that God alone is real, that a crumb is the whole universe, or that you and God are one. At the same time, the experience is somehow a grace: it is *given* and cannot be evoked by effort of will. In *Behold the Spirit* I was trying to show that the gift of the Incarnation, of God becoming man (virgin-born, without human effort), implied and fulfilled itself in this experience, and in this sense I quoted the saying of St. Athanasius that "God became man that man might become God." But I was pussyfooting, as is always the way with theologians when they try to discuss the Christology of ordinary human beings as distinct from the Christology of Jesus. For the Church's habitual assumption, having the force of dogma, is that Jesus of Nazareth was and is the only son of woman who was at the same time God. This Godhood is extended to other people by "participation in the human nature of Jesus," explained by the tortuous Greek notion that human nature is a "real universal" or "substance" in which we all share. When the *person* of God the Son assumed this nature, he assumed all our natures and became mankind, leaving, however, the person (or ego) of each man distinct and separate from his own divine person. In other words, God the Son was the person of the particular man Jesus. He assumed the nature, but not the person, of such particular men as Peter, Paul, John and the rest of us.

Looking back on this pussyfooting I find it somewhat less than a gospel—a tremendous proclamation of good news. I now find it easier to assume that Jesus was a man like ourselves who had a spontaneous (*i.e.*, virgin-born) and overwhelming experience of cosmic consciousness in which it became completely clear to him that "I and the Father are one" and that "before Abraham was, I am." But it was as tactless to say this in terms of Jewish theology as it still remains to say it in terms of Christian. Jesus had to hedge by identifying himself as the Son of Man, the Suffering Servant—or spiritual messiah—of Isaiah II. It would have been outrageous and criminal blasphemy to come right out and say, "I am God"— assuming the throne of the Cyrus of the universe. But, if we are to believe the Gospel of St. John, conviction got the better of tact—for in all those "I am" passages he came out with the simple truth of his experience and was crucified for blasphemy.

The Gospel was that "in my Father's house are many mansions," that his disciples would all be one even as he and the Father were one, and thus perform even greater works than he. It is not easy for the pious Christian to realize that Jesus was not an expert on the history of religion, and had probably never met anyone whose mystical vision was as deep as his own. The only religious language available to him was that of the legal and prophetic Hebrew scriptures which, with their image of God as the King-Father, do not easily lend themselves to a mystical interpretation. Jewish mystics—the Kabbalists and the Hasidim—have always had to read the scriptures as complex allegories in order to go beyond their literal sense. Therefore Jesus had difficulty in saying what he felt, not only because it was officially blasphemous, but also because it made no sense to say that he was consciously and personally ruling and causing every detail of the universe, and attending to all prayers from everywhere. Thus on the one hand he could say, "I am the way, the truth, and the life," and on the other, "Why do you call me good? There is none good but God." But such problems do not arise for those whose image or non-image of God is not monarchical.

The Gospel must therefore be the communication of Jesus' own experience of Godhood. Otherwise Christians put themselves in the absurd situation of reproaching themselves for not following the example of one who had the unique advantage of being God or, at the very least, "the Boss's son." It is thus that the "saving truth" of the Gospel appears, not as Jesus' experience of Godhood, but as his punishment for proclaiming it, and that sanctity in the following of Christ is chiefly measured by the degree of guiltiness felt in failing to come up to his example. Christians dare not believe that, as St. John says, they have been given power "to become the sons of God," remembering that the expression "sons of" means "of the nature of." The dubious uniqueness of the monarchical religions (Judaism, Christianity and Islam) is that they overstress the difference between Creator and creature and, by making virtues of feeling guilty and frightened, inculcate a very special terror of death—which Jesus saw as a source of life. Is it really such a profound theological paradox to be trying at once to "be not anxious" and to "work out your salvation with fear and trembling"? To substitute the fear of God for the fear of the world is to exchange a finite terror for one that is infinite—for the terror of everlasting damnation. As an inheritor of the monarchical tradition, Jesus recognized this terror, for would not the Court of Heaven also have dungeons? But he saw the possibility of overcoming it in his and our realization of divine sonship—that is, in mystical experience. Lacking such experience, religion is only a futile straining to follow a way of life for which one has neither the power nor the grace, and there is no power in a merely theoretical grace which one has allegedly been given but does not feel.

From this point of view it would seem that the Church has rendered the Gospel ineffective by setting Jesus on a pedestal of excessive reverence and making him so unique that he is virtually isolated from the human condition. By setting itself apart from the world-wide traditions of mystical religion Christianity appears, not as unique, but as an anomalous oddity with imperious claims. Thus the religion *of* Jesus became the religion *about* Jesus, lost its essence, and appeared more and more to be ridiculously aggressive as the context of world religion came into view. How can there be "one flock, one fold, and one Shepherd" unless it is recognized that there are *already* "other sheep who are not of this fold"?

As might have been expected, *Behold the Spirit* was criticized for its creeping pantheism—a point of view which, in its many forms, is so repugnant to religious monarchists that simply to be named a pantheist is enough to have one's case excluded from an intelligent hearing. I am no longer concerned to defend myself against the charge of pantheism because, from my present point of view, all doctrines of God—including atheism—are ultimately false and idolatrous, because doctrines are forms of words which can never be more than pointers to mystical vision, and not by any means the best pointers. At most I feel that some sort of pantheism is the least inconsistent with that vision, and by pantheism (or panentheism) I mean the conception of God as the total energy-field of the universe, including both its positive and negative aspects, and in which every discernible part or process is a sort of microcosm or hologram. That is to say, the whole is expressed in or implied by every part, as is the brain in each one of its cells. This view strikes me as cleaner and simpler than monotheism.

Theoretically, pantheism may blur or confuse the distinction between good and evil, but where is the evidence to show that monotheists are better behaved than pantheists—and by whose standards? Moral principles and sanctions are weakened when absolutized, for much the same reasons that respect for law is diminished by judicial torture and frantic punishment for crime. Metaphysically and intellectually, solutions to the problem of evil require far more tortuous conceptualization for monotheists than for pantheists. Furthermore, the notion that any identity of Creator and creature makes a fundamental "I-Thou" relationship of love between the two impossible is untenable for any believer in the Holy Trinity. How, then, could there be mutual love between God the Father and God the Son, since both, though different, are yet one God? And the objection that the pantheist conception of God is too vague and impersonal to inspire devotion or grace could be to the point if it were no more than a conception, but is groundless if held against the vision which the concept merely represents. Inspiring and worshipful as the character of Jesus may be, it was not what inspired Jesus himself, for he was what he was because he knew of himself that "I and the Father are one," and not—obviously—because he had accepted Jesus as his Saviour. But, from the beginning, institutional Christianity has hardly contemplated the possibility that the consciousness of Jesus might be the consciousness of the Christian, that the whole point of the Gospel is that everyone may experience union with God in the same way and to the same degree as Jesus himself. On the contrary, one who says, with Eckhart, that "the eye with which I see God is the same eye with which God sees me" is condemned as a heretic.

Small wonder, for the immediate following of Jesus was Jewish and it was as difficult for them as for him to reconcile mystical experience with Biblical monotheism. Instead of following him they worshipped him, for they still felt that—for anyone except Jesus—it would be pride, presumption, and insubordination for a mere creature to be one with the Creator. For monotheism can allow only the devotional (bhakti) style of mysticism, where Creator and creature find union in intense mutual love, never in basic identity. In the context of monarchical monotheism to say, "I am God," doesn't seem to carry the implication, "And so are you," because it has the same ring as saying, "I'm the boss around here." Within this context the mystic is always in danger of that spiritual megalomania which Jung called "psychic inflation" in which one takes one's ego for God instead of God for one's ego—and Christianity has manoeuvred Jesus into just that position. It is thus that the individual Christian frustrates himself perpetually, always finding himself guilty for not living up to the example of one who had the unique advantage of being God incarnate, and who was by definition incapable of being guilty.

The question then arises: Can Christianity abandon the monarchical image of God and still be Christianity? Why should this be of concern? For which is more important—to be a Christian or to be at one with God? Must religion be Christian, Islamic or Hindu, or could it simply be religion? Certainly there must be the same variety of style in religion as there is in culture, but the concern to preserve, validate and propagate Christianity as such is a disastrous confusion of religious style with religion. Indeed, this sectarian fanaticism (shared alike by Judaism and Islam) is all of a piece with the monarchical image and its necessary imperialism. Even such scholarly theologians as Maritain and Zaehner keep up this pitiful game of spiritual one-upmanship in differentiating the "natural" mysticism of Hindus and Buddhists from the "supernatural" mysticism of Christians, and continue to damn other religions with faint praise. If Christianity cannot be Christianity without pushing the claim to be the best of all possible religions, the world will breathe more freely when it dissolves.

The practical problem is, what are we going to do on Sunday mornings? How are multitudes of ministers to continue their work? What is to be the use of Church buildings, funds, and administrative machinery? Naturally, institutional Christianity will, in its present form, continue to supply the demand which remains for a monarchical religion. But a considerable number of ministers and even congregations—not to mention millions of reasonably intelligent young people—realize that churches must "put up or shut up," and that the chief business of religious facilities and assemblies is to provide a social milieu for religious experience. This is no mere matter of changing the externals—of having rock bands instead of organs and *Kyrie eleison* set to jazz, nor even of turning churches into social service centers with the idea that this would be practising Christianity seven days a week instead of just talking it on Sundays. Indeed, one may well hope that monarchical Christianity will *not* be practised, even on Sundays, since the dutiful spirit in which it dispenses charity breeds resentment in the giver and the receiver alike, for when the one gives with reluctance the other receives with guilt. Ministers and their congregations must instead consider what need there may be for churches as temples for contemplation and meditation, stripped of the courthouse furniture of stalls, pews, pulpits, lecterns and other equipment for throwing the Book at captive audiences. They must consider also the need for retreat houses and religious communities, and for guidance and instruction in the many forms of spiritual discipline which are conducive to mystical vision. They must further consider whether, as things now stand, they are even able to offer such services— sorely neglected as they have been in theological education. Obviously, if Christian groups cannot or will not provide mystical religion, the work will be (and is already being) done by Hindus, Buddhists, Sufis, unaffiliated gurus, and growth centers. Churchmen can no longer afford to laugh these things off as cultish vagaries for goofy and esoteric minorities—as if any intensive practice of religion had ever, anywhere at any time, been of interest to the majority of people.

This prompts me to say that I no longer set much store in the notion that we are about to enter upon some great New Age of spiritual development, or in such theories of historical epochs as were proposed by Joachim of Flora and Oswald Spengler. Fortunately, the preoccupation with these ideas in the first chapter, "The Epoch of the Spirit," is not essential to the main argument of the book. I am not saying that some great resurgence of spiritual vitality may not be coming upon us. The point is rather that such apocalyptic and messianic hopes for the future distract from the mystic's essential concern for the Eternal Now and encourage a dependence upon the mere passage of time as a vehicle of grace and growth. The concomitance of our perilous ecological crisis with the sudden expansion of mass-communication technology does indeed suggest that the world is in an apocalyptic and even eschatological situation, in a period of catastrophic revelation and imminent disaster. At times when the future appears to be failing us it is only natural that there should be a resurgence of religion and of interest in things eternal: it is our only recourse. It may amount to no more than the superstitious comforts of fantasy and magic, or of shrieking in desperation to high heaven. But, on the other hand, it may be something like the overwhelming sensation of release and peace which occasionally comes to people facing death.

For at such times there is no escaping the fact that in the pursuit of happiness, power and righteousness the human ego, with all its will and intelligence, has come to its wits' end. Even the solaces of religious hope and belief seem hollow—being no more than refined and fantastic forms of trying to save our carefully fabricated personalities from coming to an end. But the personality is a phantom even less substantial than the body, being an ephemeral work of art like a musical composition that dies away as it is played. But when it comes to silence we hear another tune, for we are reduced to the guileless simplicity of listening to what is—now. This is really all there is to contemplative mysticism—to be aware without judgement or comment of what is actually happening at this moment, both outside ourselves and within, listening even to our involuntary thoughts as if they were no more than the sound of rain. This is possible only when it is clear that there is nothing else to do, and no way on or back.

> *Wait without thought, for you are not yet ready for*
> *thought:*
> *So the darkness shall be light, and the stillness the*
> *dancing.*

For here, where there is neither past nor future, the doors of perception are cleansed, and we see everything as it is—infinite.

Of course, those who have never let themselves be reduced to this simplicity will feel that it is an arid oversimplification, that there must be much more than this—by way of doctrines, precepts and practices—to an effective religious consciousness. Here, then, will be trotted out all the old objections to the negativity of mystical ideas, to the dissolution of God our Father into the "divine darkness" or "cloud of unknowing" of Western mystics, or the featureless Void of the Buddhists. One can but reiterate the point that the mystic is negating only concepts and idols of God, and in this way cleansing the doors of perception in the faith that, if God is real, he need not be sought in any particular direction or conceived in any special way. To see the light, it is only necessary to stop dreaming and open the eyes.

Sausalito, California
February, 1971

ALAN WATTS

PREFACE
TO THE FIRST EDITION

This book is addressed to Christians of every denomination, and more especially to the thousands of thoughtful and sincere persons in the modern world who, though deeply interested in religion, find themselves unable to accept Christianity in the forms in which it is usually presented. It is not, however, a book of apologetics. It is written to introduce a strangely and disastrously neglected subject—the meaning of Christian doctrine. For the great majority of people, including even clergy and theologians of every school, confuse the meaning of religion with its form, and when asked to explain the meaning give only a more detailed exposition of the form.

The form of Christianity consists of certain doctrines and precepts based to a great extent on historical events. The meaning is God himself, the ultimate Reality, not as an idea conceived but as a reality experienced. When apprehended by man this meaning is a state of consciousness which might be called "the mind of Christ" in the sense of St. Paul's words, "Let this mind be in you which was also in Christ Jesus." This is that mystical and nearly immediate experience of God which, although ineffable and incapable of exact description, may be explained sufficiently to give its traditional dogmatic and historic expressions much more clarity and reality than they now convey to the modern mind. Without some apprehension of this meaning, Christian doctrines are not actually intelligible at all, and must remain mere formulae lacking real power to move the soul however ably their factual and historical truth may be defended. Obviously facts are of little value to us until we know something of their significance, and this lies not in the facts themselves but in the spiritual truths and principles, the eternal nature of God, which they express.

The reader, and especially the critic, should be warned against trying to fit into any familiar pigeonhole the manner of interpretation which will be used. This is not to be a "Gnostic" approach to Christianity which discounts its material, sacramental and historical elements in favour of a "purely spiritual" religion, nor yet a Modernist approach which discounts them in favour of a purely moral religion—if such may be called a religion at all. The factual truth of Christian doctrine, the form of orthodoxy, will be accepted throughout as a matter of course. The point is rather that whether this form be true or not, even a detailed and well-advanced knowledge of the form is quite distinct from a knowledge of its meaning.

This meaning, of which a considerable part is still outside the realm of the ineffable, was discussed and explained with some adequacy by Patristic writers, but receives such a minimum of attention in modern religious teaching, preaching and theological education that it scarcely ever reaches the general public. The study of Christian doctrine has come to the point where the forest cannot be seen for the trees; the "first principles" in reference to which the entire complex scheme has meaning are ignored or forgotten and Christianity will lack spiritual power until they are restored, though, because of the nature of the historic process, this restoration will be more than a reversion.

A book of this size cannot attempt to conduct such an interpretation over the whole field of Christian doctrine, and at the same time take into account the practical applications of these doctrines when their meaning is understood. It has therefore been necessary to concentrate mainly on the doctrine of the Incarnation, which is not only the most fruitful for this purpose, but is also the central and characteristic tenet of the Christian religion. Furthermore, the truth which lies behind the Incarnation is of the highest importance for a correct understanding and practice of mystical religion, which, apart from that truth, is always in danger of eccentricity. So far as I am aware, no modern writer on mystical religion has given the Incarnation its proper and adequate place.

It would be difficult to thank by name all the people who have directly or indirectly been of help to me in preparing this book, for there have been so many of them, and they have not always been aware that they were helping. But I do want to express my indebtedness to the many students of Northwestern University who have so pleasantly plagued me, hour after hour, with spiritual problems that had to be answered to the satisfaction of young, very modern and often keenly penetrating minds; to the Reverend A. A. Taliaferro, who read the manuscript and gave much time to an illuminating discussion of its central themes; to Mr. Harry Lorin Binsse for most helpful and sympathetic criticism and for the suggestion of a number of important corrections; and most of all to my wife who has not only "put up with me" during the sometimes temperamental and always abstracted business of writing, but

*also cheered me on and stayed up with me to the "wee
small hours" when I needed her help and advice in
thinking out many of the problems that arose in the
course of the work.*

ALAN WATTS

Evanston, Illinois
February, 1947

BEHOLD THE SPIRIT

INTRODUCTION

It is all too clear that our age suffers from a vast hunger and impoverishment of the spirit which the organized Christian religion, as we know it, rarely satisfies. It would be easy to blame the modern world for ignoring Christianity, to condemn it for a merely perverse heathenism, if Church religion showed any strong signs of spiritual life. The truth, however, is that with some very few and scattered exceptions Church religion is spiritually dead, and the best minds of the Church admit and deplore it openly. This is so obvious that there is no need to stress it except as a starting point for constructive discussion. There is an abundance of rather unprofitable literature by both Christian and non-Christian writers bewailing, grumbling or pointing scorn at the deadness of the Church and the general decline of religion of whatever sort. For the most part the constructive side of this literature is merely so much sermonizing and exhortation to "return" to the belief and practice of certain things which the Church knows well enough should be believed and practised but cannot find the heart for them. "To will is present with me; but how to perform that which is good I find not. For the good that I would I do not."

Outside and even within the Church, modern man is therefore indifferent to religion as he knows it, and yet his nervous restlessness, his chronic sense of frustration, his love of sensationalism as an escape, his fitful use of every substitute for religion from state-worship to getting drunk, show that his soul still desires that release from itself, that infusion of life and meaning through being possessed by a power greater than itself, which is found perfectly in union with God alone. Man's—modern man's—need of religion has been discussed and proved as much and more than the failure of Church religion to supply it. The point needs no further stress, for quite apart from all the philosophical, sociological and psychological arguments that have been put forward time after time, the fact that a creative and relatively sane society must in some way or other be dominated by religion is fully proved by the destructive and insane state of the first radically secular civilization in history—our own.

But, lest there be any misunderstanding, we do not mean that man and society require simply a code of morals, whether freely accepted or enforced from above. Morals are a by-product of religion, necessary as they are. For creativity and sanity man needs to have, or at least to feel, a meaningful relation to and union with life, with reality itself. It is not enough that he be related to a human group or a human ideal, for he knows that men and peoples die, and that beyond them is a more permanent reality—the reality of the natural universe, and still beyond that the gods or God. Religion must relate man to the root and ground of reality and life. Without this man cannot feel that his life has any actual and objective meaning. Without this he feels that reality itself is an inane vacuum, a chaos, in which he creates purely artificial and make-believe meanings out of his own head. He feels too, however dimly, that the emptiness of reality will at last engulf his make-believe, and that therefore to continue with it is mere postponement of ultimate frustration. It is seldom, perhaps, that this is realized quite consciously. Absorbed in the creation of artificial meanings it is possible, for a while, to forget reality, though the sense of futility remains as an undertone of feeling breaking out into consciousness in times of crisis. At such times man *knows* his need of religion; at others he only *feels* it as an unexplained void in the heart.

The present low ebb of Church religion consists in the fact that rarely, even for Church people, does it give the soul any knowledge of union with the reality that underlies the universe. To put it in another way, modern Church religion is little concerned with giving any consciousness of union with God. It is not *mystical* religion, and for that reason it is not fully and essentially religion.

The truth that religion, to be of any use, must be mystical has always been denied by the seemingly large number of people, including theologians, who do not know what mysticism is. They associate it with ecstatic trances, with the solitary life of the hermit, with purely negative conceptions of God, with keeping one's mind perfectly blank for hours on end, with vague reasoning, with pantheism, with a distaste for action and concrete, physical life, forgetting that all these things are the freaks or aberrations of mystical religion and have nothing to do with its essence.[1] Its essence is the conscious-

---

[1] Thus Reinhold Niebuhr quotes with approval the following from Mercer in his *Nature and Destiny of Man*. New York, 1941 and 1944, vol. i, pp. 135–136n: "By a ruthless process of abstraction they (the mystics) have abjured the world of sense to vow allegiance to a mode of being about which nothing can be said without denying it . . . it embraces everything and remains pure negation—leave us not alone with the absolute of orthodox mysticism lest we perish of inanition." J. E. Mercer, *Nature Mysticism*. p. 10. As will be explained below, pp. 97–98, this misses the point completely.

ness of union with God and this will only involve these freaks of negativism if God is thought of as hostile to the world, and not as its loving creator.

In almost any Church one cares to choose there is and has long been an absolute minimum of the teaching and practice of mystical religion. Even for intelligent congregations Church teaching and preaching is concerned almost exclusively with a multitude of minor matters having mostly to do with the smaller points of morality or, in liberal Protestant churches, with politics and vague ethical principles. One may go even further and state that the whole atmosphere and attitude of modern Church religion impresses the modern mind as having little or nothing to do with the Reality which controls and causes our universe. Science has given to our age a most impressive view of this universe, and this demands an equivalently wonderful and splendid conception of God together with an appropriate manner of worship. In comparison with this view of the universe, which, without the aid of religion, has so staggered man's thought of God as to stop it, present-day Church religion seems utterly paltry.

Whereas Protestantism has largely degenerated from religion into moralism, Catholicism[2] retains certain essential elements of religion but expresses them in theological and sacramental forms which are for the most

---

[2]As generally employed here and hereafter the term "Catholicism" should be understood as including but not confined to Roman Catholicism. A wider use of the term is necessary because certain Christian communions other than the Church of Rome, such as the Greek and Russian Orthodox and the Anglican, widely separated from the Roman Church as they may be, abide by formularies of doctrine and worship which certainly cannot be called Protestant in the modern sense of the word. In theory, if not always in practice, they are much closer to Roman Catholicism than to the various forms of contemporary Protestantism. The Anglican liturgy, for example, is easily recognizable as the child of the Latin Mass and Office, which certainly cannot be said of the normal types of Protestant service.

part uncomprehended both within and without the Church. As generally taught, Catholicism is a wonderfully interrelated system of doctrines and practices without ultimate meaning. Even the more intelligent Catholics know a great deal *about* their religion but little or nothing *of* it, because there is an immense confusion in their minds between symbols and their significance. For example, it is one thing to believe in the Incarnation as an historical event; it is another to understand, even intellectually, what it means, and still another to experience that meaning in terms of everyday life and consciousness. But because official Catholicism is little concerned either to explain or to experience the Incarnation and its other dogmatic symbols, it resembles an algebraic formula of great intricacy, internal rationality and even beauty, but with little indication of the realities to which its terms refer. Thus few Catholics are even aware that there are spiritual realities behind the celestial and historical events described in dogma, and fewer still experience those realities. The reasons for this will be explained shortly.

These defects of Church religion cannot be cured by mere surface alteration of the methods of teaching and worship, because they are symptoms of a profound spiritual defect. The repellent externals of modern Church life—organizational busy-ness, inadequate teaching, excessive moralism, doctrinal obscurantism, lack of conviction, absence of reality, the very disunity of the Church—all are rooted in the fact that the modern Christian has no sense of union with God. Naturally, then, the Church has no spiritual power either for creative morality, for speaking with the conviction that converts, for understanding the true meaning of doctrine and dogma, and still less for building a Christian culture and social order to displace the barren confusion of our present secular culture.

We are well aware that many of the most prominent and respected of our modern theologians and churchmen disagree profoundly with the view that the Church can only be revived through mystical religion. Among the rank and file of clergy a voice that proclaims this view is politely ignored, and treated as a messenger from the "lunatic fringe," as an extremist, an oversimplifier. It may be, as they say, that mysticism is not the essential wellspring of religion. But it is at least an element, and an essential element, in that spring, and because it is so singularly absent from modern Church religion quite a lot of overemphasis can be afforded. The Church has always walked forward on extremes like a man on his two legs, and you cannot walk by putting both legs forward at the same time.

The other remedies of the Church's state that are proposed have two serious defects. The first is that they are superficial—mere corrections of the external symptoms. The second is that they are panicky remedies of human origin, fearful of the Church's total collapse, bereft of faith in God and in the present operation of his Holy Spirit. They have no vision of the God-controlled design of human history, of the organic development of Christianity, and thus do not see that Christianity is about to begin a stage in its growth that is not only necessary for the Church's revival but also as nearly certain as anything can be. Modern Christians are not used, however, to thinking in this way. They speak of the Church as if it were a God-forsaken institution of purely human character which will collapse and vanish from history if men do not do something about it. While this is not the place to show the error of this view, we may simply note for the time being that the Fathers would have found it contrary to the very essence of their doctrine of the Church and termed it plain heresy. In contradiction to these sundry remedies and their two defects, it will be seen that mystical religion is in no sense superficial, and that, so far from being a remedy humanly applied, mysticism has its origin in God, in the action of the Holy Spirit.

What do our more wide-awake churchmen propose to *do* about the state of Christianity? Some would have the Church launch out boldly into the field of "progressive" politics, and sacrifice every doctrinal difference for the sake of Christian unity in a purely ethical bond; others would adapt the Church's teaching rigorously to modern thought, or provide for a more effective vocational training of the clergy, equipping them with the tools of modern psychological science; yet others would have the Church increase in numbers by any means possible and then dominate governments by pressure groups and political chicanery; these are among the more superficial and tiresome proposals. Wiser heads confine themselves to a few less flighty and more difficult demands. They ask for a ministry of higher intellectual power, familiar with modern thought and skilled in apologetics; for a vigorous campaign of instruction, explaining Christian belief in terms understandable to the modern mind; for an improved worship as to the nature of which both Catholic and Protestant liturgical reformers are in considerable agreement; and, more important than all, for saints, for Christians of deep faith and moral heroism who will do more for God, for man, and for the Church than any number of thinkers, teachers and liturgists.

To be sure, saints of God are our primary need. What

might not another St. Francis or another John Wesley do for Church and society? But merely ethical religions seldom produce saints. Sanctity is the fruit of faith, among other things, and we cannot expect saints unless Christians believe so strongly in God that they are willing to give up their lives for him. No movement, no individual, ever had power without some kind of creed, something believed so intensely as to be worth dying for. Ethical principles do not inspire such devotion, for the thing believed in must have far more reality than a mode of behaviour or an abstract social system. It must be a person, a husband, wife or child that one loves, or a group of persons, a society, or, more to be trusted than all these, the God who is reality itself. But, as we have seen, modern Church religion has not great faith in God, and less still in Jesus Christ. In practice, and often in theory, its belief in God is thin and vague, and is seldom taught and proclaimed. Sermons about God are preached but rarely.

We need, then, faith as well as sanctity, and what are we going to do about it? As for faith, the Church has the richest store of literature about the nature of God and the reasons for believing in him—the soundest and the most intellectually respectable kind of reasons. And as for sanctity, the Church has centuries of experience in spiritual disciplines, and teaches the loftiest morality in the clearest terms. Here are all the techniques, and it remains simply to practise them. But we don't. "To will is present with me; but *how* to perform that which is good I find not."

The trouble is that we are still only scratching the surface. Technique is not enough. Mere discipline is not enough. There are dozens and dozens of plodding Christians, clergy and laity, who practise their spiritual exercises every day—say their prayers, observe their times of meditation, repeat the Divine Office, make their confessions, attend or celebrate Mass, and from time to time go on retreats. Others fling themselves into social service and works of charity, giving all their time and wealth to the poor. Yet somehow the fire of the Holy Spirit does not descend except once in a great while, seemingly by the purest chance.

And though I bestow all my goods to feed the poor,
and though I give my body to be burned,
and have not charity,
it profiteth me nothing.

In practising spiritual disciplines as well as in trying to acquire faith, most of us are like monkeys. We do not understand the saint's inner state, and we are trying to attain it by the mere mimicry of its outward signs. We copy his actions and ideas, but because they do not really *mean* anything to us the task is an unproductive drudgery. For example, a monkey might, with some accuracy, describe an orchestra as a collection of people who blow through metal and wooden tubes, thump upon the skins of pigs, and scrape the entrails of dead cats with lengths of horsehair. We, of course, can give a fuller and more intelligible description of the work and nature of an orchestra because we understand its true meaning, which is music. But to a monkey music means nothing; it is simply a succession of noises produced by blowing, thumping and scraping. Yet because the monkey is envious of human accomplishments, he may readily be persuaded (until bored) to imitate human actions that mean nothing to him, to go through the motions of playing a trumpet or a violin with results far from meaningful and musical. A human being, too,

11

can learn and master all the *techniques* of music and yet never be an inspired musician.

So too, the moral splendour, the interior peace, and the spiritual power of saints and mystics are things which millions of us would like to possess. But it avails nothing to ape the exterior actions or even the interior ideas of such inspired persons unless we understand the meaning which these ideas and actions express. Apart from knowledge and appreciation of this meaning, our efforts to be like the great ones are so many attempts to produce the cause by the effect, to make the tail wag the dog. Now the meaning which saint and mystic express in idea and action is God. They think and act as they do because they are in a special way possessed by this life which is God, somewhat as the heart and mind of a dancer are possessed by the music which he interprets in bodily movement.

The *idea* of God is itself no more than an interpretation of the mysterious reality whereby the saint is moved and possessed; it is a life, a being, translated into a form of thought as one might try to represent a colour by a shape, striving to interpret beauty of tone by beauty of line. Such interpretations are the genesis of all religious doctrine, both metaphysical and moral; they are the instruments and techniques for expressing the divine meaning. But in the hands of so many persons they become like musical instruments in the hands of monkeys; they lack all inner significance to those who use them and those who watch them so used. The one hopes that this process of imitation will somehow make him a saint and a possessor of eternal life, though he knows not the true nature of these ideals. The other stands by in sheer bewilderment at so much activity without meaningful result.

12

Christian faith and practice have lost force because the enormous majority of Christians, both devout and nominal, do not know what they mean. Let it be said at once that such knowledge is not a matter of mere learning, of philosophical and theological acumen. Indeed, the theologian has often just as little grasp of the meaning of his religion as anyone else. He knows ideas; he knows the relations between these ideas; he knows the historical events—the story of Christ—upon which these ideas are based. He knows the doctrines of the Trinity, the Incarnation, the Virgin Birth, and the Atonement and can describe them with accuracy. But because he does not know, or even apprehend, what they mean, having no consciousness of union with God, his description of them—while correct as far as it goes —is as uninformative and lacking in significance as the monkey's description of an orchestra.

This theologian does not fail to grasp the meaning of his religion just because he is a pure academician without interest in its practice. For his practice, as much as his thought, is imitation. Monkey-fashion, he imitates the actions of the Fathers and the saints along with their ideas, attributing the fact that he does not become a saint to not imitating hard enough.

What interests him, for instance, about the doctrine of the Virgin Birth of Christ is *whether* and *how* it happened. These two questions are, however, much less important than *why* it happened, than the discovery of what it means. For centuries theologians have wrangled and armies have fought about what happens in the Mass—whether bread and wine can actually become the Body and Blood of Christ and, if so, how. Yet if all that energy had been turned to the discovery of what such a mystery might *mean*, what it reveals of the nature of God and of the way to the knowledge of God, the history of Europe might have been written in a somewhat happier strain.

So long as the mind of man could accept the doctrines of the Church at their face value, there seemed no urgent need of enquiring too deeply into their meaning. It was enough that certain things were true, that certain miraculous events had happened; man could be content to worship the wonderful, and the simple act of exposing and submitting himself to various mental and ritual disciplines imparted a certain sanity to his life. For the monkey that imitates man is not quite so much of a monkey as his brother in the purely natural state. But now that the truth and historicity of the great dogmas have been called in question so seriously, it is not enough to prove and affirm once more that, "These things happened." Doubts have a purpose, and by means of them we step backwards to take a better jump. And the modern doubter, if he understands correctly the void in his heart, will now say, "Yes, you may prove to me that these things are true—that there is a living God who became Man, born of a Virgin, who died for our salvation, rose bodily from the dead, and ascended into heaven, from whence he shall come to judge the living and the dead. But what then? What do all these events mean? I do not want a set of strange, though true, ideas. I am not particularly interested in the assurance that I, too, shall rise bodily from the dead, nor do I desire a code of conduct simply for its own sake. I want God himself. I want my own life to be joined and made one for ever with the meaning of all things. What connection has your complicated and admittedly picturesque religion with that?"

Today, in Church and out of Church, there are thousands of souls who realize in varying degrees of clarity that what they want from religion is not a collection of doctrinal and ritual symbols, nor a series of moral precepts. They want God himself, by whatever name he may be called; they want to be filled with his creative life and power; they want some conscious experience of being at one with Reality itself, so that their otherwise meaningless and ephemeral lives may acquire an eternal significance. Hence the vogue for every kind of mystical and pseudo-mystical cult from Neo-Hinduism for the highbrows to "Unity" for the lowbrows. They do not and cannot be expected to know that the Church has in its possession, under lock and key (or maybe the sheer weight of persons sitting on the lid), the purest gold of mystical religion. Still less do they know that creed and sacrament are only fully intelligible in terms of the mystical life. And they do not know these things because the stewards and teachers of the Church do not, for the most part, know them either. For while holding officially that eternal life consists in the knowledge of God—and in nothing else—churches of every kind are concerned with almost everything but the knowledge of God. They are concerned with the grammar, the syntax, the technique whereby the knowledge of God may be expressed. But what is the use of a mastery of language when there is nothing to say, no meaning to express? What is the use of moral principles without moral power and moral vision?

Knowledge of God, the realization of one's union with God, in a word, mysticism, is *necessary*. It is not simply the flower of religion; it is the very seed, lying in the flower as its fulfilment and preceding the root as its origin. There is no "higher religion" without mysticism because there is no apprehension of the meaning

15

of reality without mysticism. It is the *sine qua non*—the *must*—the first and great commandment, "Thou *shalt* love the Lord thy God with all thy heart, and with all thy soul, and with all thy mind." On this hangs all the Law. On this all rules and techniques depend, and apart from it mean nothing.

And here is the problem. Mystical religion is not a technique, a remedy, that may be humanly applied. It is the operation of the Holy Spirit. Mysticism is necessary; you *must* love God with your entire being—but it cannot be achieved by imitation. There is no rule, no method, no formal technique whatsoever that one may simply copy and attain the knowledge and love of God. One thing is needful—is absolutely necessary—and yet we can never say, "Do this, and it will be yours." Despite the countless attempts, the innumerable claims, to do or have done this very thing, it *cannot* be done. There are a million methods for expressing the knowledge and love of God, but not one for attaining it. And yet the thing happens—God is known and God is loved.

We can no more find a method for knowing God than for making God, because the knowledge of God is God himself dwelling in the soul. The most we can do is to prepare for his entry, to get out of his way, to remove the barriers, for until God himself acts within us there is nothing positive that we can do in this direction. We may, however, be certain that he will act—indeed, that he is *already* acting—though we have difficulty in becoming aware of this action because we are always trying to put imitations and substitutes of our own in its place. We fail to see through the window because we are painting pictures on the glass. Nothing therefore can happen until we have given up every method and contrivance for possessing God, in the faith that

16

whether we feel it or not, know it or not, God possesses us entirely and inescapably here and now.[3] For there is no other possession of God than to let oneself be possessed *by* God. Mysticism is an action in the passive.

For hundreds of years Western man has been convinced that he could ultimately solve every one of his problems by *doing* something about it. It is a beneficial exercise in humility for him to come up against a problem about which he can actually do nothing. Yet the problem has to be solved. The situation would be maddening and impossible if that were all there is to it. But that is not all, because, as we have seen, mystical knowledge is something given to the soul by God, and there is a sense in which it is already being given to the soul —now and always. In this same sense, God is the most obvious thing in the world, the most self-evident, and union with God is the primary and most unavoidable reality of our lives. Yet God is so obvious and so unavoidable and so close to us that we are not aware of him. To try to see God is like trying to look at your own eyes, for he is nearer to us than we are to ourselves.

This, however, is a truth which the human mind can hardly accept or admit, because it is too proud and self-assertive and lacks the grace to receive such a gift. Man is always trying to manufacture God, or a sense of God, for himself and therefore ignores the one that is actually given, because there is no credit to be gained in accepting a gift. And man feels guilty if he cannot pile up some credit to his account. Nevertheless, this truth is the gospel, the good news, and the basic principle of mystical religion. We do not have to seek for God;

[3] Of course this does not involve the total abandonment of spiritual discipline. It means abandoning it as a means to possess God, but continuing it simply as an act of worship.

he is already here and now, and to seek for him implies that he is not. We do not, in this sense, have to *attain* union with God; it is already given as an act of the divine love. To try to attain it by our own efforts is to slight that love and, again, to imply that the gift is not given. By the same principle, though this will require further explanation, even the mystical consciousness of God is given now, whereas to seek for it by some method or technique implies the contrary.[4]

There is a second sense in which God acts within the soul, though not at so deep a level as in the first sense. There are times in the lives of individuals, of societies, and of the Church, when the Holy Spirit gives a greater capacity for the realization of these spiritual gifts—a capacity which should not be confused with the gifts themselves. Despite the fact that the immediate signs are unfavourable, from some viewpoints, the general pattern of the history and development of the Western Church suggests most strongly that the Church as a whole is close to a period when the capacity for mystical religion will be increased to a hitherto unknown degree. Three factors seem to be combining to shape the character of this period—the pressure of external events, the general laws of the growth and development of organisms, and the interior movements of the Holy Spirit.[5]

Three questions now confront us. Firstly, what is this general pattern in the historical development of West-

---

[4]The mystical consciousness of God is, of course, distinct from the direct consciousness of the Beatific Vision. Mystical knowledge is still veiled, and St. Dionysius describes it paradoxically as the "superluminous darkness." See below, pp. 91 *et seq.*

[5]This trend has already been noted by two of the Church's outstanding lay thinkers—Nicolas Berdyaev and E. I. Watkin, whose work will be discussed below.

ern Christianity, and how and why does it require and tend towards an epoch wherein Christian life and thought will be increasingly mystical? Secondly, in what does mystical religion itself consist, what are its spiritual and psychological principles? Thirdly, in what ways can the growth of mystical religion deepen our understanding of Christian doctrine, leading us from the outward symbol to the inner meaning, and what is its contribution to and effect upon the living of the Christian life?

PART ONE

It is expedient for you that I go away: for if I go not away, the Paraclete will not come unto you; but if I depart, I will send him unto you.

JOHN 16:7.

Christian dogma is merely a symbolism of spiritual experience. . . . We cannot dispense with symbolism in language and thought, but we can do without it in the primary consciousness. In describing spiritual and mystical experience men will always have recourse to spatial symbols such as height and depth, to symbols of this or another world. But in real spiritual experience these symbols disappear; there are no symbols of height and depth, of this or another world. The primal creative act is realistic and non-symbolical; it is free from conceptional elaboration.

NICOLAS BERDYAEV, Spirit and Reality.

The one secret, the greatest of all, is the doctrine of the Incarnation, regarded not as an historical event which occurred two thousand years ago, but as an event which is renewed in the body of every one who is in the way to the fulfilment of his original destiny.

COVENTRY PATMORE, The Rod, the Root, and the Flower.

The Now-moment in which God made the first man and the Now-moment in which the last man will disappear, and the Now-moment in which I am speaking are all one in God, in whom there is only one Now. Look! The person who lives in the light of God is conscious neither of time past nor of time to come but only of one eternity. . . . Therefore he gets nothing new out of future events, nor from chance, for he lives in the Now-moment that is, unfailingly, "in verdure newly clad."

MEISTER ECKHART.

Yet in my flesh shall I see God.

JOB 19:26.

I. THE EPOCH OF THE SPIRIT

Philosophers and historians have been saying for years that the Western world is in a period of acute crisis. Today the best minds among them are agreed that this crisis denotes the end of a phase of our civilization, if not the end of that civilization itself. Beyond this, their views as to the nature of the crisis and the future which it forebodes differ widely because of their varying theories of history and of the development of cultures. We recognize that theories of history belong to a highly speculative and uncertain realm of thought, depending on the dangerous but necessary art of generalization. To interpret the "signs of the times" one is almost compelled to adopt a theory of history, and the one we have here chosen is unpopular because of the admittedly narrow and unfortunate way in which its chief protagonist—Oswald Spengler—has handled it. Because of his own exceedingly superficial philosophy of life he so misapplied the basic principles of his historical theory that the principles themselves have been attacked as widely and as bitterly as their misapplication. But the *principles* have been attacked with more oratory than reason. It is conceivable that historians would not resist Spengler's basic theory quite so bitterly if they could realize, as he did not, that the closing phases of a civilization or culture are not times of pure decadence— especially from the spiritual point of view. Age and maturity may bring the weakening of physical powers, but they also bring wisdom.

I

For reasons that will presently be given we believe that our Western culture has reached the end of its physical expansion and vigour, and is entering the latter part of its life—the period of old age and spiritual, or psychological, maturity. This is why Church religion is finding it so hard to meet the spiritual needs of modern man, for it is treating him as if he were still a child, an adolescent, or even a young adult. We are not saying that modern man is the spiritual superior of his forefathers; we are saying that in important respects he is of a different and older type of psychology. Such a view depends, of course, on the theory that cultures have a cyclic and organic pattern of growth similar to the life-rhythm of individual human beings, and that, in a general way, they pass through the stages of infancy, adolescence, physical maturity, spiritual maturity (or old age), and death.

Closely interrelated and inwardly complex as they are, it is obvious that individual cultures exist. It is certainly possible, by the analytic method, to prove that they do not exist, because almost anything will seem to vanish when sufficiently reduced to atoms. But just as there was clearly such a thing as Egyptian culture, there is clearly, to a person who uses his eyes instead of the academic microscope, such a thing as Western culture. As Christendom, it once had an almost perfect unity, though now its unity is buried beneath the excrescences of time.

It is also obvious that these individual cultures come into being and pass away. If they do not disappear entirely, they degenerate into a kind of prolonged decomposition. This fact simply cannot be disputed. Roman culture has vanished; so have the Egyptian, the Babylonian, the Greek, the Cambodian, the Indian and the Chinese. New cultures are or may be active in the areas occupied by the old and among their descendants, but they are clearly new. There is no reason at all to suppose that our Western culture is exempt from this fate. If it is to continue just as it is any longer, such a fate would be almost desirable. But to say that cultures grow old and die is no more pessimistic than to say the same of persons; they would be quite horrible if they did not, for one who does not know how to die does not know how to live.

If cultures have birth and death, it would seem probable that, like all other biological phenomena, they pass through the intervening stages of growth and decay. This is not the application of a "biological analogy" to history. There is no question of *analogy*, for cultures, being composed of men, are themselves biological phenomena, and we know that biological groups can die out as surely as individuals. Where are the dinosaurs and pterodactyls, and what is becoming of lions and tigers? Indeed, this is not even a question of biology, but rather of simple energy and movement, the patterns of which are almost invariably cyclic. The fact, indeed the beautiful fact, of cyclic movement is repugnant only to the discredited theorists of linear progress and to cultural egotists who suppose that their own culture-form is essential to the continuance of truth, beauty and goodness in the world.

Naturally there would be individual exceptions to this rule, for in every period of a culture's development there are persons both before and behind the times. We can say, for instance, that the mediaeval period represents Western culture in its childhood only in a *general* sense, for in the outstanding minds of the period there are dozens of individual exceptions, although none of them *wholly* surpass the general mentality of the age. Furthermore, this view of cultural development does not involve the idea that the mature stage is better than or spiritually superior to the stage of infancy. It is simply different in form and capacity, and no one will seriously maintain that adults are of necessity holier and better than children. The cyclic view of history involves no moral judgements whatever.

Christian historians do not in general like this theory for two principal reasons. The first is that they have a myopic tendency to identify Christian history with the history of Western culture, and the second is that they feel it to be a naturalistic philosophy of history obscuring the divine design behind human events. To identify the history of Christianity with that of a particular culture is quite disastrous—to Christianity. Already the Christian religion has belonged to two cultures, the Graeco-Roman and the Western, and the former is absolutely dead and gone, while the latter is clearly within a few centuries of its demise, if some violent accident does not end it sooner. Moreover, the divine design habitually expresses itself through natural laws, which are our description of the normal way in which God works. To be an expression of the mind of God, history does not have to move in straight lines. In all probability there will be many Christian cultures following the late Graeco-Roman and our own, all exhibiting the genius of Christianity in differing ways like so many varied jewels adorning a crown. The unity of Christian history must not be confined to a single culture, for this would not begin to exhaust the manifold possibilities of Christian civilization. Christian philosophy does not make it necessary to suppose that we are steadily advancing to some *future* perfection, for in space and time we attain relative perfections only, and the glory of Christian history consists in their sum and integration viewed from the standpoint, not of time, but of eternity.

It is not our purpose to expound and defend this theory of history in detail. Spengler, despite his limitations, has at least established its general principles, and even while following theories of history which differ from his, Christian historians and philosophers such as Berdyaev, Watkin and Sorokin have advanced views of the modern crisis which imply the same *practical* consequences.[1] But the reluctance of many to admit it is due largely to our own culture's absurdly exaggerated view of its importance and to man's natural aversion to facing the fact that one day he will die. The inability of many historians to discern the various stages of cultural cycles is due also to the confusion of the general mental-

---

[1] Sorokin's *Crisis of Our Age* (New York, 1942) is an instructive example. He describes the modern crisis as the end of the sensate phase of Western culture, and draws many parallels between the decadent symptoms of our own time and those of the latter centuries of the Roman Empire and other *dead* cultures. Yet he indignantly rejects the principle of culture cycles, and reserves to Western civilization the privilege of renewing itself entirely through a return to spiritual values. But Roman culture died despite the spiritual revival of Christianity, which was the wisdom of its old age. Western culture will likewise acquire a deep spiritual wisdom, but this will not prevent its death. But Sorokin seems almost to identify the future of Western culture with the future of man, urging the return to spirituality as "the road that leads not to death but to the further realization of *man's* unique creative mission on this planet." He fails, therefore, to grasp the peculiar character of the spirituality that is to come, and thinks of it, in effect, as a return to a mediaeval type of wisdom. "There will increasingly appear the partisans of the Absolute ethical norms, often becoming stoics, ascetics, and saints. The soul of the society in the transition will be split into the *carpe diem* on the one hand, and on the other into ideational indifference and negative attitude toward all the sensory pleasures." *Ibid.*, pp. 301–302. This *may* happen as it certainly happened before the collapse of the Roman Empire, but if Christian spirituality takes this turn again it will have learned nothing further about the Incarnation in a thousand years.

ity of a given period with that of its most exceptional minds and to exclusively analytical methods of research and study which make it impossible to see the forest for the trees.

The general characteristics of the four stages of the cultural cycle are as follows:

(1) *Thesis.* The childhood of a culture normally has its roots in an older culture, from which it receives a traditional body of wisdom which is accepted on authority and understood in a naïve, literal and external fashion. Vigorous philosophy rationalizes the tradition's external form, while mystical insight is fresh and deep but improperly related to the tradition itself and to social life.

(2) *Antithesis.* The adolescent period is characterized by a growth of individual self-awareness, and involves rebellion against the parental tradition and authority. The culture discovers its own peculiar powers and abilities, and departs sharply from the patterns inherited from older cultures. The natural mysticism of childhood disappears by degrees.

(3) *Crisis.* The culture exploits its newly found powers on the physical plane, but in its enthusiasm loses touch with its traditional roots. Imperialism and materialism flourish until they reach their practicable limits or collapse through loss of inner, spiritual meaning.

(4) *Synthesis.* When physical expansion and maturity reach the point of frustration, the culture returns to its traditional roots, and, with the aid of all the experience gathered in its course of life, understands them profoundly and inwardly. This is the wisdom of old age, which may in turn become the thesis of a new culture.

The relevance of this cultural rhythm to our particular problem—the spiritual crisis of modern man—is that if, as will be shown, we are now entering the phase of spiritual maturity, we are going to understand the Christian religion in a somewhat different way than in the past. To meet the spiritual needs of modern man, the Church will have to present Christianity in a mature form as distinct from the childhood form of mediaeval Catholicism, or the adolescent form of Reformation Protestantism. It will be shown, further, that the mature form differs from that of childhood in that it is an interior, spiritual and mystical understanding of the old, traditional body of wisdom—the thesis and mythos[2] with which the cultural cycle began. What the child understood as an external, objective and symbolic fact, the mature mind will see also as an interior, subjective and mystical truth. What the child received on another's authority, the adult will know as his own inner experience. Unless understood in this mature way, the traditional religion of the Church must seem incomprehensible and even superstitious to the modern mind.

This mystical and spiritual synthesis which occurs in the final maturing of great cultures is termed by Spengler the "Second Religiousness," though in spite of his otherwise profound grasp of cultural life-rhythms a certain emotional perversity seems to prevent him from grasping the full significance of this phase of development. After the frustration of material expansion a culture

---

[2] I wish to distinguish between mythos and myth, since the latter word has now the sense of a purely imaginary folk tale. The mythos is the original symbolic story-form of a religion, in which spiritual realities are symbolized in events of terrestrial or celestial history—events which are not *necessarily* unhistorical and imaginary. In the child state abstract or spiritual truths can only be grasped in the concrete form of symbols.

weary, reluctant, cold, . . . loses its desire to be, and, as in Imperial Rome, wishes itself out of the overlong daylight and back in the darkness of protomysticism, in the womb of the mother, in the grave. The spell of a "second religiousness" comes upon it.[3]

But the external symptoms he perceives quite correctly, showing that the Second Religiousness

appears in all Civilizations as soon as they have fully formed themselves as such and are beginning to pass, slowly and imperceptibly, into the non-historical state in which time-periods cease to mean anything.[4]

He sees that the Second Religiousness employs the "Springtime" or infancy forms of religion, but does not seem to realize that they are understood in a new, interior and spiritually creative sense. For Spengler this return to the infancy forms is purely nostalgic, and fails to grasp the inner spirit. "Nothing new is built up, no idea unfolds itself—it is only as if a mist cleared off the land and revealed the old forms, uncertainly at first, but presently with increasing distinctness."

But again he perceives the external symptoms well enough:

The material of the Second Religiousness is simply that of the first, genuine [sic], young religiousness—only otherwise experienced and expressed. It starts with Rationalism's fading out in helplessness, then the forms of the Springtime become visible, and finally the whole world of the primitive religion, which had receded before the grand forms of the early faith, returns to the foreground,

---

[3] *Decline of the West*. New York, 1926, vol. i, p. 108. The characterization of this phase as a desire to return to the womb is, of course, the Freudian predilection to explain the greater in terms of the less. Spengler's emotional incapacity to appreciate and sympathize with a spirituality of this type is more evident in his *Man and Technics* than in the *Decline*.

[4] *Ibid.*, vol. ii, p. 310.

powerful, in the guise of the popular syncretism that is to be found in every Culture at this phase.[5]

Spengler rightly states that our own civilization has not yet entered upon the Second Religiousness, but the purely regressive character which he ascribes to it is typical rather of such trends as the nineteenth-century Gothic revival and the reversion of the Roman Catholic Church at that time to an extreme traditionalism and obscurantism against the rise of liberalism.

The profoundest spirituality of the human race appears during these periods of Second Religiousness. Late Graeco-Roman culture gave us Plotinus, Origen, St. Augustine and the great Byzantine Fathers. Late Jewish culture produced the Wisdom literature, Philo, perhaps the Kabbalah,[6] and primitive Christianity itself. Indeed, the Hebrew-Judiac cycle is a particularly instructive example of the spiritual evolution of cultures, having stages that are marked with considerable clarity. Its period of infancy lies prior to 800 B.C., and comprises the establishment of the original priestly religion and the primitive law, and the founding of the nation in its Palestinian home. To the same period belongs the Hebrew religious mythos contained in the earlier parts of the Pentateuch. Between 800 and 500 we have the adolescent revolution of prophetism, followed by the diaspora, which was for the Jews an era of economic rather than political expansion, since they became the bankers of the ancient world. The Second Religiousness begins after 200 with the frustration of an

---

[5] *Ibid.*, vol. ii, p. 311.

[6] Parts of the *Zohar* are ascribed, at the earliest, to the tenth century, but it obviously embodies a much earlier tradition which existed, according to Edersheim, at the time of Christ. For a full discussion of this problem see A. E. Waite, *The Holy Kabbalah*. London and New York, 1929, esp. pp. 51–111.

attempted political independence, and is seen in the Wisdom literature, primitive Christianity and such cults as the Essenes. The important feature of this phase is that it gives a mystical and interior interpretation to the primitive religion of the law and the sacrificial worship of the Temple.

> For Christ is not entered into the holy places made with hands, which are the figures of the true; but into heaven itself, now to appear in the presence of God for us. . . . For ye are not come unto the mount that might be touched, and that burned with fire. . . . But ye are come unto mount Sion, and unto the city of the living God, the *heavenly* Jerusalem.[7]

Examples might also be cited from the Oriental cultures, for we find the immense insight of Mahayana Buddhism and Sankhara's Advaita Vedanta in the latter phase of Indian culture, and the great Ch'an (or Zen) synthesis of Taoism, Confucianism and Buddhism after A.D. 700 in China.

It is obvious, however, that not all aspects of a Second Religiousness are of equal profundity. Along with Plotinus and St. Augustine we have the complex but superficial theosophism of the Gnostics, while Philo is tedious and involved in comparison with St. John and St. Paul.[8] Thus, in our own day, the profounder Second Religiousness of Western Christianity must not be confused with

---

[7]Hebrews 9:24 and 12:18–22.

[8]According to Spengler, primitive Christianity, Philo, Plotinus, Origen and St. Augustine belong to the early or Springtime phase of Arabian culture rather than the late phase of Graeco-Roman and Judaic. But this is no more than to say that the synthesis of one culture becomes the thesis of another, for all cultures existing around the Mediterranean are closely interwined. Even so, Spengler's view of the constituent elements of Arabian culture is most questionable, and he is always anxious to prove that nothing of great profundity can come out of a Second Religiousness. For him, old age is simple decadence—not the flowering of wisdom.

the modern Gnosticisms of Theosophical "Esoteric" Christianity, Christian Science, and other manifestations of that occultism which has little in common with genuine mystical insight. Such movements are indeed early signs of a Second Religiousness, seeking an inner meaning behind traditional symbols. But the meaning which they discover is usually some form of pantheistic rationalism.

II

To understand the spiritual needs of modern man we must consider in some detail the successive phases of our own West European-American culture, which at present seems to be at the close of its physical maturity.[9] We have to see what are the factors in our life-rhythm and the elements in the modern situation that seem to lead up to a Second Religiousness, and what in terms of our rich tradition of Catholic Christianity the character of this era is likely to be. Why are there grounds for believing that in this phase Christianity will have a primarily mystical emphasis, quite apart from the fact that this is the only thing which might possibly revive and even unify the Church in Western civilization? Why, again, is it possible that this particular development in Western Christianity may constitute an epoch of the first importance in the whole evolution of Christian life and thought?

The stages through which the life-movement of Western culture has already passed are fairly easy to

<hr>

[9]It is impossible to determine as yet whether America actually belongs to the West European culture cycle. If there is to be a distinctively American culture, it is as yet embryonic and its thesis will emerge from the spiritual maturity of the West European.

distinguish. The period of infancy lies between 900 and 1400, wherein our culture receives its thesis and its particular mythos, which is mediaeval or Gothic Catholicism. Between 1400 and 1800 we have the adolescent antithesis of Protestantism and Humanism, of the Reformation, the Renaissance and the Enlightenment. The era of physical maturity runs from about 1700 to our own day, and with it the usual decline of spirituality under the dominant materialism common to this stage. Towards the end of this era there begins the sense of frustration and spiritual hunger which is the prelude of the Second Religiousness and spiritual maturity.

Mediaeval men, says E. I. Watkin,

> were always children. They were naughty, very naughty, children or good children; rough children or gentle children; children ignorant of their alphabet or children eagerly learning and poring over any book they could lay hands on; foolish children or wise children—but all alike, children. That, no doubt, is the reason why, from the Renaissance to the present day, the conceit of raw adolescence has despised them.[10]

As a child mediaeval man lived under two mothers—Mother Nature and Mother Church, both of which he took for granted, and both of which, in different ways, he failed to appreciate and understand with any real depth. Like almost every people in its primitive, peasant state, he lived close to the soil and but rarely had any eye for its beauties. The peasant home was a small, windowless hovel, made to exclude rather than admit light and air. Flowers, trees, birds, animals and stars were observed, not for their beauty, but for a fanciful

---

[10] *Catholic Art and Culture.* London and New York, 1944, p. 80.

symbolism of moral and spiritual principles.[11] The great windows of the churches were not to frame any vista of clouds and hills; they were spaces for a translucent screen of many-coloured symbols—the stained glass window. An abbot of Ely, watching a flight of water birds at evening over the fen, silhouetted against the afterglow of sunset, saw only a troupe of devils on their way to fetch the soul of a neighbouring heretic, and in the night the booming of bitterns among the reeds was heard only as the uproar of fiends. Until quite late mediaeval times art had no perception at all of natural or human beauty, and though to our eyes it glows with a supernatural beauty of its own, one may doubt whether its creators were conscious of it in the same way.[12] Crudely cut precious stones were lavished upon sacred objects—Gospel books, crucifixes, reliquaries—with an eye only for their value and their glitter, and before the work of time had mellowed them to loveliness, the polychrome of cathedral statues, screens and pillars was a gaudy riot of loud colour.

None of this is said to deprecate mediaeval culture, but simply that we may perceive and love it for what it was—the work of a child-mind spontaneously achiev-

---

[11] A possible exception to this rule is the poetry of the Celtic monks of Ireland, though they are, perhaps, too early to be included in this period and in any case too isolated from Latin Christianity and Gothic culture to be regarded as in any way typical of mediaeval tendencies. An exception might also be made with St. Francis of Assisi, but in many respects modern writers sentimentalize his attitude to natural beauty.

[12] Watkin mentions a contemporary comment on Salisbury Cathedral where the writer admires, not the graceful form of the Gothic columns, but "the polish of the Purbeck marble, so smooth that you could see your face reflected in it." He also shows that the pointed Gothic arch was no imitation of the natural arch of the forest glade but a practical device to save material by greater window space and to get rid of the inflammable wooden roof of the Romanesque Church. *Catholic Art and Culture*, pp. 80–83.

ing an unconscious beauty of form, but taking conscious delight in the brilliance of colours, stones and precious metals for their own sake. Yellow trees, green skies, blue houses, red lions are as much a feature of the stained glass window and the illuminated miniature as of the paintings of any child today, together with a crudity of outline and absence of perspective saved only from complete childlikeness by the greater muscular control of the practised artist. Yet with the wisdom peculiar to children mediaeval man saw, inadequately it may be, what modern man does not see—that man and nature are indeed symbols of God. *"Alles Vergängliche ist nur ein Gleichnis,"* said the mature mind of Goethe in a much later age. To be sure, mediaeval man stated this symbolism in the wrong way, not by analogy but by clumsy and far-fetched metaphor, but at least he grasped the all-important point that the world is intelligible only as a revelation of the mind of God.

Though he lived so close to Mother Nature, mediaeval man was far more concerned with Mother Church, though here again in childlike fashion he grasped certain essential principles with little understanding of their inner meaning. His religion was mythological—that is to say, he apprehended spiritual realities in concrete, external symbols, not, save in rare cases, as interior events in the life of the spirit. God was the majestic old man with the triple crown, seated above the spheres on his golden throne, just as he is shown on the painted roof of Ely Cathedral. Heaven was literally the golden city with saints and angels encircling the Almighty like the courtiers of an earthly monarch. Hell, situated geographically in the heart of the earth, was a torment of physical fire. Even such profound and revolutionary minds as St. Thomas Aquinas could ask in all seriousness, "Whether our atmosphere is the demons' place of punishment?"

The centre of his spiritual life was the mystery of the Mass, the miracle performed on the altar that stood in the heart of the community, the transubstantiation of bread and wine into the very Body and Blood of the risen Christ. For mediaeval man the sacred Host was an object of such awe that he hardly dared to receive it in Communion, partaking of it (unless he was a priest) but once or twice a year. This infrequency of Communion was the symptom of the fact that he did not receive the mystery of the Mass into himself, did not understand it interiorly. The miracle of transubstantiation, of the most intimate union of God the Son with physical matter, was a thing that happened externally, at a distance, localized upon the altar, but not spreading out from thence into human life and consciousness. In such a period the primacy of God's transcendence goes hand-in-hand with a mythological type of religion, that is, a religion understood in purely external terms, wherein the divine mysteries are worshipped from a safe distance. The intimate mystical communion which the sacrament actually implied was known to a small circle of monks, who, though they entered the very depths of mysticism, were never quite successful in relating it to the sacramental and physical aspect of religion. Indeed, mystical writers of the Middle Ages, and even later, always give the impression that they are dragging in the sacramental life by the heels—just because Holy Church says it is necessary. Mediaeval mysticism is always in danger of Manichaeism, of denying altogether the importance and eternal value of matter and form, and of drifting off into a realm of pure abstraction. Their mysticism was still Neo-Platonic; it was not, and

37

there has not yet been in Christianity, an incarnational mysticism which truly accepts and comes to terms with physical existence. Erigena, the Victorines, St. Francis, Eckhart, Tauler, St. Bonaventure—all were still at heart despisers of the world which "God so loved," and of the flesh which the Eternal Word became.

The fact that these great interior souls of the Middle Ages, as well as the Neo-Platonic Christians before them, so wholly despised the flesh has created the central moral problem of Christianity—how to reconcile holiness with material life. The problem still is and always has been most acute in regard to sexuality, for it was only with difficulty that they could accept the sacramental character of marriage. For St. Thomas, with all his sound, earthy common sense, marital intercourse performed simply for pleasure was a venial sin—and in such matters St. Thomas was dangerously "advanced." Nineteenth-century Roman Catholicism seems rather less "advanced" than St. Thomas. Yet the historic opposition of holiness to sexuality has given sexuality an altogether unmerited importance in the Western mind, just because of its alleged "naughtiness."[13] Neither Protestantism, nor Romanticism, nor modern Liberalism has yet solved this problem; they have only veered between extremes and compromise, which is no solution.

The entire problem of the relation of holiness to

---

[13]According to the *Visio Alberici* (12th cent.) a special place of torture is reserved in hell for married couples who have intercourse on Sundays, Church feasts or fast-days. *Op. cit.*, ch. 5, p. 17. Even an involuntary nocturnal emission required, according to Gregory III, the recitation of twelve penitential psalms. (*Judicia congrua poenitentibus*, cap. 24, in *Mansi*, xii, 293.) If, however, the act is *ex cogitatione*, twenty-one psalms are required. So, too, Gury describes as venial sin *pollutio, quae fit cum imperfecta voluntate et libertate, ut quandoque in semisopitis accidit.* (*Compend. Theol. Moralis* i, 430. 2.)

physical existence remained unsolved because the original Catholic mythos, which contains the solution, was not inwardly understood even by the mystics. Absorbed in the contemplation of God as the "divine darkness" or the "cloud of unknowing," these profound souls never really tried to penetrate the mysteries of dogma and sacrament; for the most part they left them politely on one side, and thus there was the deepest rift between the religion of the mystics and the religion of the common man. The "higher end" of the problem, the inner meaning of the dogma of the Holy Trinity, the significance of the Incarnation as the birth of Christ in the soul, was tackled by Eckhart, Ruysbroeck and Nicholas of Cusa, but the crux, the relation of spirit to matter, was barely scratched. And yet the key to the problem lay right to hand in the daily ritual of the Mass, in that most intimate union of Godhead with common material forms, and in the entire sacramental and incarnational character of mythos and Church.

The adolescent revolution of Protestantism brought no solution to the problem because instead of using the key to unlock the door it threw it away. It abandoned the very elements of the Catholic mythos which were most revealing of its inner significance—the Mass, the doctrine of transubstantiation, the Catholic philosophy of the sacraments, and, in a later stage, even the dogma of the Incarnation that in Christ true God had become true man. It was impossible for the Protestants to see wherein mediaeval man was right and wherein he was mistaken. They could not see that Catholic sacramentalism was not purely and simply magic and superstition; they could not see the profound truth underlying the very materialism of mediaeval religion, the very emphasis on the union of God with physical symbols.

And they could not see it because mediaeval man himself had not seen it; he had been right for the wrong reasons. He had indeed used the sacraments magically, for just because he was a child he mistook the concrete symbol for the whole truth behind it. He could not see that the supreme truth behind the Mass, the Incarnation and the sacraments was that union with God was *given* to the creation and the flesh here and now, and did not have to be attained by human efforts.[14] He could not see this because, for his childlike mind, the gift stopped in its particular symbols; it stopped on the altar; it did not extend from thence into his own life and experience. And yet just because he was childlike he had the humility and the grace to accept the gift, as far as he could see it, with faith and wonder. But just because the Protestant was an adolescent and not a child, he was proud, and could not understand or sympathize with a God who could give himself so readily and generously to mere dust. The Protestant inherited from the mediaeval mystic his contempt of matter without the saving corrective of a sacramental Church.

Adolescence is man's awkward age, for which reason the history of our next phase, of Protestantism and Humanism, seems unattractive and barren. But it must not be condemned as a tragic historical mistake. It was absolutely necessary for the eventual understanding of the Christian and Catholic mythos. For the mythos is like a nut—a shell containing hidden fruit, a hard, concrete symbol embracing a spiritual truth. To extract the truth the nut must be broken—with reverence and re-

---

[14]This is not, of course, the necessary and automatic union of God with the world which we find in pantheism. On the contrary, the union implied in Christian doctrine is the free and loving gift of the living God. The whole subject is discussed below in Chapter II.

spect, because without the shell's protection the fruit would never have grown. The task of Protestantism was to break the shell, though because the Protestants did not fully realize this and did not know about the fruit inside, the job has been inexpertly and irreverently done. They have hammered away with gusto; they have cracked the entire surface; they have taken whole chunks of the shell right off, and, having thrown some of them away, have taken the rest into a corner and there tried to piece them together in a different form. But the fruit has not interested them. Protestantism has simply broken up the system of symbolism, reduced it and re-formed it, and, in these later times, has practically discarded the whole thing. The time has come for us to attend to the long-neglected fruit.

Humanism and Protestantism are of one spirit, although in Reformation Protestantism that spirit was not quite so obvious as it is today. This is the adolescent spirit of revolt against nature and supernature, the soil and the Church. In this phase man's end and god becomes man himself.

> Know then thyself, presume not God to scan;
> The proper study of mankind is man.[15]

Already in scholastic philosophy mediaeval man was awakening to the power of his own reason; in every direction his cleverness was developing, and under the stimulation of newly discovered books and statues from the mature age of classical culture, man became fascinated by his own mind and form. In every aspect of life symptoms of the change appear. Dante is a map of the celestial realms, but Shakespeare of the human soul.

---

[15]Pope, *Essay on Man*. But the thought is taken from Charron's *Treatise on Wisdom*: "*La vraie étude de l'homme c'est l'homme.*"

In painting, Giotto and Fra Angelico are still concerned with man only as a symbol of the divine mysteries, but with Michelangelo, Botticelli, Raphael the centre of interest shifts to the splendour of the naked human form.[16] By degrees the agrarian culture of feudalism gives place to the bourgeois, mercantile culture of cities, where man is surrounded by his own works and absorbed in his own concerns. The expansion of man's powers and his increasing absorption in their use from the time of the Renaissance; the development of science and secularism, the Church's loss of position and strength before the rising might of nations and other purely human institutions, the unprecedented increase in man's power over nature—all this is history too familiar to need elaboration, and leads up to the special modern conceit that there is no problem too great for human reason. All this gave the nineteenth and early twentieth centuries dreams of the indefinite progress of man towards the fulfilment of the Serpent's promise—"Ye shall be as gods."

In spirit, Protestantism was also grounded in the worship of man. As a popular revolution it was principally the work of city-dwellers; Geneva, Frankfurt, Strassburg, London, La Rochelle, Edinburgh, Leyden—these were among the many cities where Protestantism, mostly of the Calvinistic type, was welcomed by the merchant class, not just because it was a less expensive religion, but because it exactly suited the psychology of the new city-mind. This was the mind of a new economic and social group, young, vigorous, despised by

---

[16]Renaissance art has little or no interest in nature as the soil. Nature is seen only in terms of man; landscape is a mere background for portraiture. The West has never produced an important school of nature-painters in the sense and mood of Chinese landscape-painting.

the old aristocracy, anxious to prove its worth and respectability, and whose power lay not in lands or titles but in trade and money. Although nature has her freaks, she is on the whole trustworthy; generally speaking, the cycle of the seasons and the crops can be relied upon, and from her the peasant learns how to have faith in mysteries beyond his control. But in business and trade we are dealing with man, who lies and cheats and robs, and thus the man of business forms the habit of trusting but little. He has to be "shown." He must "have it in writing." And the new merchant class wanted its religion in writing; it wanted to form its own judgement on Holy Writ, for the mysteries of priests were not to be trusted. The Bible, the law book, not the Host, became the centre of Protestant worship.

For the Mass made the businessman uncomfortable. What were the mysterious actions and whisperings of the priest up there at the altar? How could anyone prove that the bread, which still looked like bread, was the Body of Christ? How could one trust in such an intangible miracle? Not being able to trust, the businessman is compelled to take more and more things under his own conscious control. He felt safer, therefore, to receive the Body of Christ by the power of his own mind, by so-called "faith," rather than by an external miracle which his senses could not verify. It was inevitable, then, that the religion of the businessman should become more and more *dependent* on his own will and consciousness, and less and less dependent on the unseen action of God.

The boy who flouts his mother's advice has always a deep sense of insecurity. She was so often right; she may still be right; mother is wise. But to defend himself against this humiliating intuition he must prove her a downright old fool by every available means. Hence the Protestant attitude to Mother Church, for the thought-habits of generations cannot be thrown off in a moment without inner misgivings. Protestantism had therefore to do everything possible to convince *itself* of its own rightness and of the damnable and wholesale corruption of Catholicism. Above all things it needed to be edified, to be built up and confirmed, and from that day to this the Protestant religion has ceased to worship in the full sense. Instead it has gone in for sermons, for Bible readings, and for fulsome and oratorical prayers which are for the edification of the people rather than the glory of God.[17] And in common with the prophetism of Hebrew adolescence, though in strange contrast to their own doctrine of predestination, the Protestants have increasingly tried to make moral conduct the chief means of salvation.[18]

The Calvinistic doctrines of predestination and irresistible grace may also be seen as signs of the inner sense of insecurity. They were the theoretical means of convincing oneself of membership among the elect, of being sure that one's salvation was a foregone conclusion. Logically, the doctrine of predestination should encourage moral indifference, for if one is either damned or saved from all eternity, what can one do about it? But the Calvinist was out to prove himself saved by every possible means, theoretical and practi-

---

[17]The Protestant Reform party in the Church of England unconsciously revealed their uneasiness at having discarded the Sacrament of Penance at several points in the *Book of Common Prayer*. Thus in the Order of Holy Communion after a somewhat fervent and emotional general confession, the compilers were not content with a simple declaration of forgiveness by the priest; they must support it with a whole collection of scriptural passages.

[18]This is not so true of Lutheranism and Anglicanism, which were always ready to compromise with Catholicism, and are not, therefore, essentially Protestant.

cal, and thus drove himself to the most strenuous moral efforts to prove that he was necessarily of the elect. And thus, by an odd paradox, the eternal and inscrutable decisions of God came to depend upon human effort. God was to be compelled to have foreordained one to salvation.

Thus the man-centeredness of Protestantism may be seen in a variety of ways—the dependence of the sacraments upon human faith and of salvation upon human effort, the substitution of edification for worship, the central place of the altar surrendered to the pulpit, the growth of individualism since the authority of the Church was replaced by personal interpretations of the Bible, the multiplication of sects based on such interpretations, the disappearance of every element of mystery and symbol from the Church in favour of the drab, trivial and secular dress of the city. And perhaps above all, the adolescence, the inner insecurity, the lack of faith in God, the vast self-consciousness of Protestantism is shown in its solemnity, its seriousness, its inability to laugh. (Aware of this criticism, modern Protestantism has acquired a sort of hearty merriment which never quite rings true.) Rare indeed is the Protestant who can laugh about, or in terms of, his own religion; a Protestant Chesterton, not to mention a Protestant Rabelais, is well-nigh inconceivable.

These may seem harsh things to say about a form of religion which has meant so much to so many sincere folk; but there is no question of *judgement* here. We are not suggesting that the Protestants should have done something else, for what they did was almost inevitable at that stage of Western history. It was part of the total design of that history. It was the beginning of the Prodigal Son's journey into a far country, where, in a later time, "he would fain have filled his belly with the husks that the swine did eat." Yet when the prodigal returns he is somehow the spiritual superior of his older brother, who, because he has always stayed at home, does not really appreciate his good fortune.

As might be expected, Protestantism has given way increasingly before the march of secular philosophy, before the rationalism which analyzed and explained the universe and man until it explained the universe and man, and reason itself, clean away. For neither reason nor faith can live when they lose dependence on God, just as the plant cannot live when uprooted from the soil. Isolated from God as he had formerly been apprehended under the symbols of Catholicism, and isolated from nature in the walls of the city, adolescent Western man developed an intense consciousness of his separation from the rest of the universe. He probed it, analyzed it, reasoned about it as one who was not a part of it, as if he sat in independent judgement upon the work of nature and God. Naturally, this purely analytic mode of thought destroyed its object; it reduced the universe to its lowest terms, its disjointed elements, its smallest fragments. The process of disintegration was so complex and the varying parts and pieces so multitudinous that no one man could comprehend the entire process. Therefore specialization became necessary. Knowledge was divided into a mass of subdivisions wherein each man learned more and more about less and less, until the work of analysis and disintegration was carried to its very limits. The view of the universe which finally emerged was the necessary result of the method of investigation. It was a totally disintegrated view. The universe was merely a system, if such a thing can be called a system, in which an incredible number of particles or impulses were going through haphazard permutations and combinations for colossal periods of time. That they had produced certain "ordered" forms such as the human mind, the solar system, vegetative life, and the like, was the result of pure statistical necessity. A sufficient number of monkeys typing for a sufficient length of time on a sufficient number of typewriters would be bound, at some time, to type out a continuous series of letters and spaces identical with those of the whole Bible. But this is merely the old trick of making things absurd by reducing them to their lowest terms. It is trying to explain away the music of Kreisler as a mere scraping of cats' entrails with horsehair.

By this process reason destroyed itself. After all, man himself *was* a part of this system, and man too was the product of statistical necessity, together with his reason, his theories, his ideas—including, we may observe, the idea of statistical necessity. But if all ideas were equally the result of statistical necessity, the possibility of a true idea vanished. Reason itself disappeared in meaningless mechanism. Vision became a chance form of blindness, consciousness a special form of unconsciousness, sense a special form of nonsense, life a special form of death. But a meaningless whole cannot evolve a meaningful part; a Godless universe cannot provide a sufficient cause for a rational man. *Ex nihilo nihil fit*— you cannot get something out of nothing. To defend itself against the modern disintegration philosophy must return to the point from which it began to decay, to scholasticism, and the robust common sense of St. Thomas. For philosophy in the Humanist age has likewise been isolated from reality; it has been philosophy about philosophy, about its own method, mere epistemology—not philosophy about life. It has taken seriously the proposition that man has no certain knowledge of anything; it has questioned the very validity of sense perception and reason, and thus is in no position to laugh when the world view of modern man reaches total absurdity.

With the progress of rationalism the whole Christian system of symbols, Catholic and Protestant, was attacked from many directions—metaphysical, historical and moral—and as Protestantism watered itself down to meet the attack, while Catholicism retired into stubborn obscurantism, the rationalist movement began to deprive life of any meaning whatsoever. The opinions of rationalist thinkers became in due time the common sense of ordinary people, so that today urban man is bereft of all but habitual faith in life, which is what keeps modern man from being more crazy than he is. The mere intellectual decision that there is no God cannot wipe out the thought patterns and habits of many centuries all at once. But in time a faith based on nothing but habit will weaken, and the complete insanity of the meaningless life will take its place if man cannot be diverted with make-believe meanings—commercial enterprise, material "success," absorption in political and social reform movements, all of which can easily be maintained in an era of physical expansion. Yet when that era ends, only futility is left.

For a time, then, modern man was diverted by the free play of newly discovered powers in an expanding world. The novelty of freedom for the growing powers of the individual distracted attention from the necessary implications of rationalism. It was enough to seek freedom, and the first joy of being free made it seem unimportant to ask what freedom was for—save to assert that it was for a vague business termed "progress" and "the development of one's personality." The underlying emptiness of such a view of life was veiled by the thrill of new sensations, which, if they were to continue to thrill, must be intensified, multiplied, magnified, to the drowning out of the ever-growing presentiment of futility. Wherefore the all-absorbing concern of urban man became business—busy, busy—buzzing like a wasp trapped in a glass, busy to pass the time, busy just to make more business, to make money to make still more business, just to keep on being busier and busier—for what no one knew, except just that *action* was a good thing and idleness very dangerous. For in silence, in idleness, there was the boredom of being alone with oneself, with that inane spark of consciousness in the abyss of nothingness into which it was destined to vanish.

Humanism ended in what Berdyaev terms "the destruction of the human image," the disappearance of man in mechanism, of the social organism in the mass-state, of the human form in an art which depicted, often supremely well, abstract mechanisms or the contents of the garbage can, of human language in the tortuous utterances of a James Joyce, of melodic and aesthetic form in the purely mathematical and technological music of a Shostakovitch, of human education and wisdom in a university curriculum composed of unrelated heaps of trivial information and technological skills, and of the human mind in a system of psychology based on the reflex actions of rats and the diseased mental processes of psychotics. Bereft of creative power through loss of union with God and the meaning of life, the soul used up its resources and then produced simply belchings and vomit. Coming to the end of the statistically necessary period when they typed out the Bible, the monkeys reverted to mere type.

III

At the present time more and more of us are becoming aware of the exhaustion of Humanism, the utter shallowness of rationalism and its analytic view of life, and of the truth that the creative and meaningful life is impossible without some realization of union with God. But, as we have seen, the old forms of Christianity as presented in modern Church religion are not really attempting to meet this need. True, there is an interesting revival of Catholic philosophy, which has made many converts among the disillusioned intelligentsia. And though much may be expected of this movement, it still leaves much to be desired because for the most part it is simply a return to mediaevalism, albeit to the most exalted and permanently valuable aspects of mediaeval religion.

Beyond this there is a ferment of all kinds of small mystical and pseudo-mystical groups and movements revolving around individual leaders—many of them influenced directly or indirectly by some form of Asiatic religion, and many, such as Christian Science and Theosophy, distinctly tinged with Manichaeism, the contempt for physical existence.[19] These are so many straws in the wind. They indicate a hunger. By itself each one is too partial, too narrow in vision to appeal beyond a rather limited circle. And there is something slightly exasperating about the perennial appearance of the unholy alliance of mysticism and Manichaeism.

[19]An interesting account of some of these will be found in Rom Landau's *God is My Adventure*. London and New York, 1936.

Mysticism will only be a great cultural force when it learns to accept the world, to love it as God loves it, and to this end it must ground itself in the central principle of the Christian mythos—the mystery of the Incarnation, of the Word made flesh.

It seems, then, that some five factors will predominate in forming the Second Religiousness of Western culture:

(1) The obvious collapse of Humanism and secularism in all its aspects—philosophic, sociological, artistic and religious. In the coming years the bankruptcy of all political and economic substitutes for religion will become increasingly apparent.

(2) The growing conviction that the *basic* doctrines of Catholicism are intellectually respectable and are, furthermore, essential to reason and sanity. The work of such men as von Hügel, Maritain, Gilson, Garrigou-Lagrange, Berdyaev and Mascall, together with such popular writers as Chesterton, Noyes, C. S. Lewis, and others, has already achieved much in this direction. In comparison with modern Catholic philosophers the work and opinions of such as Bertrand Russell, Santayana, Dewey, William James, and even Bergson seem callow and superficial. When they treat of Catholic doctrine they invariably reveal an entire want of understanding and information on the subject, though towards the end of his life Bergson came into the closest sympathy with Christian belief.[20]

(3) But it will be impossible for Catholic doctrine to be widely acceptable on the purely symbolic level. Five hundred years of Protestantism and rationalism, to-

---

[20]See especially his *Two Sources of Morality and Religion.* Paris, 1932 and New York, 1935. Also the two chapters on Bergson in Maritain's *Ransoming the Time.* New York, 1941, pp. 52–114.

gether with the slow maturing of Western culture, have made it impossible for the modern mind to be satisfied religiously by mere ideas, past events (*e.g.*, the Incarnation conceived simply as an historical truth), and ritual actions. The mythos of Catholicism must be understood inwardly and mystically as well as in terms of history and theology.

(4) The general growth of interest in mystical religion since the close of the nineteenth century, and the building up of mutual understanding on the basis of the interior life between persons of widely differing denomination, religion and race.

(5) The growing influence of Oriental culture and religion upon Western life. Within a mere fifty years our knowledge of Indian and Chinese thought has increased enormously, and a vast quantity of both scholarly and popular literature on the subject has been produced in England, America, France, Germany, Holland, Switzerland and other Western countries.[21] This cannot fail to have the most profound effect on the development of our culture, and in many directions its influence is already apparent.[22] So far, however, it has made little impression on Church Christianity, where it is regarded as a dangerous and competitive tendency.

---

[21]On Buddhism alone there were in the English language, as late as 1939, well over 2000 works listed in March's *Buddhist Bibliography*. London, 1935, with supplements for 1936–1939. The *Bibliographie Bouddhique*, comp. Jean Przyluski (Paris, 1928–1933), and the *Deutsche Bibliographie des Buddhismus*, comp. Hans Ludwig Held (Munich, 1916), list as many more in both French and German, and other European languages.

[22]In the realm of literature alone the influence may be noted in the work of some of our most outstanding writers—W. H. Auden, Aldous Huxley, Somerset Maugham, Pearl Buck, and, going back earlier, Thoreau and Emerson. Several Oriental writers are widely read today, including Tagore, Lin Yu-tang, and the translations of Chinese and Japanese classics by Arthur Waley. In the realm of psychology the debt of C. G. Jung of Zürich to Oriental philosophy is well known, and through him has had a far-reaching effect on other European psychologists.

This is a symptom of the interior weakness and uncertainty of Church religion, for in the great ages of Christian thought theology has always been able to embrace and absorb alien systems much to its own enrichment. In fact, every great advance in Christian theology has involved the absorption of an alien philosophy, to mention only the debt of Origen, Clement and St. Augustine to Platonism and Neo-Platonism and of St. Thomas Aquinas to Aristotle. It is not too much to predict that the next great step in Christian theology will be due, in part, to the absorption of Hinduism, Buddhism, Taoism, and, perhaps, Mohammedan Sufiism, all of which are profoundly *mystical* religions.[23]

If these are the factors which are likely to shape the next phase of Christian life and thought, what will the general character of this phase be, and with what main problems will it have to deal? As already suggested, the nature and work of the period will be, firstly, the *synthesis* of former trends, and, secondly, the interior understanding and mystical interpretation of the original mythos—the translation of symbol into living experience. The factors at work imply this direction, the needs demand it, and the general patterns of the growth of cultures make it highly probable.

Let us look, first, at some of the trends demanding

---

[23]With the exception of the earlier Jesuit scholars, the work of Christian writers in comparative religion has been of a rather superficial character. The object of most of it has been to minimize the spiritual insights of other religions in comparison with those of Christianity. Where this is the purpose, such writers invariably reveal their failure to understand these alien religions. Thus the manuals of comparative religion studied in theological schools are full of blatant misrepresentations, such as the favourite trick of dismissing Taoism as a mere lazy quietism by translating the term *wu-wei* (which denotes the psychological character of the mystical state) as "doing nothing." The Advaita philosophy of the *Upanishads* and the Ch'an (Zen) Buddhism of China are termed mere pantheism, a conclusion which reveals nothing but the writer's ignorance.

synthesis. We begin, obviously, with the thesis and the antithesis which have dominated our culture to this point—Catholicism on the one hand and Humanism and Protestantism on the other. These represent respectively the life-giving mythos which is at the root of our culture, a symbolic apprehension of revelation of the deepest spiritual realities, and the negative movement which destroys the outward shell of the mythos in order that we may be conscious of the inner content. Within these two complementary opposites there are others, not always or necessarily coterminous with them, but none the less fundamental problems for our culture and for human life as a whole.

There is the tension already mentioned between holiness and physical existence, which is expressed in the conflict between mediaeval Catholic ascetic-mysticism and Humanism, or between Protestant puritanism and liberal romanticism. Herein lies the basic moral problem of Christian life. Related to it is the opposition of transcendentalism and immanentism, finding expression in a whole complex of conflicts—official theology versus mysticism, spiritualism versus sacramentalism, traditional Catholicism versus Humanism, Manichaeism versus the religion of the Incarnation. While it has received full attention from both mediaeval and modern philosophers, the solutions offered are of the nature of compromise rather than synthesis.

Again, there is the familiar tension between law and grace, works and faith, discipline and spontaneity, technique and inspiration, a synthesis of which is of the utmost importance for the living of the moral and spiritual life. Allied to it, as well as to the opposition of transcendentalism and immanentism, is another complex of tensions—between formal religion and formless religion, between liturgical, ritual worship and the simple "practice of the presence of God," between life lived in terms of religion and religion lived in terms of life.

Philosophy alone, theology alone, will never solve these problems; they can succeed only in so far as they are the instruments of the mystical life, of the realization of union with God. There remains, then, the supreme work of the epoch that lies ahead—the interior understanding of the great Christian symbols that the divine life which they contain may become conscious, that the Catholic mythos may reveal the secrets of union with God. Lest there be any misunderstanding, it must be made perfectly clear that in using the terms "symbol" and "mythos" we do not imply that Christian dogma is *mere* symbol and *mere* myth. We are not suggesting that the literal interpretation of the Faith should be replaced by a mystical interpretation, but that the mystical must come out of the literal and exist in addition to it. We are not concerned to discuss here the historicity of the great events of the life of Christ, nor whether or not he was in fact the incarnate Son of God. Granting all those events and all the claims which the Church makes for Christ to be factually true, they are still symbols. They are symbolic events revealing the nature of God and of the way in which man realizes union with God.

After all, the important thing about Christ was not his exterior appearance but his inner character. So, too, the important thing about events is not how they happened but what they mean. Indeed, it could possibly be maintained that even if the whole story of Christ and all the dogmas of the Church about him were pure myth, none the less it would be a myth implanted in the human soul by God, arising out of the racial unconscious under the guidance of the Holy Spirit. But it still would have to be maintained that the myth was the work of God, and not a purely subjective wish-fulfilment dream of strictly human origin.[24] An enormous amount of spiritual energy is wasted and Christian unity lost in argument as to whether these symbolic events actually happened. Granted that this is an important question; but it is so much more important to understand what they mean, and if unbelievers could be enlightened as to the inner meaning of these events they would be far more ready than otherwise to accept their factual truth.

The whole purpose of the symbol and the mythos, which is the system of symbols, is to lead us to God himself, just as the purpose of language is to convey meaning and not mere words. God—the Meaning alike of the universe and the mythos—is alive; like wind, like moving waters, like fire, he cannot be grasped in some rigid form. Thus the symbolic form conveys the life of God as the acorn conveys an oak. In time, if the acorn is alive, its shell will burst; the living tree will grow out of it, and refuse to be enclosed in a shell any more. Likewise, God gives his life to men in symbols and sacraments, but if that life is to be truly lively, it will not stay confined in those forms or in any others. It will use forms; it will express itself in forms; but it will not be held in forms.

Herein is the great difficulty in passing from the sym-

---

[24]It is strange that liberal Protestants who deny the historicity of such events as the Resurrection and the Virgin Birth as well as the actual Godhead of Christ have never made anything of this theory. They still insist on basing their religion on historical facts, however reduced in richness. Yet in order to make a case for their very impoverished form of religion (which they seem to want to do), they are logically bound to show not only that Catholicism is unhistorical, but also that, as a myth, it is not a divine revelation.

bol and the idea to God himself. It is that God is pure life, and we are terrified of such life because we cannot hold it or possess it, and we do not know what it will do to us. "It is a terrible thing to fall into the hands of the living God." Therefore we are always trying to possess God, it may be in some state of exalted feeling, or perhaps in some neat little theological formula, or even in a ritual act which we can perform—or leave alone. In just the same way we are always hanging on grimly to our own lives, protecting ourselves with all kinds of conventions, securities, habit-mechanisms, prejudices and hopes. But the more we hang on, the more we fail to live. The more sedulously we avoid death, the more certainly we avoid life. We are scared stiff to awaken to the truth that we are being swept along by the life of God as in a mighty torrent; that it sweeps us away from our possessions and our very selves to carry us out to the ocean of God himself. Therefore we cling desperately to floating logs or swim with all our might against the stream, not seeing that this effects nothing but our own discomfort and exhaustion.

The symbol reveals God, but wrongly used it hides him. An idea, a doctrine, a sacrament, a spiritual exercise hides God when we use it as a means to hold him —that is, when we use it monkey-fashion as a comfortable and convenient technique for acquiring sanctity by imitation. Used in this way religion becomes a series of conventional ideas, conventional feelings, conventional spirituality and conventional good deeds utterly divorced from real life, which is to say God on the one hand, and on the other—walking, eating, breathing, digging potatoes, writing letters, watching birds, feeling sick, loving your wife and children, and taking a bath. "Every moment," wrote Dom John Chapman, "is the message of God's will; every external event, every-thing outside us, and even every involuntary thought and feeling within us is God's own touch." But we are scared of that touch; it may burn; it may kill. Therefore let it be circumscribed in a conventional religious pattern. Instead of laying ourselves open to full mystical possession by God the reality, instead of trusting ourselves to the living Spirit as he gives himself to us in every moment, we cling desperately to these symbols and idols, setting up new ones of our own making when the old are broken.

The symbol is the seed of the divine life, and so long as man is himself a seed, a child in his mother's protection, he *must* have the symbol. And the symbol must continue to exist because there will always be souls needing their religion in this form. But for the thousands and thousands of souls living in the modern world who have passed beyond that stage, what is true of the seed in the Gospel is true of the Catholic symbolism—"Except a grain of corn fall into the ground and die, it abideth alone. But if it die, it bringeth forth much fruit." Or, in the words of St. Paul, "That which thou sowest is not quickened, except it die."

To the literalist, the obscurantist, the idolater of symbols, that is of course shocking. Yet the disciples of Christ were similarly shocked when he likened himself to the grain of corn that must die. "We have heard out of the law," they protested, "that Christ abideth for ever: and how sayest thou, The Son of Man must be lifted up?" We, too, have heard from the "law" that the Catholic faith as interpreted and understood "officially" will remain for ever the most complete exposition of the mysteries of God that may be found on earth. That is true enough if we add—the most complete *symbolic* exposition. But for countless souls—not for all—those symbols must die or have already died that they may bear the fruit which is their own meaning, that they may release the life of God which is in them. Thus the losses, the attacks, the weakening of faith, which the Church has suffered are a sharing in the Passion of Christ. The faith of Christians in the rigid symbolic forms of dogma is shaken and shattered that their living content may be discovered—that through this *bodily* death the Church and its faith may "rise with Christ" in a spiritualized body. For as the mortal body is to the body of the Resurrection, so is symbolic faith to mystical realization.

Symbols are destroyed for us through the mercy of God in order that we may not rest content with anything less than his own divine essence, however holy that thing may be. Even the divine humanity of Christ had to be destroyed on the Cross, and the dogmatic symbols of the Church are not more holy than that. When the time of destruction comes the opportunity which it offers is altogether missed if one grasps around for new symbols or tries to patch up the old. It has been necessary for Western man, for Christendom, to go through with this passion to the bitter depth of "My God, my God, why hast thou forsaken me," to the sense that his life is utterly meaningless. For just as the Church relives the life of Christ through the liturgical year, so the Church relives it again and again in the spirit. Thus as Christ was crucified, and as his divine humanity rose again and ascended into heaven, so the dogmatic symbols are destroyed only to rise again spiritualized and to ascend to a higher level of meaning. For "it is expedient for you that I go away: for if I go not away, the Comforter will not come unto you; but if

I depart, I will send him unto you. . . . When he, the Spirit of truth, is come, he will guide you into all truth."[25]

At the close of the twelfth century Joachim of Flora conceived the idea that the history of the Church was divided into three dispensations or ages—the Age of the Father, which was the age of the Old Covenant of the Hebrew, the Age of the Son, which was to run from the birth of Christ until 1200, to be followed by the Age of the Holy Spirit, an age of mystical illumination in which, as a mediaeval monk might be expected to imagine, all Christians would take to cowl and cloister. The idea was, of course, a rather crude generalization and simplification of a certain truth, namely, that in the development of cultures periods do arise which might be termed "ages of the Holy Spirit," which is to say periods of spiritual maturity. Thus the era of childhood, when man is under the rule of the parental mythos, might be called the age of the Father, and the era of adolescence, when man comes into his own and feels his independence, is in a certain sense the age of the Son, during which, incidentally, the worship of the human Jesus came into prominence. It can hardly be applied more generally than this to the whole history of the Church or of the human race, as these do not move in a linear progression, nor in a steadily ascending spiral. The Church embodies a constant mythos which evolves in accordance with the life-movement of the *culture* to which it is attached.

But in terms of Western culture and Western Chris-

---

[25]John 16:7 and 13. As originally used, the word "comfort" did not have its present meaning, for a seventeenth-century document speaks of the schoolmaster who "comforts" his boys with a stick. Thus the Holy Spirit as the Paraclete, the Comforter, is a rousing force, the one who puts fire in the soul.

tianity it does seem highly probable that in the epoch ahead we shall think of God more and more as the Holy Spirit. It is significant that thus far the theology of the Holy Spirit is in a most undeveloped state. He is, as it were, the unknown Person of the Holy Trinity, for hitherto our attention has been focussed primarily on the Father and the Son. Few indeed in the Missal and the Breviary are prayers addressed to the Holy Spirit when compared with those to the Father and the Son.[26] When we consider the enormous number of theological works on the Fatherhood of God and on the problems of Christology, it is amazing to see how few have been devoted to the Holy Spirit. Likewise, from the standpoint of popular devotion, the Holy Spirit has had little attention because his symbol is the dove, which cannot be taken too seriously. The popular mind has no concrete picture of him as it has of the Father, the Son and the Virgin Mary.

Mystical religion, however, is the special province of the Holy Spirit, and in a certain sense the God of the mystics is the Holy Spirit, formless but fiery, impossible to picture or conceive but dynamic in effect.[27] To this extent an epoch of mystical religion will be an age of the Holy Spirit. Writing of future trends in his recent history of Catholic art and culture, E. I. Watkin says:

---

[26]Thus the Latin Mass has no definite Epiklesis or invocation of the Holy Spirit in the prayer of consecration. The more mystical Christianity of the Eastern Church regards the Epiklesis as an essential part of the consecration.

[27]Cf. Pascal's *Memorial:* "The year of grace 1654, Monday the twenty-third of November, St. Clement's Day . . . from about half past ten in the evening until about half-an-hour after midnight—FIRE. God of Abraham. God of Isaac. God of Jacob, not of the philosophers and the learned. Certainty; certainty; feeling; joy; peace. . . . Forgetfulness of the world and of everything other than God." Bremond, *Histoire Littéraire du Sentiment Religieux en France.* Paris, 1916–1928, vol. iv, pp. 359 *et seq.*

God's presence and work in nature and man must be brought into greater prominence than in the past. This immanental operation, however, is, as we have seen, appropriated to the Holy Ghost. We are therefore to look for a dispensation of the Holy Spirit. . . . Catholic truth will be grasped from within, not only by a contemplative minority but generally by the members of the Church. Doctrines will no longer be accepted solely on authority and stored unused in the mind. They will be vitally assimilated and practically lived. That is to say, contemplation will be spread throughout the Church and with it mystical experience.[28]

Because this epoch will reinterpret the mediaeval mythos, Berdyaev, who observes the same tendency of events, terms it the "New Middle Ages."

Thus modern history draws to an end, giving place to a new era which I have called by analogy the New Middle Ages. And in order to integrate himself anew, man must submit himself once more to a higher power. Certain aspects of mediaeval asceticism must be revived in a new form in order to allow the human personality to reveal itself again, and in order that the Christian ideal so essentially a part of man's universal historical destiny might still prove a guiding light. *We must now experience immanently what the Middle Ages had experienced transcendentally.*[29]

The beginnings of this epoch are already among us, but because they are the work of the Spirit we cannot force their growth. At least, however, we can begin to try to understand. We can lay aside the petty pursuits, the small-minded notions, and the trifling quarrels in which modern Church religion is involved, and, through the fellowship of the interior life, cut across

[28]*Catholic Art and Culture*, pp. 201–202.
[29]Berdyaev, *The Meaning of History*. Trs. George Reavey. London and New York, 1936, p. 181. The italics are mine.

political and ecclesiastical boundaries and penetrate beneath the external surface of doctrine. At least we can stop prattling about the minutiae of polity, order and liturgy, and in our conferences make sure that we understand what we mean by the great fundamentals —God, the Incarnation, and the life of Prayer—since a thousand obvious differences about minor points are rooted in a few unconscious differences about major principles. At least we can cease from the interminable sermonizing about ethics and politics and small morality, and tell the people in human speech, as distinct from theological algebra, that the Church is where one comes to find union with God. Above all we can ask the Holy Spirit to open our minds to the realization of the truth from which all the joy and power of Christianity proceeds, the truth of the Word made flesh—that the eternal life of God is *given* to man here and now in the "flesh" of each moment's experience.

II. THE GIFT OF UNION

To be alive spiritually man must have union with God and must be conscious of it. Apart from this union his religious life will be an empty drudgery, a mere imitation of true spirituality. But there is no formal technique whereby man can attain either the union or its conscious realization. God, the infinite life, cannot be grasped in forms. Because union with God is the goal, the very meaning, of human existence, its apparent absence shows a radical defect in our nature—a defect whose clear symptom is precisely our attempt to *possess* God in so many different ways. When the finite tries to embrace the infinite it must be radically selfish and proud, not to say ridiculous. Yet the very fact that we desire God so urgently is the sign that we are made for him, however twisted and perverted the desire may be. Here is the essence of our spiritual problem to which, as we have said, the Christian solution is the Incarnation.

Throughout the history of Christianity the implications of the Incarnation have, relatively speaking, been so little understood and so consistently resisted that its true meaning is largely obscured. The inner meaning, the spiritual reality, which the Incarnation expresses, is of the essence of true spirituality wherever it may be found and under whatever external form it may be apprehended. The Christ is a cosmic and omnipresent reality which is always involved in higher religion under whatever name he may be known. For the real Name of Christ, the only Name under heaven whereby men may be saved, is not, of course, the literal composite of sounds J-E-S-U-S, but the spiritual and universal reality incarnate in Jesus. We have to see, then, why this reality is necessary for man's union with God and what is its nature.

I

Human desire differs from animal desire in that it is at root insatiable. Man is characterized by a hunger for the infinite, for an eternity of life, love and joy which, whether he knows it or not, can be nothing other than God. Assuming that God exists, it will follow that God is man's true end, for the appetite of a living organism shows its function. The stomach hungers for food because its function is to digest food. As physical taste and hunger may often be mistaken as to their true object, desiring nothing but caviar instead of a balanced diet, man is often mistaken as to the goal of his life, desiring wealth, power or physical pleasure instead of God. But his real appetite continues to be God, for which these lesser goals are always unsatisfactory substitutes. Those who set their hearts on finite goals are always discontented; they must always have more and more and more of what they desire, and failing this are frustrated and miserable. Profound content is only enjoyed by animals and primitives, in whom infinite hunger has not been awakened, and by the saints and mystics who have realized union with God. Thus it is that, known or unknown, God is the ultimate object of human desire, whether that desire is highly spiritual or grossly sensual. "Even in the midst of the lowest pleasures, the most abandoned voluptuary is still seeking God; nay more, as far as regards what is positive in his acts, that is to say in all that makes them an analogue of the true Love, it is God Himself who, in him and for him, seeks Himself."[1]

Assuming, further, that God is love, the goal of love is always union with its object. If man is therefore a creation and an object of the divine love, union with God is likewise the true end of man from the divine standpoint. From this same standpoint, the true end of all creatures—not man alone—is union with God, but only in man has the end become conscious. Only man can love God consciously; other creatures are drawn towards him blindly, and have no will in the matter.

The conscious love of God is only possible for a free soul. In one sense man loves God inevitably because the finite naturally and necessarily hungers or moves towards the infinite. But by its own power it can never reach or embrace the infinite; however far you may climb and soar, you can never touch the sky. Though natural love (*eros*) points to God, he is beyond its reach. But man is capable of another kind of love which can reach to God, and this, following Nygren's useful distinction, we will call *agape*.[2] The difference between the two is that whereas *eros* is a possessive hunger, a desire to swallow God, *agape* is the free, conscious and deliberate desire to give oneself to God. Man is capable of both *eros* and *agape*, for he desires both to magnify

---

[1] Etienne Gilson, *The Spirit of Mediaeval Philosophy*. London, 1936, p. 274.

[2] The use of the terms *eros* and *agape* to denote these two kinds of love is purely modern. In both classical and *koine* Greek the words do not carry this distinction, and in the Johannine literature *agape* is used of both types of love. Cf. John 3:16 and 1 John 2:15. For the full discussion see Nygren *Agape and Eros*. 3 vols. London, 1932, 1938 and 1939.

himself and to lose himself, to swallow the infinite and to plunge into the infinite. But such absolute self-surrender is a power of freedom alone. Love under compulsion is *eros*—never *agape*—which is why a successful marriage could never be contracted under the influence of an aphrodisiac. The consent for so deep a union of souls must be willing. Since, therefore, man is capable of *agape*, the type of union with God for which he is destined is of a peculiarly high order, a union of mutual love, a spiritual marriage. The union of man with God is to be voluntary on both sides. The union of lesser creatures with God is voluntary on God's side alone. But *eros* cannot reach its goal without *agape*.

When we say that man is made in the image of God, we mean that he is free. This is one of the deepest of human intuitions, and it can only be denied at the price of surrendering rational thought. If you argue that you have no freedom, you imply that you are *compelled* to argue in this way, and that thus your opinion is not a free and rational decision but a compulsive mechanism of no more significance than a nervous tic. All rational thought and action assume a relative freedom of will.

The freedom to love God, to give oneself to God, involves also the freedom not to love. If the free soul refuses *agape*, it gives itself up to the domination of *eros*, which, though not evil in itself, becomes evil when chosen freely in preference to *agape*. Man falls when he chooses natural hunger instead of spiritual love as the principle of his life; he subjects his freedom, his very spirit, to the insatiable, ever-frustrated yearning of his natural soul, and becomes temporarily incapable of *agape*. For *agape* is God; *agape* in man is God in man, and once God is refused it is impossible to love

God, since God can only be loved with his own power and his own love, dwelling in the human soul.

All the problems, all the evil of human life rise from this refusal to love God, and we can no more say when this first happened than why it happened. We only know that we are now in a state of evil, that our freedom to love God is inhibited and is completely under the power of *eros*. We cannot possibly say why man chose not to love God because, when we ask this question, we are looking for a sufficient and necessary cause for the refusal. But the refusal was a free act, and in the realm of freedom there are no necessary causes because there is no necessity, no determinism. The principle of evil, the refusal to love God, is an entirely free, spontaneous and original action.[3] To say that it is caused by pride is only to say that it is pride.

This, of course, is not a solution to the problem of the origin of evil. There is no known solution to that problem, and speculation concerning it is of no practical consequence. To understand the origin of evil is not to be free from evil. The origin lies within ourselves, and we can no more seek it out and examine it than we can turn round and look straight into our own eyes.

Our concern is with the present results of this refusal, and these are all too familiar. We know from experience that there is absolutely nothing which we ourselves can do to love God, to surrender ourselves with absolute trust and devotion into his hands. For every attempt we make to give ourselves to God is frustrated by a selfish motive. All our efforts at a spiritual life are prompted by self-interest.

---

[3] It is analogous to God's own creative action, since man's freedom is a delegation of the very freedom of God. Evil is an act which the creature commits with God's own power. He must use God to refuse God.

The original sin—pride, refusal to give ourselves to God, self-love, putting ourselves in God's place at the center of the universe—immediately confronts us with the gulf, the opposition, between ourselves and all that is not ourselves. When man tries to usurp the throne of God, all creation, all other men, strive to drag him down. Thus in the Eden myth, as soon as Adam had eaten the fruit he became aware of his own loneliness and nakedness, and God pronounced upon him the curse which was simply a description of the inevitable conflict between self-centered man and nature. "Cursed is the ground for thy sake; in sorrow shalt thou eat of it all the days of thy life; thorns also and thistles shall it bring forth to thee."

The consequence of pride is therefore fear, fear of losing one's beloved self. God and nature seem to conspire together to deprive us of ourselves, the one out of love and the other out of obedience to God, and in fear of the loss we cling to ourselves with all our might, strangling the breath out of our bodies in the effort. But fear is suffering; fear threatens our pride; we would like to be without fear and suffering. The saints tell us that fear may be overcome by faith and love, by giving ourselves wholly to God. And so we try to follow their advice, but pride remains the motive. We give ourselves to God in order to protect ourselves, in order to flatter ourselves not only with the possession of God's power and glory, but also of his love and humility. Ambition ceases to be worldly and becomes spiritual; but it is still ambition.

Thus we find ourselves in a vicious circle. Our nature is selfish, and we can no more change this nature than we can lift ourselves up by our own belts. We are the "wrong man," and as is said in a Chinese treatise on the spiritual life, "When the wrong man uses the right means, the right means work in the wrong way."[4] Trying to escape fear, we run into the vicious circle of being afraid of fear—worrying because we worry because we worry; trying to escape pride we become proud of our humility; trying to escape sin we repent because guilt injures our self-conceit. Hence all our attempts at spiritual life end up as imitation and monkey business because we do not have the one thing that makes spiritual life possible and meaningful—union with God. And we do not have it because we have refused it. How are we to accept it? Why do we want to accept it? It always comes back to pride.

Egoism is like trying to swim without relying on the water, endeavouring to keep afloat by tugging at your own legs; your whole body becomes tense, and you sink like a stone. Swimming requires a certain relaxation, a certain giving of yourself to the water, and similarly spiritual life demands a relaxation of the soul to God. Thus Hindu philosophy speaks of egoism as *sankhocha*, a contraction or tension in the soul, and if it is hard to relax the superficial tensions of jumpy nerves and insomnia, it is impossible to relax by any contrivance of our own a tension which grips the very core of our being. This entire state of inescapable selfishness, blended of pride and consequent fear, this total inability to give ourselves without reservation to God is what the Church terms the fallen state of man—bondage under the sin of Adam. Those who have developed any profound degree of self-knowledge are so acutely aware of this predicament that it brings them often to utter despair.

⁴Jung and Wilhelm, *The Secret of the Golden Flower*. London and New York, 1931, p. 70.

The formal teaching of the Church is that we are released from the sin of Adam by the Incarnation, which is the assumption of our human nature by the Logos, God the Son, who as Jesus of Nazareth lives a life and dies a death wherein this human nature is perfectly surrendered to the divine will. As a result of this perfect surrender, the humanity of Jesus is transfigured and wholly informed by the Godhead, and, united with Life itself, it rises from the grave and ascends into heaven. The Incarnation is of effect for us men because Christ's human nature is our nature, and because Christ introduced a new life, a new power, into that nature which made it capable of perfect surrender to God. We become possessors of that power by incorporation into the new human race which he began, the race which is his own divinized humanity extended in his Mystical Body the Church. In Christ, God did for man what man could not do for himself: God as man offered our human nature to the Father in a perfect sacrifice which effected the union (At-one-ment) of man with God, making us heirs of his own eternal life and his adopted sons. Generally speaking, the modern mind finds statements such as these almost wholly meaningless. They seem to bring a mythological complexity into the spiritual life which, even though it may have some deep meaning, is more of a nuisance than a help, and to involve the study and acceptance of a mass of historical details which we are in no position to verify. Surely, if God is in fact love and wills our salvation with his whole being, he could have contrived our redemption in a less tortuous way.

It is obvious, however, that in the past this same story has been of the highest significance for innumerable souls. The reason, as we have seen, is that at certain stages of his development and at certain levels of his nature man can only grasp spiritual reality in terms of mythos. But when the time comes for him to understand the naked reality behind the symbol, the symbol itself appears confusing and unessential. When, however, the inner reality is seen, the symbol again appears logical and meaningful although its function changes. We have therefore to discover the meaning of the Incarnation.

I I

There are two ways of reaching the house next door. One is to travel all the way round the globe; the other is to walk a few feet. There are two ways of finding the heavens. One is to journey upwards and upwards in quest of an ever-receding firmament; the other is to realize that here on earth you are already in the heavens and that our planet is in fact one of the company of celestial bodies. It is easy to get lost on the way round the world to the house next door, and easier still to fall into despair at the hopeless task of climbing to an infinite height. These two ways of approach are exemplified again and again in the history of man's spiritual life. There have been religions such as Primitive Buddhism, Neo-Platonism, certain forms of Yoga, Gnosticism, and the like which have stressed the arduous ascent of man to the divine state. These are religions of *eros,* of man's infinite hunger for God. Their ideal state is normally an attainment of identity with the ultimate Reality in which the soul, as it were, swallows God. On the other hand, there are religions which stress the *given-ness* of union with God, and these conceive the spiritual life as the acceptance and affirmation of a present reality. Such are religions of *agape, religiones naturaliter Christianae*, and include many forms of Mahayana Buddhism and of Hinduism, early Taoism, and, of course, Christianity itself. Where these religions tend to a pantheistic theology they contain no explicit statement of the given-ness of union with God since pantheism implies that union with God is necessary and automatic. They do, however, state that union does not have to be attained but realized, because it is a present reality from the very beginning. In other words, they have experienced the love of God for man, but lack a theology to express and interpret it.

Quite frequently the first type of religion turns into the second. The soul striving to attain the divine state by its own efforts falls into total despair, and suddenly there dawns upon it with a great illuminative shock the realization that the divine state simply IS, here and now, and does not have to be attained. For example, the Zen Buddhism of China and Japan has produced an entire technique of meditation involving these two phases, and terms the sudden shock wherewith the first turns into the second *satori*, or sudden awakening.[5] The Incarnation, the coming of Christ, is *satori* on the plane of human history, the sudden change from the old order of striving for redemption through obedience to the law, to the new order of redemption through the gift of divine grace.

> While all things were in quiet silence, and that night was in the midst of her swift course, thine Almighty Word, O Lord, leaped down out of the royal throne, alleluia.[6]

---

[5] D. T. Suzuki has reproduced many interesting first-hand accounts of this process in his *Essays in Zen Buddhism,* vol. ii. London, 1933. Essay on "The Koan Exercise," pp. 1–165.

[6] Antiphon on the Magnificat at Vespers on Sunday within the Octave on the Nativity.

In the midst of the soul's dark night of despair at the frustration of *eros*, there dawns the *agape* of God—the realization that although the soul is powerless to attain union with God, God out of unchangeable and infinite love has given union with himself to the soul.

The meaning of the Incarnation, therefore, is simply that we do not have to *attain* union with God. Man does not have to climb to the infinite and become God, because, out of love, the infinite God descends to the finite and becomes man. Despite man's refusal of God, despite his pride, his fear, his helpless and hopeless involvement in the vicious circle of sin, God's nature remains unalterably love—the *agape* which consists in giving oneself wholly and without reservation to the beloved. Therefore the eternal Word, the Logos, becomes flesh, making our nature his nature; he assumes our limitations, suffers our pains and dies our death. More than this, he bears the burden of our sins: that is, he remains in union with us even though we crucify him and spit on him; he continues to dwell within us and to offer, or sacrifice, our lives to God even though we commit every imaginable form of depravity. In short, God has wedded himself to humanity, has united his divine essence with our inmost being "for better for worse, for richer for poorer, in sickness and in health" for all eternity, even though we elect to be damned.

If I ascend up into heaven, thou art there;
If I make my bed in hell, behold, thou are there also.

All that remains for us to do is to say, "Yes—Amen" to this tremendous fact, and this is still within the power of our fallen nature. Our motive for saying it, however perverted by pride and fear, makes not the least difference, because the fact is the fact: we have been given union with God whether we like it or not, want it or not, know it or not. Our flesh has become his flesh, and we cannot jump out of our own skins. And once we realize the futility of our pride, that we can neither ascend to God nor, by reason of pride, prevent his descent to us, the proud core of egoism is simply dissolved—overwhelmed by God's love. The function of Christian morality and spirituality is not to earn or deserve this gift of eternal life, but rather to appreciate and express it. The saint is holy not to attain union with God, but to give thanks for it. For this union is not, as in pantheism, a necessary and automatic and inherent fact of our being; it is an entirely free, spontaneous and unnecessary gift of the living and loving God, since the heart of Being is not law and mechanism but life. Hell consists not in being deprived of union, but in wilful failure to appreciate it; in a state of soul so perverse that the love and the gift of union are so repulsive that they appear not as the light of glory but as a terrible and consuming fire. The flames of hell are, in fact, the inescapable love of God.[7]

This truth of our given union with God is precisely the "good news," the Gospel, of Christianity, however much it may have been weakened and obscured through theological timidity and obscurity in the passage of time. "As many as received (*i.e.*, accepted) him," says St. John in the prologue to his Gospel, "to them gave he authority to be the children (or, sons) of God." The phrase son or child of God does not mean creature of God but one who is of the same nature as God, in St. Peter's words, "partakers of the divine na-

---

[7]This is the clear implication of St. Catherine of Genoa's eschatological doctrine. See von Hügel's *Mystical Element of Religion.* London, 1927, vol. i, pp. 281–294. But see below, pp. 243–244.

ture." Still more plainly is the nature of the gift described in St. John's report of Christ's prayer at the Last Supper: "That they all may be one, as thou, Father, art in me, and I in thee, that they also may be one in us. . . . And the glory which thou gavest me I *have given* them; that they may be one even as we are one: I in them, and thou in me, that they may be made perfect in one; and that the world may know that thou hast sent me, and hast loved them as thou hast loved me . . . for thou lovedst me before the foundation of the world. . . . And I have given them knowledge of thy Name, and will make it known, that the love wherewith thou hast loved me may be in them, and I in them."[8]

That nothing can be done to escape from this union is the meaning of St. Paul's celebrated words: "For I am persuaded that neither death, nor life, nor angels, nor principalities, nor powers, nor things present, nor things to come, nor height, nor depth, nor any other creature, shall be able to separate us from the love of God, which is in Christ Jesus our Lord."[9] The gift of union with God, known as the indwelling Holy Spirit who makes his temple in our bodies, was the major source of the tremendous enthusiasm of the Primitive Church—an enthusiasm lacking in our own day because the whole force of this truth has been obscured. For so many centuries Church teaching has said little or nothing about the gift of union with God to each

---

[8]John 17:21–26. The "glory" which Christ has given them is of course the *shekinah*. which in the later Judaism of the time of Jesus had come to mean something very close to the divine essence. "It does not indicate the radiance or brilliance, but *the central cause of the radiance.*" Marshall in *HDB*, vol. iv, art. *Shekinah*. Note also that they have been given God's love which in Johannine theology is God himself, and further that they have been given knowledge of the Name of God, which, in later Judaism, again signified God himself. To know the Name of God is to share in the divine power and life.
[9]Romans 8:38–39.

individual soul and body, that the Christian religion has become a horribly timid and watered-down affair. We are given only "grace," considered as a somewhat arbitrary hand-out of an impersonal power for goodness from a distant deity. Or else the union is watered down by distribution, as when it is said that it is given only to the Church as a whole, rather than to each individual member of the Church—in absolute contradiction to Christ's clear teaching that every individual soul is an object of the Father's love. "Are not two sparrows sold for a farthing? And one of them shall not fall on the ground without your Father. But the very hairs of your head are all numbered. Fear ye not therefore; ye are of more value than many sparrows."[10] Salvation, heaven, eternal life has been discussed as something to be bought and sold at the price of so much virtue and merit, something which you may possibly "get" in the future because, propitiated by Christ's sacrifice, God has at last agreed to sell it to you for a stiff fee. Christianity has thus degenerated into a system of morality with remote eschatological sanctions, and in practice is therefore a religion largely bereft of joy and power.

The Incarnation is of effect for each and all, in every time and place, because as an historical and local event it is the projection into time and space of an eternal and universal reality. It occurs not only at a distance of two thousand years in Palestine, but within all human nature, all human beings, past, present and future. In the words of St. John's prologue, the Logos "was the true light which, coming into the world, enlightens *every* man. He was in the world, and the world was made by him, and the world knew him not." For this reason,

---

[10]Matthew 10:29–31.

whenever and wherever men have known or glimpsed the gift of union with God, the power of the Incarnation has been at work. The predisposition and action of God towards humanity is ever the same, for his nature does not change, and an event in time and space does not alter his attitude to us; it simply reveals his attitude. B.C. and A.D., the grace and power of the Incarnation was always available, the truth of given union with God was always true. But to be communicated fully to creatures with spatial and temporal minds it had to be projected into a spatial and temporal event, and as such it had, of necessity, to be projected into some *particular* place and time.

The vast majority of human beings have always had very concrete and childlike minds, and there are levels at which even the most highly intelligent people are still children. To get an abstract, universal or spiritual truth into the understanding of a child one must make it concrete, and the best way to do so is to illustrate it with a story. Because God intends the gift of union and its realization for *all* men, and not merely for an esoteric elite, he therefore embodies the gift in a story, a mythos, which is acted out in real life—in Palestine under the governership of Pontius Pilate. Universal realities are hard to perceive because of the vastness of their extent; to be brought to our attention they must be localized. The air is all around us, but we do not notice it until the wind blows.

The Christ, the gift of union, was made concrete flesh for a still deeper reason: not only that it might be grasped by our concrete minds, but also to demonstrate that union with God is given to us as material as well as spiritual beings, to the body as well as to the soul. Physical life is therefore not at all inconsistent with spiritual life. Almost without exception the religions of *eros* have despised the body, and Christianity has despised the body to the extent that it has been contaminated with Gnosticism, Neo-Platonism and Manichaeism, to the extent that Christians have resisted the Incarnation and fallen back under the spell of *eros*. For the infinite hunger of *eros* eventually finds the body an intolerable limitation. When physical pride and ambition give place to spiritual pride, man longs to *be* the infinite and tries to throw off the chains of matter. This is why all *eros*-mysticism is world-despising and has no place in a sacramental and incarnational religion.

But God, being without any trace of pride, loves the material element which he has created, and finds it in no way inconsistent with his spiritual dignity and purity to stoop to unite himself with the earth, with flesh and blood. Thus to accept the gift of union we do not have to cease to be men and become angels; we do not have to throw off our material limitations, denying our senses and bodies, for the Word was made *flesh* and our *bodies* are temples of the Holy Spirit.

This strongly materialistic aspect of Christianity has always been a stumbling block to those who prided themselves in having "purely spiritual" religions, and, as we have seen, this kind of pride has appeared so repeatedly in the history of mystical religion that in many minds mysticism is necessarily associated with it. But if mysticism is the consciousness of union with God, this is in no way inconsistent with physical life if it is true that God has given himself to our flesh.[11]

[11] The materialism of Christianity is of course quite different from the supposed "materialism" of modern civilization, which is in fact not materialism at all but sensationalism—the quest for psychic thrills. The modern

These two essential principles of the Incarnation—the localization of the universal and the union of God with matter—are continued as a witness to and extension of the Incarnation in the sacramental system of the Church. The whole mystery of the Mass, for example, the intimate union of the Godhead with simple bread and wine, revolves around these two truths, and is of course despised as a "materialistic" and superstitious rite by those who do not appreciate God's love of the material world. Bread and wine are employed in the Mass because they are, or used to be, our staple food and drink, the sources of our material life, and thus the representative symbols of that life. By the Incarnation this life, together with the pain and death involved in it, is made one with God and taken up into heaven. Thus the Mass is an *anamnesis*, a re-calling from eternity to the present, not only of Christ's death and passion, but also of his "glorious resurrection and ascension." The Body of Christ, the Host and the Church, is his risen and ascended Body.

For the gift of union with God means that our mental and physical space-time life is given the dimension of eternity. Death is the end of our life in terms of space and time, just as the head of a hammer is an end of the hammer in terms of space. But as the hammer endures through time, with both ends present, so, despite our "ends"—our birth and death in time, we endure through eternity because God has added that dimen-

<hr>

world is, on the contrary, highly contemptuous of matter and treats this holy substance disgracefully. It indulges in vast material waste, covers the earth with hideous material structures, and eats, dresses, works and lives with a minimum of material refinement. It should be noted that the real alcoholic, for example, drinks for the sake of a psychic stimulation and not because he enjoys the taste of his liquor, which he swallows at a gulp. True materialists, such as the Chinese, admire a good drinker but despise a mere "soaker."

sion to our lives. It is the gift of his own eternal nature. Thus our eternal life, our ascension with Christ into heaven, does not lie in the future any more than the temporal endurance of the hammer increases its spatial length. We confuse the whole doctrine of eternal life when we speak of it as "future life." Eternity is not unending time; it is an indestructible present, for Christ did not say, "Before Abraham was, I was," but, "Before Abramham was, I *am.*" Material death and resurrection involves, therefore, the translation of consciousness into an eternal present, not into an everlasting future. In this state the pain and death of temporal life are seen *sub specie aeternitatis,* that is, transfigured by divine understanding, somewhat as in music chords that would be dissonant in isolation are woven into a perfect harmonic sequence.

In sum, therefore, Christ is the gift of union with God to humanity in general and to human beings in particular. He is born in us; he lives in us a life of perfect abandonment to the divine will; he dies in us; and in and with us he rises and ascends into heaven, into the eternal life of the Divine Trinity. Only through realization of this truth as a present and already accomplished fact can our outward and conscious lives reflect the inner process, which reflection is the life of Christian holiness—the fruit, not the cause, of union with God.

III

It is notorious that scripture can be quoted to prove almost anything, and it may be asked what solid authority exists for maintaining this particular view of the meaning of the Incarnation and the doctrine of God which it involves. Setting aside, for the moment, certain theological and metaphysical problems,[12] it is sufficient to say here that it is in line with the deepest mystical and spiritual insights which man has been given, and that it involves a vision of the divine love and humility which human thought can hardly surpass. If God is less loving than this, we have conceived an idea of God more noble than the reality, which would make us, quite illogically, the moral superiors of God.

The fact of a given union with God, given without respect to virtue or holiness, has been the central and secret joy of many a great mystic, Christian and non-Christian, in all times and places. The profoundly mystical writings of the Byzantine Fathers speak of it constantly in the boldest language. "The Logos," wrote St. Gregory of Nyssa, "was already Christ and Lord. He that is assumed (into membership of the Church) becomes it."[13] Or in the words of St. Simeon Neo-theologos, "We become Christ's limbs or members, and Christ becomes our members. . . . Unworthy though I be, my hand and foot are Christ. I move my hand, and my hand is wholly Christ, for God's divinity is united inseparably to me. I move my foot, and lo! it glows like God himself."[14] And again, "I thank thee O God that thou, who reignest over all, art now in very truth and unchangeably one spirit with me," following St. Paul's "He that is joined unto the Lord is one spirit."[15]

The point could hardly be made more strongly than in the following from St. John of Damascus:

---

[12]On which see below, Part Two, Chapter I, pp. 127–147.

[13]*Antirrh. adv. Apollin.*, 53.

[14]*Divine Hymns of Love,* quoted in *Orthodox Spirituality.* Anon. London, 1945.

[15]1 Corinthians 6:17.

But we hold that to the whole of human nature the whole essence of the Godhead was united. . . . He in his fulness took upon himself *me* in my fulness, and was united whole to whole that he might in his grace bestow salvation on the whole man. For what has not been taken (*i.e.*, assumed to the divine nature) cannot be healed. . . . Further, the mind has become the seat of the divinity united with it in in subsistence, just as is evidently the case with the body too.[16]

Parallel sayings on the given fact of union with God from the mystics of the Western Church are familiar enough, and so numerous that it will be sufficient to quote as typical the following from Ruysbroeck:

But our nature, forasmuch as it is indeed like unto God but in itself is creature, receives the impress of its Eternal Image passively. This is that nobleness which we possess by nature in the essential unity of our spirit, where it is united to God according to nature. This neither makes us holy, nor blessed, for all men, whether good or evil, possess it within themselves; but it is certainly the first cause of all holiness and blessedness.[17]

But throughout Christian history two fears have always tempered the boldness of this kind of language

---

[16]*De Fide Orthodoxa, iii,* 6.

[17]*Adornment of the Spiritual Marriage,* ii, 57. Trs. Dom P. Wynschenk in his *John of Ruysbroeck,* London, 1916. For the whole passage and others of a similar nature from Western mystics, see below, pp. 133–136. Von Hügel, *Mystical Element,* vol. ii, pp. 151–152, quotes the following interesting passage attributed to St. Thomas Aquinas: "Already in this life we ought continuously to enjoy God, as a thing most fully our own, in all our works. . . . Great is the blindness and exceeding the folly of many souls that are ever seeking God, continuously sighing after God, and frequently desiring God: whilst, all the time, they are themselves the tabernacles of the living God . . . since their soul is the seat of God, in which he continuously reposes. Now who but a fool deliberately seeks a tool which he possesses under lock and key? or who can use and profit by an instrument which he is seeking? or who can draw comfort from food for which he hungers, but which he does not relish at leisure? Like unto all this is the life of many a just soul, which ever seeks God and never tarries to enjoy him; and all the works of such an one are, on this account, less perfect." *De Beatitudine, iii,* 3.

and held this sublime truth under a cloud. One was the fear of pantheism, of abolishing the ontological distinction between Creator and creature, and the other the fear of presumption, of laying claim to salvation apart from holiness of life. Of the first, we need only say here that the distinction between a *given* union and a *necessary* union of man with God renders this view entirely different from pantheism. The second fear is in fact a false humility; presumption itself lies hidden under the fear of presumption.

The truth is that the gift of eternal life is an insufferable blow to our spiritual pride, because the ego desires at all cost to be able to claim some of the credit for its own salvation. Even in avowedly pantheistic religions this pride sometimes manifests itself in attempts to conceal or soften the fact of union with God. Thus the ego increases the distance between itself and God in order to flatter itself with the thought of bridging that distance by its own efforts. By every conceivable subtlety it ignores the gift of union in order to have the satisfaction of manufacturing its own union with God.

Three things must therefore be emphasized:

(1) There is an infinite natural distance between man and God. Being finite, and also fallen, man cannot possibly shorten this distance by his own power. However high he may climb by his own efforts, he does not begin to approach the holiness and transcendence of God.

(2) Because God is love, he himself annuls this infinite distance and gives his eternal life to man without regard to man's moral and spiritual attainments. "For he maketh his sun to shine upon the evil and upon the good, and sendeth his rain upon the just and upon the unjust." Or in the words of St. John, "This is love, not that we loved God but that he loved us."

(3) Holiness of life is the consequence and appreciation of this truth, and brings it to full realization. Of course it is possible, and almost inevitable, that one takes pride in appreciating the gift, but this pride is eventually dissolved in the realization that the gift simply IS, pride or no pride, appreciation or no appreciation. Naturally, however, a gift not appreciated is a gift not enjoyed; it is of no good to you, and, as the Lord's Body received unworthily in Communion, works only to your condemnation. "For God sent not his Son into the world to condemn the world; but that the world through him might be saved. . . . And this is the condemnation: that light is come into the world, and men loved darkness rather than light."

Human freedom has still, therefore, its part to play in the scheme of redemption, not as freedom to attain union with God but as freedom to appreciate, affirm and realize it. In contradistinction to quietism, human action has also its part, not, however, as effort to earn the divine state, but as effort to express it and give thanks for its bestowal.

All this is simply to say that the motive power of any vital religion is the divine love. Christianity exists to reveal that love to the world in all its overwhelming and almost outrageous fulness. Only by contemplation and realization of the love which is God can we have any love for him and for our neighbours, just as a mirror has brilliance—power to reflect light—only when turned towards the sun so that it receives the image of the sun within itself. It is absolutely useless for the Church to moralize, to deplore the sinfulness and irreligion of the world, to rant and rave about God's wrath and judgement like the prophets of old, and summon men with a solemn voice to return to religion or be damned, unless it attends to its principal business, which is to extend the Incarnation and reveal the love of God. Moralistic bombinations never have effected and never will effect in the human soul anything other than a temporary conversion through fear. Had they any lasting value it would have been enough for God to send Amos and Jeremiah with the implementation of Sennacherib and Nebuchadrezzar; there would have been no need for Christ. God's judgement of the world is primarily and essentially his love, which is poured out with such extravagant generosity that whoever fails to respond to it is simply self-condemned by contrast.

Nor will the revelation of the divine love create the least appetite in hungry souls if interpreted as this distant well-wishing, this simple opportunity to buy our way into a remote heaven, this vague extension of a "hand of fellowship" from eternity to help us to be good. Nor will it be sufficiently revealed in elaborate, archaic and unexplained symbolisms about our incorporation into the Mystical Body of the Church whose Head is Christ ,[18] about being partakers of his Body and Blood, about being infused by divine graces as if they were so many fitful winds, about becoming children of God as if we were as distant from him as the subdued and timidly respectful offspring of the legendary paterfamilias of the Victorian era.

Love, in the divine sense, is the giving of one's whole being to another, and when we say that God is love we mean that he gives his entire infinite Self to every single object of his love, to every creature that he has

---

[18]While formerly somewhat of a cliché, the term "Mystical Body" is now being given intelligible content by the Catholic liturgical reformers, and to many Catholics it is now a meaningful expression, though the same can hardly be said in other quarters.

made. Of course the gift is received in varying degrees by different creatures as the light of the sun, shed with equal brilliance upon all parts of the earth, is reflected more perfectly by a mirror than by a brick. Man can reflect God's love more perfectly than an animal. To reflect it with absolute perfection, one would have to *be* God.[19] But while the degrees of reception differ, the gift is always infinite in fulness. To man and to atom, to star-cloud and to earth, to sun and to snow crystal, to mountain and to worm, to sage and to fool, to saint and to sinner, God, to whom size and number offer no obstacle, gives eternal and inescapable union with his very Self. For in God to exist, to create, to love and to redeem are all one pure and simple act; they are himself. And the gift of union with God's own Self is the Logos, the eternal Word, incarnate in history and incarnate in the souls and bodies of men as Christ.

"God, who is rich in mercy, by reason of his great love wherewith he has loved us even when we were dead through our sins, made us alive together with Christ, by whose grace you have been saved, and raised us up with him, and made us sit with him in the heavenly places in Christ Jesus: that in the eternal ages to come he might show the immeasurable riches of his grace in kindness towards us in Christ Jesus. For by grace you have been saved through faith; and this is not your own doing—it is the gift of God."[20]

---

[19]As are the members of the Holy Trinity, the Son and the Holy Spirit reflecting the Father's love completely and eternally.

[20]Ephesians 2:48.

III. THE REALIZATION
OF UNION

To be told that union with God is given to us here and now is one thing; to realize it in experience is quite another. Without realization this truth can neither be an effective force in human life nor yet a statement of real meaning. To say that the Incarnation symbolizes the gift of union with God is in fact to interpret one symbol by another and perhaps more understandable symbol. All theological statements, sacramental forms and divine revelations are symbols having one object— to lead us to the actual knowledge of God, of the union itself, and it must be remembered that the very terms "God" and "union" are themselves symbolic. But these ideas and terms denote a reality which defies verbal description and yet is none the less offered for our experience by the love of God.

The very fact of mystical experience belies the oft repeated assertion that human consciousness can never rise above the level of formal religious symbolism; as is maintained by those who hold an exclusively sacramental viewpoint in religion. Thus in the one-sided sacramentalism of popular mediaeval and much modern Catholicism, mystical experience is regarded as an abnormal freak—a special and extracurricular grace vouchsafed quite arbitrarily to a chosen few.[1] This

---

[1]This would seem to be the opinion of Poulain whose *Graces of Interior Prayer* (London, 1910) is a standard manual of spiritual direction. Garrigou-

viewpoint, however, is perhaps to be expected in periods when the religious consciousness is passing through the stages of infancy and adolescence, for then indeed, save for some rare souls, the symbolic mode of understanding is the only possible way. But in later stages of the religious consciousness the mystical approach becomes not only generally possible but generally necessary—not by reason of any growth in sanctity, but by reason of a natural growth of the soul. Christianity as a complete or catholic religion is both sacramental and mystical. When the sacramental side of religion is followed exclusively, there comes a time when it obscures truth instead of revealing it.

Not only is this true of the sacramental aspect of religion in its strict sense, but also of its dogmatic, doctrinal and historical aspects—of its whole symbolic structure. For all these figures and images of God are means and not ends. They exist to give us sufficient intellectual and emotional courage, sufficient faith of the will, to venture beyond figures and images to Reality itself, and at first sight this realm beyond symbols is empty, arid and terrifying, an unaccustomed territory where all familiar landmarks are left behind. Plunged into it against their will, souls for whom the symbolic aspect of religion is especially dear refer to it as a Dark Night, a Valley of the Shadow, wherein one experiences bitter desolation and comes close to absolute despair.

LaGrange, however, in his *Christian Perfection and Contemplation* (London and St. Louis, 1937) allows that the mystical state is the normal end of the spiritual life, extraordinary in the sense that relatively few souls attain to it. Saudreau takes a similar position. See his *Mystical State*, London and New York, 1924, pp. 10–13 and 199–201. St. Teresa, *Way of Perfection*, c.xx, says, "Yet our Lord has not said, Let some come by way of contemplation, and the rest by other paths; on the contrary, so great is his mercy that he will not hinder any from coming to drink at this fountain of life."

Thus the Dark Night is a recurrent feature of later Catholic mysticism where maturing souls who still cling hard to symbolic religion are forced beyond it against their will. Deprived of intellectual and emotional consolations they feel deserted by God, and some even believed that they were lost souls. Significantly, Dom John Chapman points out that the Dark Night often involves temptations against faith, for what is actually happening is that the Church's dogmatic and doctrinal symbols of God are losing force, are being shattered until and in order that their inner content may be known. But in types of Christianity where the mystical element is better understood, such as the Byzantine, and the late classical spirituality of St. Augustine and St. Gregory the Great, the symptoms of the Dark Night are found hardly at all.[2] The approach of the "divine darkness," the "cloud of unknowing," is expected and welcomed.

There is a general misunderstanding to the effect that a spirituality which passes beyond formally religious symbols is of necessity acosmistic, despising form and matter, finding the contemplation of God wholly incompatible with any interest in sense experience as well as with theology, philosophy, and even creative morality and social action. While there have been pseudo-mystics who adopted this view, it is well known that truly great contemplatives such as Plotinus and St. Teresa of Avila were souls with a high degree of wisdom and skill in the management of material affairs and of practical charity towards others. The mystical state is no more incompatible with form and matter than a mirror is incompatible with the images which it reflects. The mirror transcends, is other than, its images,

[2] See the interesting discussion of this type of spirituality in Dom Cuthbert Butler's *Western Mysticism.* New ed., London, 1946.

and for this very reason is able to reflect them perfectly and clearly. As Eckhart says, "If my eye is to discern colour, it must itself be free from colour."

I

God is the most obvious thing in the world. He is absolutely self-evident—the simplest, clearest and closest reality of life and consciousness. We are only unaware of him because we are too complicated, for our vision is darkened by the complexity of pride. We seek him beyond the horizon with our noses lifted high in the air, and fail to see that he lies at our very feet. We flatter ourselves in premeditating the long, long journey we are going to take in order to find him, the giddy heights of spiritual progress we are going to scale, and all the time are unaware of the truth that "God is nearer to us than we are to ourselves." We are like birds flying in quest of the air, or men with lighted candles searching through the darkness for fire.

The self-evidence of God is the result of his love, and is one with the gift of union with himself which he bestows upon us. For God is not niggardly in his self-revelation; he creates us to know him, and short of actual compulsion does everything possible to present himself to our consciousness. In saying that God gives us union with himself here and now, we are saying also that here and now he exposes himself right before our eyes. In this very moment we are looking straight at God, and he is so clear that for us complex human beings he is peculiarly hard to see. To know him we have to simplify ourselves, and the mind is so dominated by the complexity of pride that it will resort to every conceivable subtlety to resist and avoid a truth so wholly simple.

God and union with God are Reality; nothing is more real, more concrete, more actual, and more present. At the same time, Reality is infinitely alive. It, he, cannot be grasped in any finite form, whether physical, mental or emotional. Therefore, as long as we *try* to grasp God, we shall never realize him. Life itself, as we experience it moment by moment, proceeding as it does directly from God, is the perfect analogy of this truth, for to grasp life is to kill it, or rather, to miss it, and more than ever is this true of God—the Life of life. Pluck a flower, and it dies. Take up water from the stream, and it flows no longer. Pull down the blind, but the sunbeam is not trapped in the room. Snatch the wind in a bag, and you have only stagnant air. This is the root of every trouble: man loves life, but the moment he tries to hold on to it he misses it. The fact that things change and move and flow is their very liveliness, and the harder man hangs on to his life, the sooner he dies of worry.

Religion, as it is generally practised, is simply an attempt to hang on to life and the still more lively mystery which informs it—God. Hence religion as generally practised is idolatry. God cannot be held in theologies; theism, deism, pantheism—none of them can grasp his truth. Nor can states of mind and feeling contain him; ecstasy, rapture, quiet, *samadhi*—these are only the secondary and unessential effects of his presence. Our various intellectual and emotional idols, our doctrines, holy books, sacraments, religious feelings, creeds and churches, are of use so long as they are understood as approximating and pointing to God. But when we try to possess him within them, they must sooner or later become millstones about our necks.[3]

---

[3]In the past it has often happened that souls who recognized this left the

God, and the living creation which proceeds from his hands, cannot be possessed. To enjoy and to know Reality we must let go of it and realize that it possesses us. Beauty grasped turns into pain, for God is the source both of the beauty and of the pain of life. In its beauty he calls us to him; in the pain which comes from grasping he warns us that we cannot come to him in a possessive spirit, because in so doing we shall miss the very thing that we desire. To clutch the splendour of flame is to be burned. To enjoy anything living, whether it be fire, water, air, earth, flesh and blood, our own lives, or God himself, we must let go of it and let it be free to be itself. This is true detachment.

This is why there is no method, no formal technique, for attaining the mystical state and realizing union with God. For a method is an attempt to possess, and has its origin in pride and fear. And as there is nothing that we can *do* to realize God, we must not fall into the error of quietism, which is trying to realize God by doing nothing; for inaction is merely an indirect form of action; it is trying to possess God by doing nothing instead of by doing something, and neither course will succeed since he cannot be possessed at all.

Apparently this leaves us in a hopeless and impossible position. Doing something about it is wrong, and doing nothing about it is wrong. Seeing thus far and no further we fall into desolation, and undergo the

---

fellowship of the Church and ceased altogether from the sacramental life. This, however, is still an adolescent procedure. Whatever individual members of the Church may think, the Church herself is complete and catholic enough to retain the loyalty of these souls. But when the mystical life results in external protests, such as abstaining from the eucharistic fellowship and publicly despising sacramental forms, there is clearly something immature and uncharitable about it. The true mystic discovers in these forms altogether new depths of meaning. Only sheer spiritual pride could stop him from worshipping at an altar with souls lacking his own insight.

experience of impasse, of reaching a blind alley.

But we have to return to this point: the Reality which we term union with God simply IS, whether we realize it or not, whether we are doing something about it or nothing about it. Any attempt to grasp it, by action or by inaction, suggests that it is not absolutely present. The moment we look for union with God, we imply that we do not already have it, and this is true even when we look for it by not looking.

Like unto space it knows no boundaries;
Yet it is right here with us ever retaining its serenity and
*   fulness;*
It is only when you seek it that you lose.
You cannot take hold of it, nor can you get rid of it;
While you can do neither, it goes on its own way;
You remain silent and it speaks; you speak and it is silent;
The great gate of charity is wide open with no obstructions
*   whatever before it.*[4]

The focal point of Reality is now—this present moment, this elusive image of eternity, so small that it has no temporal length and yet so long that we can never escape from it. Here in this present moment life is most lively; here alone do we really exist. The past is dead; the future as yet is not. The moment assumes a hundred different forms—moments of pleasure, moments of pain, moments of elation, moments of depression, moments of quiet, moments of agitation; but it will not stay, it cannot be grasped, in any of its forms. This moment is our life, but the more we try to hold it, the faster it slips away. We look for it and cannot find it because it is too small to see, too slippery to hold, and yet this is where we are given union with God. If we do

---

[4] Hsüan-chiao's *Cheng-tao Ke*, xxxiv. Trs. D. T. Suzuki in his *Manual of Zen Buddhism.* Kyoto, 1935, p. 115.

not discover it in this moment, we shall never discover it.

> O all ye who thirst! Know that you have not far to seek for the fountain of living waters; it springs close to you in the present moment. . . . The present moment is the manifestation of the Name of God and the coming of his Kingdom.[5]

But while we cannot grasp the moment, arresting that flow of life which we call time, there remains the fact that we cannot get away from it. It seems, as we cling to it, to slip away, but what slips away is only its outward form. In reality it stays with us. However hard we may fight to retain the past or to hurry on into the future, we cannot get out of the present moment. The more we try to hold it, the more we fail to perceive that it holds us. The moment always carries us in its embrace, and wherever we go or whatever we do, it cannot be escaped. To understand this is simplicity itself.

And here is the perfect analogy of our union with God—a reality which possesses and holds us as surely and as presently as the moment, a reality which in some sense *is* this moment. For the moment is not its forms; it is not space; it is not time; it is infinitesimal and thus infinite; it is Reality, Being, the eternal presence of God. In this moment we live and move and have our being, and nowhere else. What we have to realize, therefore, is not the getting of union with God, but the not being able to get away from it. It is in, it *is* this Eternal Now, wherein God so lovingly holds us.

---

[5]De Caussade in *Abandonment to the Divine Providence*, ii, 9 and 10. Trs. E. McMahon. New York, 1887, pp. 99–101.

Whither shall I go from thy spirit? Or whither
shall I flee from thy presence?
If I ascend up into heaven, thou art there:
if I make my bed in hell, behold, thou art there.
If I take the wings of the morning, and dwell in the
uttermost parts of the sea; even there shall thy
hand lead me, and thy right hand shall hold me.
If I say, Surely the darkness shall cover me;
even the night shall be light about me.
Yea, the darkness hideth not from thee; but the night
shineth as the day: the darkness and the light
are both alike to thee.[6]

Union with God is here and now; here and now is
union with God. Surely God in his love could have
made nothing more simple, but the Old Adam in us
raises every possible objection to seeing the point. To
begin with, we are all unconscious pantheists, trying to
grasp the moment, the Eternal Now, in and as its various forms, trying to identify God with something *in* the
moment. It may be, as in avowed pantheism, that we
try to grasp and hold him as the concrete material life
which occurs in this moment. More generally those
inclined to the mystical and spiritual life will try to
identify him with some profound state of feeling, some
rapture or ecstasy, some special state of mind, which,
again, occurs in but does not embrace the living moment. Such ecstasies frequently proceed from the realization of our inescapable union with God, but as soon
as we try to hold on to them as if they were that union
we have missed the point. Strangled by our grasp, the
ecstasy vanishes.

He who fondly imagines to get more of God in thoughts,
prayers, pious offices and so forth, than by the fireside or
in the stall: in sooth he does but take God, as it were, and

---

[6]Psalm 139:7–12.

swaddle his head in a cloak and hide him under the table. For he who seeks God under settled forms lays hold of the form while missing the God concealed in it. But he who seeks God in no special guise lays hold of him as he is in himself, and such an one "lives with the Son" and is the life itself.[7]

Or again, we object that the whole thing is too simple and too easy, as some object that it is too easy to receive the Body of Christ by going up to the altar, kneeling down, and opening your mouth or holding out your hands for Communion. Why then it is possible for immoral and sinful people to get it! They are, of course, the very people for whom it is intended. Union with God is easy, for "my yoke IS easy and my burden light," but we do not want this kind of ease because it isn't flattering; it leaves us no attainments to brag about. To realize union is indeed a very simple and childlike affair, but, as we have seen, pride loves complexity, avoids the obvious, and will always, when alternative routes are offered, choose the longer and more circuitous.

There is then the objection that the Eternal Now is too much of an abstraction, an infinitesimal point too coldly mathematical, a thing too devoid of colour, content and life to be the source of mystical inspiration, of love, courage, wisdom and all the virtues of Christian sanctity. Surely more fire is to be gained from contemplating the figure of Christ, or reading the lives of the saints. No one will deny that very great fire may be had from these latter sources, especially for those whose religious consciousness is still wholly dependent on images and symbols. But there is always the danger that the imitation of Christ may become monkey business,

---

[7]Eckhart, sermon, xiii, in Pfeiffer's *Meister Eckhart.* Tr. C. de B. Evans. London, 1924, vol. i, p. 49.

and what is important for us is not so much the outward form of Christ as his inner spiritual state. Humanly speaking, his inner state, the cause of his outward glory, was precisely his realization of the inescapable presence (here-and-now-ness) of God and union with him. It is from the Eternal Moment that the saints derive the *momentum* and power of holiness.

When we try to speak of the Now in words and ideas it naturally appears abstract and empty for the very reason that the mystery of God wholly transcends thought. Apparently there is nothing in God, and yet everything comes out of him. Sun, moon, stars, mountains, trees, men—all have their being in and emerge from the Now, from something which, when we try to think about it and examine it, instantly seems boundless and void. This is why there is so much negative language in mystical writings. In the words of St. Thomas:

> In treating of the divine essence the principal method to be followed is that of remotion. For the divine essence by its immensity surpasses every form to which our intellect reaches; and thus we cannot apprehend it by knowing what it is.[8]

And again:

> We know God by unknowing, by a manner of uniting with God that exceeds the compass of our minds, when the mind recedes from all things and then leaves even itself and is united with the super-resplendent rays of the Divinity. . . . In this state of knowledge of God, the mind is enlightened from out of the depths of the divine wisdom which defy our scrutiny; for to understand that God is not only above all that exists but even above all that we can comprehend comes to us from the divine wisdom.[9]

[8] *Summa Contra Gentiles*, I. xiv.
[9] *Comment. de Divinis Nominibus*, VII. 1. iv.

Looking at it from an intellectual and emotional point of view, the Eternal Now certainly seems dry and empty. From this standpoint, entering into it amounts to a kind of death, and the surrender of cherished intellectual and emotional consolations is indeed a sharing in the death of the Cross, from which the whole power of the Resurrection flows.[10] From this same standpoint it does, of course, seem incredible that creative love and life can come out of the seeming Void, and that God can move us to sanctity when we have no inspiring image of him. But this fear of the Void is lack of faith in the reality of God. In the mystical state, virtue proceeds not from an image but from God himself, because in the Now we meet Reality itself even though it wholly surpasses our comprehension. There seems no reason why creative life should come out of it, but it does because there is God himself. If faith and courage are weak we shall, of course, prefer to depend on an image of Reality crowded with ideas and concepts and precepts. In meditation we shall cause our minds to buzz with holy considerations for fear of entering into the silence, where God might not exist after all.

Full of mysterious and infinite life, the Eternal Now lies beyond every concept and image, but is yet the source of all images. The very idea, the very word "God" may indeed distract us in the process of realization because it is still a symbol, a concept, standing between us and the Reality—Now! When we say, the Eternal Now is God, our minds are apt to start equating the Now with an idea called "God" and thus we are

---

[10]Part of this "death" is the sense of unworthiness which constantly beset so many of the Christian mystics, as for example St. Francis of Assisi. The simplicity and absolute given-ness of union with God made them feel acutely undeserving of it and inadequate in their response to it.

distracted from the real and present Now. At this stage the *idea* of God becomes unnecessary. Abandoning all concepts and conventional feelings *about* Reality, letting go of all devices and methods for realizing union with God, we approach the Now just as it is. And this becomes possible through the understanding that methods for grasping Reality, for getting God into our consciousness, are as absurd and as confusing as putting red paint on red roses or as trying to kiss your own lips. The fact of union with God simply is, whether realized or not, and no amount of striving to possess it will get rid of it. You live and move in the Now, and though you try to grasp the moment or flee from the moment until the end of time, it holds you unchangeably in its embrace. The realization comes and the possessive will surrenders itself when you are thoroughly convinced that, struggle as you may, there is no escape from the love of God.

> The person who is not conscious of God's presence, but who must always be going out to get him from this and that, who has to seek him by special methods, as by means of some activity, person, or place—such people have not attained God. . . . Of what does this true possession of God consist? It depends on the heart and an inner, intellectual return to God and not on steady contemplation by a given method. It is impossible to keep such a method in mind, or at least difficult, and even then it is not best. We ought not to have or let ourselves be satisfied with the God we have thought of, for when the thought slips the mind, that god slips with it. What we want is rather the reality of God, exalted far above any human thought or creature. Then God will not vanish unless one turns away from him of his own accord.[11]

---

[11]From Eckhart's "Talks of Instruction," in Blakney's *Meister Eckhart*. New York, 1941, pp. 8–9.

The consciousness of union with God thus realized is mystical, that is, veiled, rather than beatific; it is not an absolutely direct and full consciousness, but resembles to some extent the consciousness which we have of our own selves. For while we cannot perceive our own egos directly, we know that we exist. We do not know what we are, but we know ourselves as existing, and this knowledge is present as an undertone in all other knowledge. Similarly, the mystical knowledge of God is a knowledge of God in the act of his presence and union with us, but is not immediate vision and apprehension of the divine essence.[12]

To return to the analogy of the mirror: no one has ever seen the true nature, or colour, of a mirror. A mirror is only present to our eyes by reason of what it reflects, whether light or darkness, white or black, shape or colour. But we are none the less aware that there is a mirror transcending and underlying the reflections. The colour of a mirror, being a "no-colour," does not distort or contest place with the colours it reflects. In the same way, the mystical awareness of God does not contest place with other experiences and states of mind. Mental states, such as joy, sorrow, exaltation, dejection, pleasure and pain, are as a rule mutually exclusive. But the mystical state is inclusive, just as God and his love include the whole universe. There is no conflict between experiencing the Now and things which happen in the Now. But the Now, God, the mirror, is not known in isolation, apart from the events and images which it produces or contains, although something very close to this may sometimes break upon the

---

[12]Presumably this is only possible when actual death has removed the ego from standing in its own light.

mind in an ineffable flash. Such rare moments of vision do not, however, become the mystic's habitual and constant state of soul.

Many people are under the impression that the mystical state is one of constant ecstasy, and for that reason seek the realization of union as ecstasy. But as Père Lallemant says:

> Without rapture, a soul will sometimes have a more sublime light, a clearer knowledge, a more excellent operation of God, than another with extraordinary raptures and ecstasies. . . . Our Lord enjoyed beatific vision without ecstasy. The blessed in heaven will enjoy the perfect use of their senses.[13]

Saudreau likewise explains that the exaltation of the feelings or the rapture of the senses is not

> the "rough sketch," so to speak, of this union, nor even its prelude: it is possible to conceive a person who, without ever having been in ecstasy, might be favoured with this permanent union.[14]

While it will be seen from the above that there is some uncertainty as to the precise use of the terms ecstasy, beatific vision, and the "sublime light" which comes without ecstasy, the principle is clear: the latter is the characteristic of the mystical state, and differs both from ecstasy and from sudden apprehensions of the beatific vision.[15] In this present world-order God does

---

[13] *Spiritual Doctrine*, princ. VII, c. iv, a. 7.
[14] *The Mystical State*, pp. 99–100.
[15] I have used "ecstasy" in a very loose and popular sense to cover all experiences of an ineffable character which involve an exaltation of the feelings or a suspension of the mind's normal activities, including sudden flashes of the beatific vision—which would certainly stun the ordinary human mind. But in Catholic mystical theology the term ecstasy is restricted to the suspension of mental faculties, which, according to Catholic theologians, does not occur to the blessed in heaven who behold the beatific vision. At the same time, they do not permit any confusion of the beatific vision with the mystical state.

not normally intrude the full light of his glory upon our minds, but rather reveals himself as the mysterious Void whose content wholly transcends normal thinking and feeling, and can only be known to the intellect by analogy. We may transcend images, ideas and symbols, but we are then confronted with a Reality which we experience but do not comprehend, a living mystery which imparts life, power and joy, though we cannot say how. When we stop to examine it, there seems to be nothing in it, but in use we find it inexhaustible.

The fact that we may apprehend Reality beyond images, but know it as living mystery, is the reason why so many Christian mystics speak of knowing God by "unknowing" or "mystical ignorance." For what we experience teases us out of thought, and the more vividly and thoroughly we experience it, the more we grow in wonder at the mystery of God, and the more acutely we are aware of his incomprehensibility.

Now the realization produces definite effects, though no amount of striving for and imitating these effects will produce realization. It infuses our life with a deep undertone of love, joy, peace and spiritual freedom, and these come in part from the certainty and security of our union with God. From the negative standpoint, the surrender of the possessive will cuts at the very root of evil. Living to so great a degree in the present, we are delivered from "anxiety for the morrow." And the vital, lively nature of the Eternal Now imparts a certain *joie de vivre* that expresses itself naturally and spontaneously like the song of a bird. It issues in a profound and joyous acceptance of the will of God as this is expressed in the circumstances of each moment, for we realize that all these circumstances are included in and governed by the Eternal Now, the love of God. Above all it appears in love, for God and for man, because we are consciously united with Love itself. Just how all this happens cannot be said, and if it could there would be no point in saying it since none of these effects can be produced by mimicry. We have to discover first our total dependence on and union with God, and then "all these things shall be added unto you."

II

So much has been said about the surrender of devices, methods and techniques, that this must not be allowed to lead to a misapprehension. This does not mean that we are to cease entirely from prayer, meditation and worship in their formal sense; it means that we are to cease using them as ways to possess God. Formal religion has two functions. For those who *cannot* at present understand anything beyond forms, it is a way of speeding up and intensifying the attempt to possess God until they become quite convinced by experience that he cannot be possessed. In addition, it imparts a symbolic, analogical knowledge of God which, as we have seen, gives them courage to venture into the Reality beyond symbols. For those who *can* go beyond forms, it is a way not of getting but of expressing, of making incarnate and concrete, their spiritual realization and its effects. It is language and grammar at the disposal of inner meaning. It incarnates their love of God as works of mercy incarnate their love of men.

But between these two uses of formal religion there is a difficult intermediate state—the state of those who can go beyond forms but hesitate to do so through fear or ignorance, and the state of those for whom the forms have lost all real meaning, or for whom they have become positively misleading. Little recognized but extremely prevalent is the problem of those who have at some time acquired repugnant emotional associations from the terms and form of the Christian religion. This is a very real problem for the Church, because it means that thousands and thousands of souls are outside her fellowship, not because of any wilful heresy or insincerity, but because the Church *insists* on the acceptance of certain particular analogies of God which, divinely revealed though they may be, cannot always and invariably be meaningful and helpful.

Because the supremely important thing is God himself and not his analogies, the Church in this case should be great and catholic enough to lead these souls to God without the use of formal religion. Like St. Paul, the Church must be "all things to all men," instead of trying to impose a uniform procedure on all souls alike, which is, of course, the easiest and laziest way of going about the teaching of religion. The dropping of formal religion in certain cases is not the proper work of a sect; nor is it something to be done universally for the whole flock of Christ. This is no mere question of dispensing with ritual, and trying to present the Christian religion in up-to-date terms. It is a question of suggesting, of indicating, the very essence and reality of religion by dropping religious forms and terms altogether in certain special cases and circumstances. Of course this cannot be done unless the essence is there to be indicated, unless there are a sufficient number of teachers who have adequate spiritual insight.

It is quite possible to do this for the reason that the reality of religion and the reality of life are one and the same, though to many Christians this is not sufficiently clear. When Catholicism is exclusively sacramental it is far from clear, because the forms of the sacraments seem, to the modern mind, utterly remote from the forms of everyday life so that the problem of relating the two is difficult indeed. However much the worship of the Church may thrill the emotions and senses with its beauty, there are thousands of people who find it so "out of this world," so archaic, so intensely symbolic, that it is impossible to relate it to prosaic, everyday affairs. Heaven forbid that the Church should cease this worship; but, again, there are cases and circumstances where she should work otherwise.[16]

The apparent rift between religion and life appears also on the doctrinal side. Exposed to the normal presentation of Christian doctrine, a person who is not deeply read in theology and mysticism receives an impression of the Christian religion which is extremely remote and unreal in every sphere save the ethical. Instead of focussing his attention on the *presence* of God in everyday life, it draws it away to the past and the future—the "mighty acts" of God in distant history and the promises of God in regard to a future life. He learns of God and Christ as impalpable presences alongside his life rather than in it, though St. Paul says, "To me, to live is Christ. . . . Christ liveth in me."

The same remoteness and unreality characterize the usual methods of prayer and meditation, which, from this point of view, have altogether too much religiosity

---

[16]The Quakers have here a great contribution to make to the catholic wholeness of the Church, for a far greater use should be made of their worship in corporate silence. The retreat house or "school of wisdom" has great possibilities as an alternative and supplement to the formal church building, for here meditation may be carried on in normal and informal surroundings without the distraction of noise.

and formality to become that "prayer without ceasing" which is St. Paul's ideal of spirituality. Prayer considered simply as talking to or at God, and meditation practised largely as thinking *about* God, are all too apt to set him at a distance rather than to realize his presence. Furthermore, their form and content distract the mind far too readily from the living reality of God as the Eternal Now, because they comprise so much mental busy-ness, so many sentiments, considerations, resolutions, notions, imaginations, so much wordiness and conceptualism.[17]

It is perfectly possible, under certain conditions, to indicate the present reality of God, and that with great effectiveness, without resorting to formal religious terminology. It has been done for centuries in a type of Buddhism from which we have much to learn, since any truth, wheresoever found, is Catholic truth. We have spoken already of Zen Buddhism in connection with the experience of *satori*, or sudden realization.[18] The characteristic way of teaching employed in Zen is simply to demonstrate the Eternal Now, Reality itself, by forms derived from everyday life rather than philosophy and religion. But like Christianity, Zen also uses

[17]The fact that this kind of prayer is still so widely taught in the Church is the result, firstly, of the revolt of Roman Catholic officialdom against mysticism in the 17th and 18th centuries, described by Dom John Chapman as an entire "reversal of tradition," and secondly, of the Protestant concentration upon what Heiler terms "prophetic prayer," which is essentially self-conscious in content, being concerned almost exclusively with petition, resolution and repentance. On this whole subject see below, pp. 229–238.

[18]The word "Zen" is the Sino-Japanese form of the Sanskrit *dhyana*, untranslatable into English, but signifying the state of consciousness involved in mystical experience. Originating in India, the Zen school of Buddhism was brought to China by Bodhidharma in the 6th century A.D., and was there influenced by Taoism and Confucianism. Zen as known today is a distinctly Chinese creation, modified by its long sojourn in Japan. For a complete account see D. T. Suzuki's *Essays in Zen Buddhism*, 3 vols. London, 1927, 1933 and 1934. Also my *Spirit of Zen*. London and New York, 1936.

the usual externals of religion—scriptures, ceremonies, laws, images and symbols, though there are times when it departs from them surprisingly, which is what gives Zen its unique character. This departure is effective and startling for the very reason that it goes along with formal religion, because, as we have already seen, there can be no kernel without shell.

Zen is largely a monastic religion, although the monks do not as a rule take life vows since their stay in the monastery is often only temporary—for purposes of instruction. These monasteries are run somewhat on Benedictine lines, the rule consisting of both meditation and manual work, and the spiritual life is directed by a *roshi* or "master" distinct from the abbot, who attends to administrative affairs. The following instances of the Zen way of teaching are dialogues between masters and their monks or lay inquirers:

"Ever since I came to you," a monk complained, "I haven't been instructed at all in the study of Reality." "Ever since you came to me," replied the master, "I have always been pointing out to you how to study Reality." "In what way, sir?" "When you brought me tea, did I not accept it? When you served me food, did I not eat it? When you made bows to me, did I not return them? When did I ever neglect in giving you instruction?" Seeing that the monk did not understand, he concluded, "If you want to see, see directly into it; but when you try to think about it, it is altogether missed."

In answer to a question about the meaning of Reality an old master simply held up his fly-whisk, and another master asked one of his monks to explain the action. "The master's idea," replied the monk, "was to elucidate the spiritual along with the material, to reveal truth by means of an objective reality." "Your understanding," said the master, "is all right as far as it goes. But why are you in such a hurry to make theories about it?" At this the monk asked, "What, then, will be your explanation?" The master held up his own fly-whisk.

Sometimes these exchanges were very brief and to the point:

> "What is the real meaning of religion?"
> "A refreshing breeze is stirred in the blue sky."
>
> "What is the Tao (i.e., God, Reality)?"
> "Walk on!"
>
> "What is Realization?"
> "Your everyday thoughts."
>
> "What is the one ultimate word of truth?"
> "Yes."
> "I asked, what is the one ultimate word of truth?"
> "I'm not deaf!"
>
> "I have just come to this monastery; please give me some instruction."
> "Have you had your breakfast?"
> "Yes."
> "Then wash your dishes."

At times Zen is violently iconoclastic in its attitude to revered religious symbols and personages:

> "What are the characteristic features of your household (i.e., school or teaching)?"
> "A table, a tray, a chair, a fireplace and windows."
>
> "What is the religious life?"
> "In early morning, 'How do you do?' At night, 'Good night.'"
>
> "What is the teaching of Buddhism?"
> "The Buddha is a bull-headed jail-keeper, and the Patriarchs are horse-faced old maids."

The above incidents may perhaps be clarified by the following extract, freely translated, from one of the greatest Chinese Zen masters:

The truly religious man has nothing to do but go on with his life as he finds it in the various circumstances of this worldly existence. He rises quietly in the morning, puts on his clothes and goes out to work. When he wants to walk, he walks; when he wants to sit, he sits. He has no hankering after becoming a Buddha (*i.e.*, one who has attained Realization), not the remotest thought of it. How is this possible? A wise man of old says, If you strive to become a Buddha by any conscious contrivances, your Buddha is indeed the source of eternal bondage.[19]

The secret of the above quotations is simply that they have to do with a mystical state wherein religion and everyday life are identical. Religion is no longer something in a water-tight compartment; it has become so released from special forms that it fills all forms. God is here and now, and thus we turn our attention to here and now, though this must not be understood in any sentimental, naturalistic and pantheistic sense. When, in answer to questions about Reality, the masters wave a fly-whisk, point to a bush or make some casual, everyday remark, they are most decidedly not to be understood as saying that the whisk, the bush or the ordinary affairs of life are God. No conceptualism of this kind is involved here. The point is rather that Reality, God, the Eternal Now, is entirely beyond speech and understanding and attainment, but at the same time is right here. If you try to catch hold of it, you will miss it. But go straight ahead with your ordinary life, "Walk on!", wash your dishes, think your everyday thoughts, and you will see that you can't get away

---

[19]That is, a "bull-headed jail-keeper." From the *Lin-chi Lu*, after the translation by Suzuki in *Essays in Zen*, vol. ii, p. 260. All the above quotations have been taken from the various works of Suzuki, though in certain cases his translation has been adapted for the benefit of those who have no technical knowledge of Chinese Buddhism.

from it. Yet this is already too much conceptualism![20]

In Zen this way of teaching has been established for over a thousand years, and thus has reached a point of refinement, subtlety and allusiveness such that a thorough understanding of it is quite beyond the average Occidental. These dialogues between masters and their disciples have been accumulated into a large body of literature, and are used as subjects *(koan)* for meditation. Through the years the original spontaneity of this way of teaching has been to some extent hardened and modified, yet none the less it remains one of the most effective and stimulating means of presenting the inner essence of religion that the world has ever known.[21] The metaphysical background of Zen is the philosophy of Mahayana Buddhism, and deficient as this may be from a Christian standpoint there can be no doubt whatever that this kind of Buddhist *mysticism* is as genuine an experience of God as that ineffable mystery known in Christian mysticism as the "cloud of unknowing" or the "luminous darkness."[22] Christians cannot feel that the Buddhist's philosophical explanation of the experience is adequate, because it goes no further than the experience itself, describing God as the "pregnant Void" *(sunyata)*. It remains a total mystery as to how or why this Void should have produced the universe or have inspired such a loving and lofty moral concept as

[20]Pai-chang was asked, "I have been seeking for Reality, but do not yet know how to go on with my research." He answered, "It is very much like looking for an ox when you are riding on one."

[21]It remains to this day by far the most vital and spiritually mature form of Buddhism, and has had a profound influence in moulding the higher culture of the Far East.

[22]These terms are first found in St. Dionysius pseudo-Areopagite, whose mystical writings are the root of Catholic mystical theology. See my *Theologia Mystica of St. Dionysius*. West Park, N. Y., 1944.

the Bodhisattva ideal.[23] But to Christians, who know that God the Holy Trinity is love itself, this is somewhat less of a mystery.

But whatever the subtleties of Zen in its present form, the principle of its way of teaching is clear, and whatever the deficiencies of Mahayana philosophy from the Christian standpoint, this principle is certainly applicable in Christianity. One cannot help feeling that something of this kind would be a refreshing and invigorating relief from the interminable explanations of theologians and sermonizings of moralists, necessary as these may be. It would, of course, be absurd to apply the principle generally as a popular stunt, but in the spiritual direction of individuals and small groups it would be of the highest value. There is no thought here of determining just how the principle should be applied, for this would at once lead to artificiality and affectation; it must spring naturally and immediately from the realization of union with God. It will doubtless develop in its own time, but when it does the Church should be wise enough to accept it.

It is almost certain that something of this kind will arise as the inner consciousness of Christianity realizes a union with God beyond formal symbols and becomes free from excessive religiosity. This *must* be the ultimate development of the religion of the Incarnation, since the final end of the Incarnation is the realization

---

[23]According to Buddhist philosophy one who attains the supreme Realization or Enlightenment is freed from the process of reincarnation whereby the unenlightened are born again and again into the world. He may then enter the transcendental state of bliss and peace called Nirvana. But the Bodhisattva is one who renounces this state out of love for all other creatures, and submits to reincarnation again and again through vast periods of time in order to be of service to the world. Anyone familiar with the Buddhist conception of time, rivalling the modern astronomical calculation of light-years, will realize what a tremendous renunciation this involves.

of God's union with the entire universe. As the Breviary hymn says:

> *From that Holy Body broken*
> *Blood and water forth proceed;*
> *Earth and stars and sky and ocean*
> *By that flood from stain are freed.*

The Incarnation and the Mass have as their logical end the transubstantiation, the inclusion within the Divine Humanity, of the whole creation. Thus far the Incarnation process has been circumscribed to actions that are formally spiritual (*i.e.*, prayer and meditation), sacramental and moral—that is, to specifically religious actions. But while the historic Incarnation and the formal sacraments will remain the energizing centres of the process, the process itself will expand beyond spiritual and moral actions to art, literature, music, athletics, engineering, eating, drinking, conversation and amusement—to every single aspect of life from the most important to the most trivial. The Western world has not thus far evolved a Christian art at all. That is to say, it thinks of religious art in terms of liturgical art—painting, literature and music having formally religious subject matter There is no conception yet of painting a landscape, a group of flowers, a portrait, a street scene, in a Christian and incarnational way.[24] There must even be a Christian way of making shoes and washing one's hands, and by that we do *not* mean that there should be a crucifix and two candles beside the washbasin!

In speaking, therefore, of a religion which goes

---

[24]The special type of Chinese and Japanese painting directly inspired by Zen almost invariably selects "secular" things for its subject matter. See the reproductions in Ernst Grosse's *Die Ostasiatische Tuschmalerei*. Berlin, 1923. Also in Binyon's *Spirit of Man in Asian Art*. Cambridge, Mass., 1936.

beyond symbols, we are thinking primarily of theological, liturgical and moral symbols. In a very strict sense the human mind can never go beyond symbols of some kind, since in the most rigorous sense of the word even the Eternal Now and the mystical state themselves are symbols of God.

> With the growth of spirituality these mediating symbols tend to become more abstract; but this does not mean that they are left behind. The "emptiness," the "darkness," the "nothing," the "Cloud of Unknowing" of the mystic, though they be negative statements, are still symbols drawn from his sensible experience, in and through which he seeks to actualize his obscure experience of God.[25]

A knowledge of God entirely transcending symbolism would amount to the Beatific Vision itself, and, as we have seen, the mystical and the beatific modes of consciousness are different. The point is that the "symbol" of the Eternal Now relates God more effectively to every aspect of life. The very fact that Christianity, as modern Church religion, is not related to the whole of life shows its inner weakness and its unfaithfulness to the Incarnation. It renders it repugnant and unsatisfying to mature minds, and reveals its failure to realize union with God, which is the reason why it lacks both vision and power. "Who sees not God everywhere sees him truly nowhere."

---

[25]Evelyn Underhill, *Worship.* New York, 1937, p. 38.

PART TWO

We are obliged to preserve the concept of the "otherness" of God from ourselves even though we cannot use it without distorting or at least wrongly stressing it. . . . It is an otherness which not only does not exclude but positively (just because it is what it is) includes and demands *oneness* —a oneness, indeed, which is actually more real and intimate than what we normally would describe as identification.

R. H. J. STEUART, S.J., *World Intangible.*

> *He taught them laws and watchwords,*
> *To preach and struggle and pray;*
> *But he taught us deep in the hayfield*
> *The games that the angels play.*
>
> *Had he stayed here for ever,*
> *Their world would be wise as ours—*
> *And the king be cutting capers,*
> *And the priest be picking flowers.*
> G. K. CHESTERTON, *The Song of the Children.*

Let me ask you to remember some day that I have told you that the hatred of evil strengthens evil, and opposition reinforces what is opposed. This is a law of an exactitude equal with the laws of mathematics.

RONALD FRASER, *Bird Under Glass.*

Eschew as though it were a hell the consideration of yourself and your offences. No one should ever think of these things except to humiliate himself and love our Lord. It is enough to regard yourself *in general* as a sinner, even as there are many saints in heaven who were such.

CHARLES DE CONDREN.

Our father holds it for better that in all things one should endeavour to find God, rather than that long continuous periods of time should be applied to prayer, . . . in conversation, in walking, seeing, tasting, hearing, thinking, and in fact in all kinds of activity, for of a truth the majesty of God is in all things. This kind of meditation, in which one finds God in everything, is easier than the other, and prepares the soul to receive great graces from God, without it being necessary to spend a long time in prayer.

ST. IGNATIUS LOYOLA.

115

I. THE BEING OF GOD

In its fulness, the realization of union with God is the end of human life. But because God himself is eternal life and is infinitely creative, this end is no mere conclusion; it has immeasurable results and is for ever fecund because the infinite can never exhaust itself in finite expressions of its nature. Even though the full content of mystical experience can never be set down in finite forms of ideas, words and actions, those who have glimpsed it in any degree will try to express it and to share it with others. This is why mystical religion involves both doctrine and action, for the teachings and principles of religion, in so far as they are true at all, invariably begin with an experience of God. Thus the deeper our experience of God, the more profound and effective will be our understanding of doctrine.

It is certain, therefore, that the coming of an incarnational mysticism and of a mature understanding of the Christian faith will bring a deeper comprehension of the being and the character of God, requiring doctrinal expression, and will also have important effects upon the moral and spiritual life. We turn, then, to the possible effects of such an awakening upon these four central aspects of the Christian religion—the theology of the divine Being, our conception of God's character, the life of moral action, and the life of worship and contemplation.

I

A way of life and thought which denies or ignores the existence of God is bound to end in dissolution and self-contradiction. If this is not sufficiently proved by the state of futility to which Humanism and rationalism have brought us, a state of inhumanity and irrationality, all that remains necessary is to reason the matter out. From the standpoint of *reason* the conclusion that God exists is absolutely unavoidable; to demonstrate this truth was the greatest and perhaps the most permanent achievement of mediaeval philosophy, and in particular of St. Thomas. The only way to escape this conclusion is to deny the validity of reason, which is merely to make argument, philosophy, and almost every form of discussion and thought impossible.

Although our purpose here is the interpretation of Christian doctrine and not its evidences, this much must be said. Either the living God is, or he is not. Either the ultimate Reality is alive, conscious and intelligent, or it is not. If it is, then it is what we call God. If it is not, it must be some form of blind process, law, energy or substance entirely devoid of any meaning save that which man himself gives to it. Nobody has ever been able to suggest a reasonable alternative. To say that Reality is quite beyond thought, and therefore cannot be designated by such small, human terms as "conscious" and "intelligent" is only to say that God is immeasurably greater than man. And the theist will agree that he is infinitely greater. To argue that Reality is not a blind energy but a "living principle," an "impersonal super-consciousness," or an "impersonal mind" is merely to play with words and indulge in terminological contradictions. A "living principle" means about as much as a black whiteness, and to speak of an "impersonal mind" is like talking about a circular square. It is the result, of course, of misunderstanding the word "personal" as used of God—as if it meant that God is an organism, form, or composite structure like man, something resembling Haeckel's "gaseous vertebrate." But the word is not used at all in that sense. From many points of view the term "personal" is badly chosen, but it means simply that God is alive in the fullest possible way.

If the ultimate Reality is indeed a blind energy or process devoid of inherent meaning, if it is merely an unconscious permutation and oscillation of waves, particles or what not, certain consequences follow. Human consciousness is obviously a part or an effect of this Reality. We are bound, then, to come to one of two conclusions. On the one hand, we shall have to say that the effect, consciousness, is a property lacking to its entire cause—in short, that something has come out of nothing. Or, on the other hand, we shall have to say that consciousness is a special form of unconsciousness—in short, that it is not really conscious. For the first of these two conclusions there neither is nor can be any serious argument; not even a rationalist would maintain the possibility of an effect without a sufficient cause. The main arguments against theism follow, in principle, the second conclusion—that the properties and qualities of human nature, consciousness, reason, meaning, and the like, do not constitute any *new* element or property over and above the natural and mechanical processes which cause them. Because Reality itself is a blind mechanism, so is man. Meaning, consciousness, and intelligence are purely arbitrary and relative terms given to certain highly complex mechanical structures.

But the argument dissolves itself. If consciousness and intelligence are forms of mechanism, the opinions and judgements of intelligence are products of mechanical (or statistical) necessity. This must apply to *all* opinions and judgements, for all are equally mere phenomena of the mechanical world-process. There can be no question of one judgement being more *true* than another, any more than there can be question of the phenomenon fish being more true than the phenomenon bird. But among these phenomena are the judgements of the rationalist, and to them he must apply the logic of his own reasoning. He must admit that they have no more claim to truth than the judgements of the theist, and that if rationalism is true it is very probably not true. This is intellectual suicide—the total destruction of thought—to such a degree that even the rationalist's own concepts of mechanism, unconscious process, statistical necessity, and the like, also become purely arbitrary and meaningless terms. To hold such a view of the universe consistently, one must separate oneself, the observer, from it. But this cannot be done, for which reason a contemporary philosopher has complained that man's subjective presence constitutes the greatest obstacle to philosophical knowledge!

Now this is pure nonsense. Man's subjective presence is, of course, the very condition of knowledge both of the universe and of God. It is precisely the existence of man in the universe as a conscious, reflecting self that makes it logically necessary to believe in God. A universe containing self-conscious beings must have a cause sufficient to produce such beings, a cause which must *at least* have the property of self-consciousness. This property cannot simply "evolve" from protoplasm or stellar energy, because this would mean that more consciousness is the result of less consciousness and no consciousness. Evolution is, therefore, a transition from the potential to the actual, wherein the new powers and qualities constantly acquired are derived, not from the potential, but from a superior type of life which already possesses them.

What is this superior type of life? Taking as his basic principle the fact that something cannot come out of nothing, or, to state it positively, that every effect demands a sufficient cause, St. Thomas both demonstrates the necessity for its existence and outlines its general character in five ways.[1] He shows that it must be the First Mover, the First Cause, the Being which exists necessarily, the possessor of the perfect degree of every positive property to be found in things, and the origin of order, whereby all things are directed to their proper ends. The gist of the whole argument is simply that the universe requires an origin or cause other than itself, and that this cause must be absolutely self-sufficient. Everything in the universe is the effect of some prior cause; every movement is the result of a prior movement; every being is derived from some prior being. The universe is always depending on something prior to itself, and at any "moment" it can only be a cause, can only exist, by virtue of being an effect. It is therefore primarily an effect. The chain of causation cannot be extended back infinitely, for then we should have a system which is an effect without any primary cause. This is nonsense, like the Cheshire Cat's grin suspended in empty space with no cat. It does not make it any less nonsense to increase its size, to carry the effects causing

---

[1] *Summa Theologica*, I. Q. ii, a. 3.

one another back and back and back. It only becomes a bigger and bigger absurdity. Carry it back to infinity, and you have an infinite absurdity—an infinite grin without cat. You must, then, arrive at an origin, a cause, which is *not* an effect, which exists in its own right—necessarily—and does not derive being from something else just because it *is* Being.

It follows that this necessary and self-sufficient Being will have some astonishing properties. Because it must be the sufficient cause of the whole universe (otherwise it would not be the *first* cause), it will have in the most complete degree every positive property to be found in the universe—including life and consciousness. It will be utterly free from other than self-limitation, for there is nothing prior to it to impose any limits upon it. It will not, therefore, be limited by time and space, and thus will be entirely present in every place and at every moment. It will not be a body, because all bodies have spatial limitations and are *subject* to change and motion. It will not be a world-soul, considered as the form of the universe-body, because form and body are mutually dependent whereas the first cause is necessarily independent. It will not be the universe itself considered as a *Gestalt*, a whole organism greater than the sum of its parts, because every organism is a dependent system which does not originate itself.[2] It will not even

---

[2] The *Gestalt* or configuration theory of the universe is perhaps the only serious alternative offered to the various systems of mechanism or vitalism in the whole field of modern philosophy. It explains the development of organisms very satisfactorily until it tries to reach a final, or first, organism —the universe-as-a-whole, greater than the sum of its parts. But such a universal organism would be self-originating, and therefore utterly unlike all other organisms—utterly different in principle. Yet the *Gestalt* theorists assume it to be the *same* in principle, and reason accordingly. For a brief exposition see R. H. Wheeler, *The Laws of Human Nature*. New York and Cambridge, 1932, esp. pp. 1–66.

be divisible into parts, since parts involve spatial and temporal limitations.

In sum, reason can show that God exists, and that he *is* the unlimited fulness of life and being. Yet he is quite other than what we normally term life and being, that is, the universe, for whereas things *have* life and *have* being, God *is* life and *is* being. Otherwise, reason alone tells us what God is not, for beyond these great generalities its description of him is negative.[3]

The fact that all life has its origin as well as its continued existence in a Being of this kind raises many problems, though not so many or such serious problems as it solves. It raises the possibly insoluble problem of evil, but solves what would otherwise be the far more remarkable problem of the existence of good. It raises the difficult question of how an imperfect universe can be the effect of an infinitely perfect Being, but at least it gives us the exceedingly welcome assurance that there *is* a perfect Being. It implies properties and qualities in this Being which bring thought to the limits of its power, not by their complexity, but by their astounding simplicity, and yet by disclosing such a property as God's entire presence at every point of space and time, it brings him from a distant realm of abstraction to a realm "nearer to us than we are to ourselves." The argument can be shown to imply, too, that every process, every movement from the circling of stars to the vibration of a gnat's wing, is not only under the complete control of God, but also occupies his entire con-

---

[3]The foregoing is intended as nothing more than a résumé of the basic philosophical argument for belief in God. For the detailed argument see *Summa Theologica*, I. QQ. 1–26; E. L. Mascall, *He Who Is.* London, 1944; Farrell, *A Companion to the Summa*, vol. i, chs. 2–5. New York, 1941. Mascall's work is a particularly valuable discussion of the argument in relation to recent philosophical trends.

sciousness as if it were the only thing that was happening. And while this makes the problem of evil even more acute, it gives the splendid knowledge that life is utterly to be trusted, however painful, and that nothing is easier than to have communion with God.

But the argument raises one particularly serious problem which is both practical and theoretical—a problem of the greatest importance for mystical religion and for the whole work of realizing union with God, a problem for which Christian philosophy, Thomist or otherwise, has not yet found a satisfactory answer. It is the problem of the true relation between God and the universe, the Creator and the creature.

From the purely philosophic standpoint the problem is that while the Thomistic argument works perfectly backwards, in reasoning from the universe to God, it does not work so well in reasoning forwards from God to the universe. It is shown quite clearly that the universe demands a Cause such as has been described. But it is not shown at all clearly how the Cause produces the universe. Two possible solutions have to be rejected. The first is that God created the universe out of some primordial, chaotic matter which had existed from all eternity along with but apart from God himself. But if this matter is not caused by God he is not the first cause, and we have to look for God elsewhere, because if we are not dealing with the first cause, we are not dealing with God. The second is that God created the universe out of his own "substance," by a process which should be called emanation rather than creation. But if God is indivisible this involves pantheism, since every "part" of the indivisible God is equal to the whole—is God himself. If every single creature is absolutely identical with God, all differences, all grades of perfection, all values, become illusory. In fact the universe, as we understand it, does not exist at all. The problem of creation, of the origin of the universe, is abolished by saying that there is no creation. There is only God. There is also a completely unexplained illusion of a diversified universe. To say that God caused the illusion is in effect to return to the problem of creation, and we have to begin all over again. To say that man created it is to say the same thing, because man is God; or else it is to say that God as man became *subject* to the illusion. And again, God is not the first cause.

Rejecting these two solutions, orthodox theology maintains that God created the universe out of nothing.[4] The universe, together with its time and space, was not. And then, by a fiat of the divine will, it was. Of course, this is not really a solution. It is simply a description of what must have happened if there was no pre-existing material and if God did not make the universe out of himself. God caused the universe by some other means, but we don't know how. Reason here has to jump a gap, seeing no way out of the dilemma. The gap does not lie between God and the universe; it lies in reasoning, for theology knows no rational principle which can account for the action. It can only say that whereas creatures cause things out of themselves or out of pre-existing material, the Creator causes things in the manner proper to a first cause—independently of pre-existing material. But the point upon which orthodox theology wishes to insist is not just that there was no pre-existing material; it is that the universe, definitively and absolutely, is *not* God. For in ordinary logical

---

[4]This does not, of course, mean that the "nothing" was in any sense a material out of which the universe was constructed, nor yet should we imagine it even as an empty space apart from God within which it was made.

terms the identification of the universe with God involves pantheism, which renders all moral distinctions unreal.[5]

We could well afford to leave this problem alone as one of the unfathomable mysteries of the Godhead were it not that mystical experience, both Christian and non-Christian, glimpses, or intuits, an answer deeper than this, an answer for which theology has no proper terms of expression. When expressed in theological terms, the answer *sounds* like pantheism, for which reason official theology has always looked upon mysticism with suspicion. The mystic, on his side, is often somewhat dissatisfied with theology, because it seems to set a gulf between God and man which love cannot tolerate because it desires the most intimate kind of union. We are raising, in fact, the crucial problem of transcendence and immanence, the One and the Many, a problem that has always been troublesome for Christian theology because the seeming *dualism* of God on the one hand and the universe on the other has not been adequately resolved. While it remains unresolved the mystic must either go his own way and leave theology alone, or else he must be for ever wrestling with the adaptation of experience to theology and theology to experience, forever tempering his language with caution and taking care not to be a heretic. For the mystic knows that in some mysterious and indescribable manner God and his universe are one.

---

[5]The term pantheism is commonly used much too vaguely, and here must be taken in its strict sense, namely that God and the universe are two names for the same thing, that God − universe=0. Sometimes confused with pantheism is emanationism, the doctrine that the universe is a finite form of part of the divine substance. But the argument which follows assumes that the infinite is indivisible and can have no parts.

No system of philosophy or theology, no precise intellectual structure, can ever fully embrace the mystical experience of God. Not only is the divine Spirit as living and ungraspable as the wind, but the experience itself contains paradoxical elements which no ordinary logical procedure can reconcile. While we cannot hope for a theology which explains it, we may be able to find one which neither suspects nor conflicts with it—a theology in real sympathy with mysticism. Among the reasons for which the prevailing theology has been dubious of mysticism is that theology sets so great a value upon precise and definite beliefs and their necessity for salvation. This is partly due to the fact that a certain type of mind is frightened by the mutability, the elusiveness, and the mystery of life, and thinks of salvation as a state of everlasting fixity and certainty from which the disconcerting elements of spontaneity, surprise and mystery are largely removed. Yet in these same elements another type of mind discerns the activity of a living Spirit. For him salvation is an entire union with and acceptance of this mysterious Spirit, and with the expression of its liveliness and spontaneity in the elusive flux of life as we experience it from day to day. For this type of mind fixity is death, and instead of trying to catch and possess the wind of the Spirit, he lets it blow freely around and through him, finding peace, joy and salvation in its very movement. He surrenders the desire to possess it in any fixed state or form, and lets it possess him, affirming and joining in its unceasing and ungraspable movement as in some divine dance or melody.

It is not that Spirit comes or goes, shifts or changes in

itself. Like the present moment, it is elusive when the mind tries to pursue and hold it. The true movement is in its creative expressions, in the activity of Spirit rather than the agent, and this movement is not so much the quest for an attainment as a dance celebrating fulfilment. God is himself "unmoved, all motion's source," and in union with him the mystic feels with Dante that

> *ma già volgeva il mio desiro e il velle,*
> *sì come rota ch'egualmente è mossa,*
> *L'amor che move il sole e l'altre stelle.*[6]

Sometimes the mystic feels that this Spirit, this ultimate Reality, is inseparable from the immediate contents of daily experience, and on the basis of this intuition is often erected the theology of pantheism or immanentism. At other times he experiences Reality as something immeasurably other than himself and all created things, as a Being infinitely great, holy and splendid, before whom the world as we know it appears ugly, gross and evil. From this intuition comes the theology of transcendence, or else the common corollary of pantheism—the doctrine of the illusory universe. Again, there are times when Reality presents itself to him as something so alive and intelligent that he feels himself to be in communion with a person. At other times he is so impressed with its infinitude and mystery that anything so suggestive of man as personality seems an unthinkable limitation.

All of these apparently paradoxical elements will have their place in a truly complete mysticism, in a full

---

[6] *Paradiso*, xxxiii. 143–145. "But now my desire and my will were revolved, like a wheel which is moved evenly, by the Love which moves the sun and the other stars." (Norton.)

experience of union with God. If the union is to be perfect, God must be in the most intimate and inseparable union not only with the soul but also with its entire experience of life and the world. But if that with which the soul is united is to be God, he must at the same time be infinitely above, beyond and other than the soul and the world. Furthermore, if God is the source and height of liveliness and creative power, he cannot be anything less than a person, since a law or principle is simply an automatic, mechanical and dead mode of behaviour. On the other hand, if God is the ultimate Reality, the one source of all things, he must be free from the limitations of personality as we know it, and must not be subject to the mutability and the limitations of the forms in which his creative activity is expressed.

To these essential paradoxes or antinomies of religious experience must be added another, both mystical and philosophic. The human mind is profoundly dissatisfied with any form of absolute dualism, with a religion or a metaphysic for which ultimate Reality is not one and undivided. The dissatisfaction is not only felt with such crude dualisms as the Zoroastrian contrast of ultimate light and ultimate darkness, Ormuzd and Ahriman, or the Manichaean dualism of Spirit and Matter; as we have seen, it is even felt with the monotheistic "dualism" of Creator and creature *ex nihilo*. On the other hand, reason and the moral sense rebel at pantheistic monism which must reduce all things to a flat uniformity and assert that even the most diabolical things are precisely God, thus destroying all values.

No forms of compromise or *via media* can resolve these antinomies because mystical experience presents them to us in the most extreme and contrasted manner.

Compromise would altogether destroy their vitality and power over human life. Nor can we divide these elements as the sheep from the goats, and term some of them "true" mysticism and others "false," for this would be a ridiculous simplification. Yet compromise or division has been the traditional method of Christian theology. There are two reasons for this. Firstly, the "theological mind," which above all things seeks definition, precision and fixity, has the most intense difficulty in accepting the mystery of paradox and the terrible uncertainty as to ultimate truth which it seems to involve. Secondly, the reasoning processes of the Western mind, grounded as they are in Greek logic, can never be happy with a profound antinomy. A proposition must be true or false, and x cannot at the same time be both y and not y.

On the whole, traditional theology has leaned principally to the theology of transcendence, of God's holiness and otherness. After the Renaissance, to meet the rise of Humanism, it combined the stress on transcendence with an increased emphasis on the personality of God as this was revealed in the divine humanity of Jesus. Theology and spirituality became more and more Christocentric, and at the same time quite alien to the traditions of Christian mysticism! Contemplation, as understood by the mediaeval mystics, was replaced by affective and imaginative devotion to the humanity of Jesus.[7] From the standpoint of mysticism this was a disaster based on a misunderstanding of the Incarnation, for it made the divine humanity transcendent and humanized the mystery of God. It frustrated the very purpose of the Incarnation because, in practice, it did

[7] See on this the excellent article "Roman Catholic Mysticism" by Dom John Chapman in Hastings' *Encyclopaedia of Religion and Ethics.*

not raise humanity to union with God; it raised only the historic Jesus.[8] God was made at once transcendent and anthropomorphic, and with such a God mysticism is impossible because it makes him as remote, or rather, infinitely more remote than another human being.

Mediaeval mysticism as we find it in *The Cloud of Unknowing,* in Eckhart, Tauler, the Victorines, Ruysbroeck, and even as late as Denis the Carthusian, St. John of the Cross and Augustine Baker is little concerned with devotions to the humanity of Jesus. Yet the intensity and intimacy of the union with God which it experiences can only be justified in a Christian context by the doctrine of the Incarnation. For, in the words of St. Athanasius, "God became man that man might become God,"[9] and it is precisely on the basis of the Incarnation, its revelation of the eternal function of the Word,[10] and its realization of God's union not only with Jesus but with man and all creation, that there is room for a complete mysticism in Christianity.

When, however, theology tries to achieve a compromise between immanence and transcendence, both are deprived of their effect. God is not quite immanent and not quite transcendent; the world conceals his omni-

---

[8] The dogma of the Incarnation insists that in Christ God became man, not *a* man. That is to say, in Christ there are two natures, but only one person. The person is divine—God the Son—but it is in hypostatic union with a complete human nature, though not with a human person. Thus the humanity of Christ is representative of *all* humanity, and by this means the gifts of the Incarnation are bestowed upon the whole race and not upon the historic Jesus alone.

[9] *De incarn. verbi,* 54. iii. Some would prefer to translate, "God became man that man might become divine." Cf. Irenaeus, *"non ab initio dii facti sumus, sed primo quidem homines, tunc demum dii."*

[10] Cf. Irenaeus, *Adv. haer.,* 3. xvi. 6. "His only-begotten Word is always present with the human race, united to and mingled with his own creation, according to the Father's pleasure." Again, *ibid.,* 3. xviii. 7: "And unless man had joined to God, he could never have become a partaker of incorruptibility. . . . Wherefore also (the Word) passed through every stage of life, restoring all to communion with God."

131

present Being like a veil; he is "in" all things, but not thoroughly united with them, just as water is not fully united with the jar which contains it because the substance of the water and the substance of the jar are mutually exclusive. In this sense God and the world are simply mixed. They may even interpenetrate to some degree like air and dust, but still they are mutually exclusive. But if God and the world are mutually exclusive, God does not actually transcend the world, because mutually exclusive entities must belong to the same order of being. For example, different shapes are mutually exclusive, and although a square can be put inside a circle, it cannot be fully united with it. A square can in no sense *be* a circle. But colour is wholly other than shape, and there is no mutual exclusiveness between a circle and redness. Colour can no more be described in terms of shape than God can be described in terms of created things. Yet although the colour red is quite other than the shape circle, there is a sense in which a circle can *be* red.[11]

The analogy of colour and shape goes some way to solving the problem, showing us that the completeness of God's union with a creature depends on his very transcendence. But the analogy, and the solution to the problem which it suggests, has three disadvantages. Firstly, it leads us to think of God as a substance out of which things are made as figures might be cut out of paper or wood. It would follow from this that creatures are so many forms of God (shapes of colour). This gives us, secondly, the disadvantage of suggesting that

---

[11] For clarity of thought here, one must avoid the mental picture of uniting the colour red with a white circle outlined in black. The shape circle must be thought of as quite abstract until the colour gives it substance. In rather the same way creatures are purely abstract until God gives them being.

God's immanence in creatures circumscribes him. Thirdly, a transcendence or otherness of this type would seem to eliminate all possibility of God having any influence on the creature, or even of creating it. Colour is not a sufficient cause of shape. Beauty or intensity of colour would in no way be able to effect beauty or clarity of shape. The two orders of being touch; they may even coincide; the presence of the latter may even be shown to depend on the former. But there the relationship ends. There can be, as it were, no understanding, no communion, no passage of influence between the two. Here we have, in principle, the same difficulty that we found in the idea of the creation of the world *ex nihilo.* We do not see how it can possibly be done, but we are doing our best to safeguard the transcendence of God!

For practical purposes mystical religion has always tended to insist that man and the world must be utterly united with God, must in some sense *be* God. In the words of the unknown author of *The Cloud:*

> For he is thy being, and in him thou art what thou art, not only by cause and by being, but also he is in thee both thy cause and thy being. And therefore think of God in thy work as thou dost on thyself, and on thyself as thou dost on God: that he is as he is and thou art as thou art; so that thy thought be not scattered nor separated, but oned in him that is all; evermore saving this difference betwixt thee and him, that he is thy being and thou art not his. . . . He is being both to himself and to all. And in that only is he separated from all—that he is being both of himself and of all. And in that is he one in all and all in him, that all things have their being in him, as he is the being of all.[12]

[12] *The Epistle of Privy Counsel,* ch. 1, in *The Cloud of Unknowing.* Ed. Dom Justin McCann. London, 1943, p. 96.

Or as St. Catherine of Genoa put it, "My Being is God, not by simple participation, but by a true transformation of my Being"; and again, "My *me* is God: nor do I know my selfhood except in God."[13] "The eye with which I see God," said Eckhart, "is the same eye with which God sees me. My eye and God's eye is one eye, and one sight, and one knowledge, and one love."[14] And again,

> When a man goes out of himself to find or fetch God, he is wrong. I do not find God outside myself nor conceive him excepting as my own and in me. A man ought not to work for any why, not for God nor for his glory nor for anything at all that is outside him, but only for that which is his being, his very life within him.[15]

Upon the certainty of this union with God depends the entire joy, power, and world-transfiguring character of the mystical experience. Here, too, is the source of the mystic's vivid sense of spiritual freedom: he is one with God, and "neither height nor depth, neither principalities nor powers" can break this union. The mystic knows that he has it in spite of himself; that it is God's gift, and that it is given quite irrespective of his merits and despite his total unworthiness.

Yet his very gratitude for the gift will demand expression in worship and self-oblation, acts that can only be directed to a transcendent God, to One other than himself and infinitely exceeding him in holiness and glory. The attractive feature of pantheism is just that it imparts this sense of certain and unbreakable union with

---

[13]From the *Vita e Dottrina*, quoted in Underhill's *Mysticism*. London, 1930, pp. 129 and 396.

[14]*Meister Eckhart's Sermons*. Trs. Claud Field. London, n.d., p. 32.

[15]Pfeiffer's *Meister Eckhart*. Trs. C. de B. Evans. London, 1924, vol. i, p. 163.

God. But its danger and falsity is that it excludes any basis for worship and gratitude, for in pantheism union with God is an automatic necessity; it is not a gift. On the other hand, the extreme of transcendental theism reduces the divine gift to mere "justification"—that is, the chance for a new start after the remission of past sins—coupled with the "grace" to imitate the divine life more perfectly. God is here assisting man to become one with him by analogy only; there is no union of natures.

Thus for the theology of pure transcendence, union with God is a goal not yet achieved save in rare instances of great saintliness and grace. It implies that those who have attained it have done so either through their own merits and efforts, or else that they are special objects of divine favouritism. Not only does this view encourage spiritual pride, but it raises the question as to how a human soul can rise to God unless it first *has* God. "Console thyself," wrote Pascal, "thou wouldest not seek Me if thou hadst not found Me."[16] But in the view of the mystics, union with God is a present fact to be realized rather than attained. It is neither to be earned nor is it a result of special favouritism; it is given to all to be realized, appreciated and used, just as God "maketh his sun to rise upon the evil and on the good, and sendeth his rain upon the just and upon the unjust." Almost all mysticism, whether Western or Eastern,[17] has the sense of the *given-ness* of union with God, of its eternal reality which has to be accepted and recognized—not achieved. In the words of Ruysbroeck:

[16]Cf. St. Bernard, *De diligendo Deo,* cap. 7: *"Nemo te quaerere valet, nisi quod prius invenerit."*

[17]On the sense of given-ness in Eastern mysticism see my article "The Problem of Faith and Works in Buddhism" in the Columbia University *Review of Religion* of May, 1941.

In its created being (the soul) incessantly receives the impress of its Eternal Archetype, like a flawless mirror, in which the image remains steadfast and in which the reflection is renewed without interruption by its ever-new reception in new light. This essential union of our spirit with God does not exist in itself, but it dwells in God and it flows forth from God and it depends upon God and it returns to God as to its Eternal Origin. And in this wise, it has never been, nor ever shall be, separated from God; for this union is within us by our naked nature, and, were this nature to be separated from God, it would fall into pure nothingness. And this union is above time and space and is always and incessantly active according to the way of God. But our nature, forasmuch as it is indeed like unto God but in itself is creature, receives the impress of its Eternal Image passively. This is that nobleness which we possess by nature in the essential unity of our spirit, where it is united to God according to nature. This neither makes us holy, nor blessed, for all men, whether good or evil, possess it within themselves; but it is certainly the first cause of all holiness and blessedness.[18]

This extreme immanentism or quasi-pantheism of the mystics only becomes a problem when we try to consider the mystical experience from the strictly logical standpoint of theology. In practice the mystic does not find any conflict in his experience of God; nor, save in comparatively rare instances, does his sense of being one with God destroy his sense of values. This remains true even when mysticism is related to such an extremely immanentist theology as Hindu Vedanta or Mohammedan Sufiism. He may say to himself with the *Upanishads*, "Thou art Brahman!" but he does not then proceed to claim omnipotence and omniscience. Even supposing this to be pure pantheism, the moral blind-

---

[18] *Adornment of the Spiritual Marriage*, Bk. II, cap. 57. Trs. Dom P. Wynschenk in his *John of Ruysbroeck*. London, 1916.

ness which most theologians attribute to the pantheist is largely theoretical. It might well arise if the pantheist were not a mystic; but a mystical pantheist is scarcely ever a consistent and logical pantheist, because he is trying to describe a relationship to God which is not in fact pantheism although it seems to be when he uses theological terms.

But formal and official theology will take cognizance of his views and attempt to pass judgement upon them as if they were statements of dogma. The mystic, however, knowing that he cannot describe his experience exactly, has not tried to make a *dogmatic* statement. He uses theological language only because he is talking about God, because there is no other language available and appropriate. His statements are poetic rather than dogmatic, and it is as absurd to take them literally as to imagine that the poet really means that his beloved has cherries for lips and ravens' wings for hair. Theology, however, is always reluctant to admit the limitations of its language, and disturbed to see it used with such alarming liberty.

> The very foundation of mysticism [writes Berdyaev] is an inner kinship or union between the human spirit and the divine, between creation and the Creator. It implies the overcoming of transcendence, and that sense of God and man being external to one another. Thus mysticism is always concerned with the immanence rather than the transcendence of God, an immanence, moreover, which is actually experienced. This is why mysticism always employs terms which differ from those of theology, and why in theological circles mysticism is always suspected of heretical tendencies. But mysticism is of such a profound nature that we cannot apply to it the more superficial criteria of heresy. Mystics are always suspected of pantheistic leanings and indeed, when an attempt is made to

137

understand them rationally and to translate their experience into the terms of theology or metaphysics, they certainly do come very near to pantheism. Yet while pantheism is in reality a highly rationalistic doctrine, mysticism uses paradoxical and apparently contradictory expressions, because for the mystics both the identity between the creature and the Creator and the gulf which separates them are both equally facts of existence. Mysticism cannot be expressed either in terms of pantheistic monism or of theistic dualism.[19]

Unless, therefore, we can find some terms other than pantheistic monism or theistic dualism there can be no vital relationship between mysticism and Christian theology. The highly desirable goal of a presentation of Christian doctrine interpreted by mystical religion will be impossible. The two must simply agree to leave one another alone; the mystic must agree not to give the impression of speaking dogmatically, and the theologian must agree not to judge mystical pronouncements by his own standards, and yet permit the mystic to use theological terms in his peculiar alogical and paradoxical manner.

Fortunately, however, the terms can be found, and although they may not *completely* bridge the gap between mystical and theological pronouncements, they give a more satisfactory result than anything hitherto employed, and far more satisfactory than mere agreement to remain aloof. Language and intellectual thought, we must repeat, can never so embrace and describe the mystical experience that it may be communicated from one soul to another by mere words and ideas. But theology can adopt a principle of thought

[19]Berdyaev, *Freedom and the Spirit*. Trs. O. F. Clarke. London, 1935, p. 242. The entire chapter is a most competent and suggestive discussion of the problem.

which will in great measure resolve the antinomy of transcendence and immanence, monism and dualism, without resort to compromise. This will not involve the acceptance of any new dogma, but of a new method, a new type of logic and technique of thought, which will not only resolve the antinomy, but will also illumine the very rationale of mystical experience.

The root of the difficulty is that Western theology and philosophy, grounded as it is in Greek thought, has an inadequate conception of the unity of God. Our logic, our method of reasoning is entirely dualistic, and therefore cannot without contradictions treat of a Being who surpasses duality. The unity of God is therefore seen as *opposed* to multiplicity in God. God has no opposite, and yet we apply to him the term unity in a sense which has an opposite, for unity as we conceive it is unthinkable without the contrast of multiplicity. But we find in Indian thought a method which surpasses dualism in so far as the intellect is capable of so doing. This method is developed in Sankhara's Advaita Vedanta and in Mahayana Buddhism.

Neither of these two systems carry the method to a conclusion which would satisfy the Christian because they are working with basic material (*i.e.*, revelation) which he would deem inadequate. But this need not concern us, for what is important is the method itself, and not the use which Vedantists and Buddhists have made of it. To some extent the quest of Vedanta is the same as that of Christianity, namely, the transcending of dualism, the realization of union with God. Both are agreed that God is the one supreme Reality, and that no second reality stands over against him on an equal footing, imposing any limitation upon him. God has no opposite. This is a sufficient basis of agreement for the

Indian method to have relevance for Christianity. Our difficulty is that, while admitting the non-duality of God, we apply terms to him in a dualistic sense. We speak of him rightly as one, but then go on to reason from the term as if it were to be used in an exclusive and privative sense.[20]

The method itself (which is an intellectual analogy of the mystic way) is a process of reaching as nearly as may be to the idea of pure non-duality, which, as will appear, is not at all the same thing as one-ness in the monistic sense. It is at the same time a searching critique of the dualism of every idea of unity that falls short of pure non-duality, a critique which very swiftly disposes of pantheistic monism. It starts with one item of data, one "revealed dogma" which is the same for Vedanta as for Christianity: God is That which has no opposite; he is One-without-a-second.[21] All created things have opposites whereby they are conditioned and limited; all creatures are of a mutually exclusive character in their relations to each other, for *this* is not *that, I* am not *thou, light* is not *darkness, red* is not *blue.* But God transcends creatures in the sense that nothing has power to exclude him, to set any boundaries to his being and power. He is absolutely free of

---

[20]Cf. *Summa Theol.*, I. Q. xi. a. 3: "Although in God there is no privation, still, according to the mode of our apprehension, he is known to us only by way of privation and remotion. Thus there is no reason why certain privative terms should not be predicated of God, for instance, that he is *incorporeal,* and *infinite;* and in the same way it is said of God that he is *one.* " But terms of privation are used to show God's freedom from limitation. The term *one* as used here does not do this. It confines God within the dualistic and mutually exclusive opposition of one and many. If St. Thomas had substituted the term *non-dual* for *one,* he would have had a term analogous to incorporeal and infinite.

[21]"The Lord our God is one God."—Deut. 6:4. "Before me there was no God formed, neither shall there be after me."—Isaiah 43:10. "Is there a God beside me? Yea, there is no God; I know not any."—Isaiah 44:8.

every external restraint. In a peculiar and profound sense God is all-inclusive; there is nothing "outside" him, for had he any "outside" he would have limitations and would not be infinite. It may be shown, then, that God has a power which no creature, as such, possesses —the power to be what he is not, to "other" himself.

If this can be shown, it will, on the one hand, entirely fulfil the mystic's intuition that God is "all in all" and that the universe is one with him. On the other hand, it will also account for the other aspect of his intuition, which is that individual things are not lost and obliterated in the unity of God but transfigured, seen as more perfectly and uniquely themselves. For if the unity of God is truly all-inclusive and non-dual, it must include diversity and distinction as well as one-ness; otherwise the principle of diversity would stand over against God as something opposite to and outside him. This inclusion of diversity is impossible for the God of pantheism, who cannot comprehend *real* diversity. The universe of the pantheist is *unreal*.

Thus the logic of non-duality makes short work of pantheism. If all things are in reality one thing, God, such one-ness is exclusive, dual and limited, because it excludes real multiplicity. The very concept of one-ness is a term of duality, because it is inconceivable apart from the idea of two, or of many, or even of none. Therefore if in our quest for non-duality we state that all things are one God, we are limiting God; we are implying that he is not free to make or be something truly different from himself, and such a God is still dual, and for that very reason is in no way superior to the realm of duality or creation.

On the other hand, the statement that all things are *not* God is, by itself, as dualistic as the statement that

141

they are God. The God so conceived still fails to transcend the creaturely realm of duality. Orthodox theology, and especially theology in the tradition of St. Thomas, failed to see that God could include and even be many as well as one, *because it regarded multiplicity and diversity as a privation and not a perfection of being*. It saw diversity as the subjection of unity to division and disintegration. Particular things—men, trees, stones and stars—were particular just because they *lacked* the fulness of being, and expressed only a fragment of the divine Being. But this was a wholly negative idea of particularity. It did not realize that particularity was a great and positive good, that God's expression of himself in particular things neither added to his being nor disintegrated it. It expressed the splendour of the divine unity in the splendour of variety, which, as the proverb says, is the spice of life. But the Neo-Platonic background of mediaeval thought, tinged as it was with Manichaeism, held a prejudice against variety and multiplicity. It was the old story of world-hatred, so inconsistent with the religion of the Incarnation.

Thus God's "othering" of himself in the creation is not, as in pantheism, a *maya*, an illusion. The multiplicity is as real as the unity, since the creature is one with God in the very act of being other than God. Thus we must change the meaning of the statement that God made the world out of nothing, and understand the nothing as the no-thing *(sunyata)*, the unutterable mystery, the divine darkness, which is God himself as he appears to human sense and thought and feeling. For this seeming void, this no-thing intelligible to the human mind and its dualistic mode of thought, is God as he is absolutely in himself, beyond all duality—neither one nor many, nor both one and many, and yet with equal reality one and many, and both one and many.[22] Human speech cannot surpass its own inherent duality!

The attempt to conceive a Being beyond all duality swiftly brings thought to the limits of its power and reduces philosophy and theology to silence before the mystery of God. But it does leave us with some positive concepts, as true as any idea of God, any formulation of the infinite, can be.

Firstly, it lays greater stress than ever upon the divine *freedom*. For every form of pantheism God's manifestation of himself in the universe is necessary, because the universe, if simply identical with God, must be as eternal as God. But to say that God is non-dual is another way of saying that he is free—absolutely. He is free to be One, not bound to be One. He is free to include diversity in his unity, free to "other" himself. This "othering" of himself is the free gift of his Being to creatures who otherwise might not have existed. And these creatures are *in reality* other than God; if they were not, God could not be said to *give* his Being to others, and would not be free to include *real* diversity in his unity. Thus non-duality means that God is entirely free from the essential limitation of finite existence, which is that a creature cannot at once be itself and another. More than ever, the creature may thank God for the free gift of life and being, not only because it might not have been given, but also because the gift is God.

Secondly, the idea of God's non-duality is a new way of understanding his *love*. For love is not simply, as St.

---

[22]Cf. St. Dionysius pseudo-Areopagite, *Theologia Mystica*, cap. 5: "Neither is he . . . one, nor oneness, . . . neither is there any entire affirmation or negation that may be made concerning him."

Thomas suggests,[23] the willing of another's good; it is giving oneself entirely to another being.[24] God's creation of a being is one and the same act as his love for it. In truth he becomes one who is in truth other than himself. Thus a creature fulfils God's love and will for itself not by being, or trying to be, God—but by being itself. This is true cooperation with God, because in that creature God is not being himself; he is being another. If by this means the creature fulfils God's will and love, the more it is truly and distinctly itself, the more it is truly God; for in so doing it is affirming and manifesting God's non-duality, his freedom to be what is not himself, his freedom to be more than mere one-ness. Thus one of the most interesting traits of mysticism is that those who have experienced most keenly their union with God are intensely real and unique personalities.

This corrects one of the most usual perversions of mysticism—the attempt to become one with God by mere flight from everyday life and experience. It is a perversion because it is a half truth. Certainly mysticism begins with the contemplation of God as transcendent. Because God is the maker of all sensible and intelligible things, he himself can neither be sensed nor known. As transcendent, he can never be an object of experience or knowledge, and, conversely, no particular experience or state of mind can be the immediate

---

[23] *Summa Theol.*, I. Q. 20, a. 2: "To love anything is nothing else than to will good to that thing."

[24] "Greater love hath no man than this, that a man lay down his life for his friends."—John 15:13. To lay down one's life is, of course, to give oneself entirely, which is precisely what God does in the Incarnation and Atonement. So too St. Dionysius, *De Divinis Nominibus*, IV. 13: "On behalf of the truth we must dare to affirm that the Cause of the universe himself, by his abounding love and goodness, is placed outside of himself in his providence toward all things that have being . . . and so is drawn from his transcendent throne above all to dwell within all, through a transcendent and ecstatic power whereby he yet remains within himself."

knowledge of God.[25] For all experiences and states of mind belong to the realm of duality, and are mutually exclusive. Thus the mystical experience is neither a particular state of mind nor (for this, too, has an opposite) mere blankness of mind. Like the mirror which reflects all images yet is not itself an image, the mystical experience underlies and is one with all experience, as is God himself. When St. Dionysius speaks of knowing God through *agnosia* or "unknowing," he means that we may know God in all things through not knowing him in any. The mystic, he explains, "by the very fact of not seeing and not knowing (God), truly enters into him who is beyond sight and knowledge; knowing this, too, that he is in all things that are felt and known."[26] The state of union, like God himself, has no opposite; it is all-inclusive, for which reason any experience may participate in it.

Therefore we discover the union of ourselves and of the creation with God through the very realization that they are themselves and not God. His very transcendence effects his perfect immanence, for "he ascended up far above all heavens, that he might fill all things."[27] The distinct, individual reality of things is the very measure of their union with God, of their fulfilment and expression of his freedom to include diversity, to love and be what is other than himself. For this reason, and not because he is a pantheist, the mystic apprehends all

---

[25]This same "apophatic" approach to God may be found in Advaita Vedanta. All things sensed and known belong to the realm of *dvaita* or duality, for they have opposites and thus are not God. So to each of them the seeker says, *"Neti, neti,"*—"Not this, not this." Cf. St. Dionysius, *Ep. ad Gaium Therapeutem:* "And if anyone, seeing God, were to understand what he saw, he would not have seen God, but some one of his creatures that exist and may be known."

[26]*Ep. ad Dorotheum Liturgum.*

[27]Ephesians 4:10.

things as one with God. He does not see the reality of God behind the illusion of the creature; he sees God in the very reality, entity and uniqueness of the creature, in its very distinction from God.[28]

Any view which stresses the unity of the universe with God will in some quarters be termed pantheistic, and any formal denial of pantheism will be called "merely verbal." But, strictly speaking, pantheism is the very definite doctrine that God and the universe are coterminous; that God is solely immanent, and that God minus the universe equals nothing. Such a doctrine is not only inconsistent with Christian dogma, but also with the theology of the Vedanta and Mahayana Buddhism, all of which insist that the ultimate Reality is infinite, free from all necessity and limitation, and that its existence would in no way be affected by the dissolution of the universe. True pantheism holds, furthermore, to a *necessary* identity of God and the universe, whereas all doctrines holding the infinity of God do and must maintain that the very existence of the universe is absolutely *unnecessary* (which is probably the real meaning of the Hindu concept of *maya*). Since by definition the infinite cannot be subject to any constraint, the existence as well as the union of finite beings with it must be entirely gratuitous. Thus the essential distinction between the doctrines of non-duality and pantheism is that the former, conceiving God as infi-

---

[28]Probably the nearest thing to the concept of God as non-dual to be found in Christian philosophy is the work of Nicholas of Cusa, Cardinal Bishop of Brixen (1401–1464). But he seemed to find the unity and multiplicity of God *necessary* aspects of the divine Being, even though the necessity of creation was internal and not external to God. Otherwise the parallel is close. Thus, *"Idem ipsum Deus et creatura: secundum modum datoris Deus, secundum modum dati creatura." De dato*, II. p. 286. See his *Vision of God.* Trs. E. G. Salter. London, 1928. Also Henry Bett, *Nicholas of Cusa.* London, 1932, esp. Part III, chs. 1 and 2.

nite, regards his union with the universe as a free act of grace, whereas the latter, conceiving him to be no more than a universe of finite and composite beings, regards it as necessary. Certainly there is the danger that men may presume upon this freely given union, but in the hands of evil men any truth may be dangerous.

III

Underlying the element of dualism in Christian theology is the problem of evil, and obviously the concept of God's non-duality will be unacceptable if it offers the same answer to this problem as pantheistic monism. Attempts have been made to escape the dualism of a God who utterly excludes evil through the idea that whereas God is Being, evil is essentially non-being, and having no ontological reality cannot stand over against God as an equal and opposite power conditioning him. But if evil is non-being, it offers no real problem; it is a mere illusion. The more realistic theologians therefore describe evil as a tendency in the direction of non-being, a desire, a mode of action, which is quite real although directed to an unreal goal. If God absolutely opposes and excludes this desire, it would seem that we have a clear dualism. But if we try to resolve this dualism by saying that this desire is, like everything else, an aspect of God, the whole realm of values will become illusory.

From the standpoint of non-duality, evil is not and cannot be the opposite of God. Yet this is just what evil wishes to be, opposing God in the entirely futile hope that it can exclude him, stand over against him, and limit him as an equal; this is its tremendous conceit.

Therefore the supremacy of God over evil requires that it should never be allowed to achieve this aim. Evil *tries* to oppose God, but if God were to oppose evil, he would not only be acknowledging it as an equal and opposite, but allowing it to fulfil its purpose. Hence it is not by opposing evil that God renders it futile; he overcomes it through his non-duality, his all-inclusiveness, his love, which is unconquerable and supreme because it does not oppose and cannot effectively be opposed. Evil is the attempt to pick a quarrel with God, and because it cannot, it wears itself out with exasperation. Although evil struggles to exclude and oppose God, it never succeeds because he always embraces it in his all-inclusive love. To evil this love *appears* like wrath and opposition, though this is its own wrath and opposition projected on the "mirror" of God and inflamed by perpetual frustration. It tries to mar the purity of the mirror by making it reflect its own loathsomeness. But the loathsomeness is simply reflected back to its origin with perfect clarity, and serves only to demonstrate the inherent purity of the mirror.

Not only is evil unable to oppose and exclude God, but it also achieves the very contrary of its aim. In spite of itself, it achieves greater and greater demonstrations of the divine love, just as in trying to destroy Christ, Judas achieved unwittingly the salvation of the world. This was because Christ accepted the injury done to him with the all-inclusive love of God. "Father, forgive them, for they know not what they do." The greater the evil, the greater it proves the love of God to be, because that love simply "enlarges" itself to include and embrace it.

Evil originates, not in God, but in the real otherness of the creature, to which God is giving his own Being.

He permits it to originate, because in refusing he would destroy the real individuality, the very freedom, of the creature. He would then be making the creature one with himself by identity instead of distinction. He permits it, also, because he knows that it cannot truly oppose him and, in the long run, can only demonstrate his glory and holiness. Theology, however, can never admit that God is responsible for evil. Yet although God is not responsible for evil, he makes himself responsible. Evil, to its own fury and confusion, finds itself adopted by God, finds that it cannot escape from union with him, finds it impossible to alienate itself from the love of God. "If I make my bed in hell, behold, thou art there also!" Thus God renders the evil desire futile by his very immanence in it; yet if he were only immanent, this would amount to his condonement of and subjection to evil. But because at the same time he transcends evil, and is in himself perfect goodness and holiness, he can give himself to evil without subjection as the pure mirror is untainted by a vile reflection.[29] Thus evil is overcome by love and acceptance when the One who loves is in principle greater than evil. But love and acceptance become condonement and subjection when applied to evil by one who is *not* greater in principle, which is why man is incapable of overcoming it by his own efforts. For man is involved in a dualistic relationship with evil. Evil is the opposite of creaturely goodness, but not of the goodness of God. It destroys

[29]Cf. Faber, *Creator and Creature.* London, 1928, p. 71: God "distinctly permits and actually concurs with every exercise of them (our faculties) in thinking, loving or acting. This influx and concourse of God . . . gives a peculiar and terrific character to acts of sin. . . . Everything is penetrated with God, while his inexpressible purity is all untainted, and his adorable simplicity unmingled with that which he so intimately pervades, enlightens, animates and sustains."

creaturely being, but not the Being of God. Of himself, man can only condone evil or fight it. But to fight it is like trying to smooth raging waters with a flatiron, or to drown out an abominable noise by singing hymns; the result is only an increased turbulence and discordance.

Man can only overcome evil by grace, by realizing his union with God. Through this he awakens to the transcendent immanence of God in his own evil, which effects the forgiveness of sins. He discovers that to whatever depths of depravity he may descend, he can neither escape nor separate himself from that given union with God which he has by distinction as a creature, as an "othering" of God himself. Because of this he participates in the divine Being over which evil has no power. If this does not move him to such gratitude for the gift of union with God that he sets his will firmly against evil, he shows himself incapable of appreciating the gift, incapable of appreciating an eternal and unbreakable unity with Love itself. And lacking appreciation he excludes himself from the Beatific Vision, which is precisely hell.[30]

In practice the truth of the non-duality of God is difficult to accept for psychological rather than moral or theological reasons. Man is slow to accept union with God as a living fact. It involves high responsibilities. It involves an unwelcome deflation of that pride whereby man is always trying to attain union with God by his own efforts and merits. But union with God is a gift, a reality already achieved by the love of God. Man can only realize this when he ceases his proud effort to be God and wholeheartedly accepts his manhood, his very

[30]On the implications of the foregoing section for practical morality, see below, pp. 200–212.

separateness, individuality, and limitation. In this sense only is he one with God.

Again, non-duality designates something essentially free, alive and ungraspable, which eludes all precise definition. It indicates the impossibility of possessing God, the mystery of life, in any fixed form of thought or feeling, or in any particular state of mind and activity, or in any graspable mode whatsoever, of which one may say, "Now I have it." Yet man is frightened of this living, ungraspable mystery, and is always trying to have it securely boxed up in some philosophical, ethical, theological, or psychological formula, where its vitality is destroyed. Thus when mystical union is understood as some special state of mind or feeling that may be imitated, some particular experience that may be gotten and possessed, this is a false and devitalized mysticism. In trying to hold God in one fixed form, we exclude him from all others, and, so far as our apprehension of him is concerned, "devitalize" him in the one that we hold. We lose his immanence because we try to grasp and draw down his transcendence.

Pride, and fear of the living spontaneity and mystery of God, together contribute to an intellectual and spiritual rigidity which deadens Christian life and keeps God and man safely apart. Theistic dualism, which preserves the scheme of values but frustrates the union of man and God, is as much a petrifaction of the spiritual life as pantheistic monism, which affirms the union but invalidates the scheme of values. Compromise, which is in practice the usual solution, virtually puts God into the same order and hierarchy of being as man, only in an immeasurably superior position. Under such conditions the union of God and man is at best a mixture, and can be little more complete than the union of two human persons. None of these views fit the facts of mystical experience, of which the predominating type is the sense of union so complete that the mystic feels himself to be of one life and one being with God, and yet somehow still man, lacking the omnipotence and omniscience of Godhead and laying no claim to it.

No more do these partial conceptions of God harmonize with the doctrine of the Incarnation. Salvation is the union of man and God, and the Incarnation is the means of salvation because it achieves the union of man as man with God as God. It does not involve the conversion of man into superman or demigod, because union with God is given to man as he is—in his creaturely nature, as an individual human person distinct from the divine Person. The consistency of distinct human personality and perfect union with God is only possible in terms of the non-duality of God. For this union is more than a harmony of wills or a contact of beings absolutely external to one another. It is a union beyond the realm of duality where to be and not to be God presents no contradiction, where the creation in all its creatureliness is yet one with God.

II. THE HEART OF GOD

"If we may credit certain hints contained in the lives of
the saints, love raises the spirit above the sphere of
reverence and worship into one of laughter and dalliance: a sphere in which the soul says:—

> 'Shall I, a gnat which dances in Thy ray,
>   Dare to be reverent?' "

In these words Coventry Patmore[1] expressed a truth
which is of the very essence of union with God and
which, on the surface, seems contrary to the whole
mood of the Christian religion as we have known it. As
the mystical experience illumines our conception of the
Being of God, so too it gives us a deeper knowledge of
his character, and as the former kind of knowledge is
expressed in the symbols of metaphysical thought, the
latter is expressed in symbols of moral qualities. Of
necessity our symbols of God's character will be the
more anthropomorphic of the two, and, since we are
men, we shall always be to some extent compelled to
talk, think and feel about God in our own image. This
manlike symbol of God has, in the history of Hebrew-
Christian religion, undergone many changes parallel to
the growth of moral ideals. Like every other form of
religious symbolism it will deteriorate and become ob-
structive when not informed by mystical insight and
when we outgrow it in mental and emotional develop-

---

[1] *The Rod, the Root, and the Flower.* "Aurea Dicta," 39. London, 1907.

ment. For just these two reasons the moral image of God largely prevalent in modern Church religion is inferior, and all too often inspires us with feelings quite other than those implied in Patmore's words.

In general it may be said that our moral image of God is more or less good and true, but not particularly beautiful. It is lacking in Beauty and Beauty's hand-maidens—joy, laughter and, in its sublimest sense, play-fulness, a virtue which is at the very root of creative art. Of that trinity of virtues, the Good, the Beautiful and the True, the Beautiful has always been somewhat problematic for Christian thought, since it has felt that so many things are beautiful which are neither true nor good. The restoration of Beauty to its proper place in our image of God is one of the more important results of an incarnational mysticism, for Beauty is at once the most spiritual and the most material of the three virtues.

It is the most spiritual because it is the least serious and the least necessary; it is thoroughly gratuitous and entirely characteristic of God's loving freedom. A dead and mechanical God could be true in the sense of real and good in the sense of existing; such a God would be blind necessity itself. But only a living God can be inherently beautiful, because, as our civilization bears witness, beauty is not necessary for mere existence. However, in its freedom, its gratuitousness, its playful absence of ulterior motive, beauty is of the essence of spiritual life.

Spirit lacks all gravity and in so far seriousness. Seen from Spirit, nothing is heavy; it takes all things lightly. Not only the concept of toil, even that of suffering finds no object in it. There is toil only from the viewpoint of Gana (the flesh); and man knows pain and sorrow only as a crea-

154

ture of feeling and emotion. . . . Thus, in the first place, spiritual man must needs impress man of the earth as wanting in seriousness. This is true already of the man of courage, for he puts his life to the stake; that is to say: he plays with his life, which is indeed the current French and German way of expressing the same. But the believer, above all, must appear most sadly deficient in seriousness to the man of heavy earthliness. Consciously, he stakes on what is uncertain. He trusts most rashly despite the opinions of the sententious and the objections of the grave.[2]

On the other hand, beauty is the most material because it expresses itself in perfection of form, a perfection which is unnecessary from the standpoint of a limited truth and goodness. To Christians infected with Gnosticism beauty is suspect just because it is associated with matter and especially with woman, the symbol of Mother Earth. But because the Incarnation expresses God's love of the earth, and began its historical manifestation in God's love for a woman, this suspicion must be heretical from a truly Catholic viewpoint. Obviously, any one of the trinity of virtues can be perverted— goodness by self-righteousness, truth by lack of charity in the telling, and beauty by licentiousness.

But the three virtues are essential to each other's perfection, and a God not seen as fully beautiful is for that reason less good and true, and, above all, less living. In the Eternal Now we experience not only the love and the mystery of God but also his liveliness and creative joy which, expressing themselves in the beauty of nature, reflect the inherent beauty of God. *Ex divina pulchritudine esse omnium derivatur.*[3]

Beauty is, too, the object of our most spiritual as well

<hr/>

[2]Keyserling in *South American Meditations.* London, 1932, p. 373.
[3]St. Thomas, *De Divinis Nominibus,* iv. 5. "The being of all things is derived from the divine beauty."

as of our most material perceptions, of mystical vision and of sense and feeling. Because man is so powerfully controlled by the latter, an image of God deficient in beauty is of small appeal to him; and this is especially true of that stratum of the modern mind which we have been considering throughout this book—the educated, sincere, thoughtful and spiritually hungry pagan. He is repelled by the downright ugliness and joylessness of so much that passes for Christianity. This cannot be changed by mere external adjustments in ecclesiastical art and manners, or of the mere tone and style of teaching and preaching. It must proceed from an inner experience of the beauty and the joy of God.

I

Western man has attained a far greater degree of culture and discipline in his thinking than in his feeling— so much so that the idea of evaluating religion from an aesthetic as well as from an intellectual standpoint seems to him quite frivolous. He considers the beauty or ugliness of religious symbols and concepts quite irrelevant to their truth, and, of course, it is truth which matters. Yet however much their truth may matter, their power lies more than we care to admit in their effect upon our feelings. Mature and disciplined feelings have as much right to evaluate the worth of a religion as the intellect, since they reflect upon an aspect of reality which is hidden from pure thought—a fact almost incomprehensible to the overdeveloped intellectualism of Western philosophy. But if our feeling were as highly developed an instrument as our intellect, the acceptance of certain ideas would depend both upon their being thought true and felt true. Only because of the disproportionate growth of our thinking do we consider it a more reliable judge of spiritual values than feeling which, for us, is as unreliable as primitive man's intellect. Our feelings mislead us just as the primitive's thinking misleads him—simply because it has never been developed. There is no inherent deficiency in the faculty itself.

It is otherwise with a people such as the Chinese. From our standpoint their strictly intellectual development leaves much to be desired, for we find their philosophical reasoning, for instance, lacking in coherence. But in feeling and aesthetic judgement they are so far beyond us that we cannot really translate much of their philosophic literature into any Occidental language. They have, for example, more than a hundred words expressing nuances of aesthetic experience for which we have absolutely no equivalents. While we may regard this as a decadent overrefinement of culture, we must not forget that our own high degree of intellectual subtlety could give them a similar impression. But the Chinese "aesthete" is not at all decadent, for he has what the Occidental aesthete usually lacks— strength of character and amazing emotional control. He is a philosopher of feeling as distinct from a philosopher of thinking. Not only in art but also in religion and morals his standards of judgement are aesthetic rather than intellectual. This has seldom been taken into account in presenting the Christian religion to the Chinese. The best minds of China find it unconvincing and repellent because of an entirely unnecessary ugliness which we have had neither the wisdom nor the imagination to avoid, giving them, to cite one illustration, translations of the Bible so atrocious in style that they look upon the best efforts of Christianity as we look upon uncouth religious cults from the backwoods.

In view of our emotional immaturity it is not surprising that we have given little serious consideration to the aesthetic aspect of our image of God. Just because of their lack of cultivation, most theologians are apt to regard the feelings and emotions as the special province of the devil, since they yield so easily to his temptations, and to pass over all the objections of feeling to our image of God as unworthy of attention. But in neglecting these objections we overlook one of those great opportunities for the amplification and profounder understanding of Christian truth which, when neglected, estrange so many from the Faith.[4]

In the last thousand years Western man has undergone a development which has made certain primitive notions of God unacceptable to him. Christian thought has kept pace with this development, constantly deepening and purifying the intellectual conception of God so that no one is asked to think of him as an old man with a white beard sitting upon a cloud-borne throne among the stars. But so far from there having been any parallel deepening of our aesthetic conception, most theologians consider such sensitivity to the beauty of an idea a sign of a womanish softening of the brain, thinking that when confronted with a logically sound truth the duty of the feelings is simply to "take it," as if there were some salutary medicine in the very pain of the feelings. This attitude denies the divine intention of the union of the *whole* man with God, wherein man contemplates him perfectly with *all* the faculties of the soul. Those, therefore, who neglect the aesthetic con-

---

[4] The growth of sects and cults is nearly always a sign that the Church is falling short of catholicity. Christian Science, for example, is the result of the Church's neglect of spiritual healing.

templation of God are remaining insensitive to him, and even at discord with him, in an important part of their souls.

There is a reciprocal relation between the aesthetic image of God and the response of our feelings towards him. And since, whether we like it or not, the quality of feeling dictates the whole atmosphere of piety, generations of immature feeling build up a collective image which, although it has many slight variations, permeates Christian piety as a crude perfume will linger in the draperies of a house. Many people who might be capable of a mature response of the feelings of God come into contact with this collective image (one can hardly avoid it), with the result that it calls out from them an infantile and immature response and perpetuates the bad tradition. Popular Christian piety of the post-Renaissance period is as awkward, sentimental and self-conscious as an adolescent boy's first love affair.

The spell of this bad atmosphere is tremendous and, to a great degree, unconscious. Undeveloped as our feelings are, they are none the less powerful, and in practice they mould our religion to a far greater degree than our thinking. Saturated in this atmosphere, otherwise mature souls are retarded in their growth and remain content with a piety which, lacking the genuine naïveté and unaffected simplicity of the child, has rather the bad infantilism and maudlin emotionalism of prolonged adolescence.

This problem is particularly acute for Christianity because it knows God as a person and not as a principle. A person, a living being, affects the feelings much more violently than an impersonal Absolute. In Christianity the personality of God is more strongly emphasized even than in Judaism and Mohammedanism because of its central belief that the highest symbol of God is the human character of Jesus. Intellectually, we know that while God is a person he is not a man, or even an infinitely glorified, cosmically proportioned superman. He transcends entirely the hierarchy of created forms and natures. But this lofty intellectual discernment of God, having no parallel in the realm of feeling, has little effect upon piety, which still responds to God as to a man, often as crude in conception as vast in proportion.

Our collective image of God is frequently inferior to accepted human standards of perfection. Such inferiority would be understandable if it were caused by unavoidable limitations of vision. But the limitations of our image of God are by no means unavoidable. There is no reason at all why we should not recognize in God the beauty which we perceive in nature and create in art, and why we should avoid such recognition on the poor excuse that the beauty of God is so great as to be inconceivable. For while it is equally true that God is intellectually inconceivable, we have not therefore refused the task of intellectual contemplation, which, although it can never be more than the merest approximation to truth, has certainly deepened our understanding of God and even increased our love. Devout and thoughtful Christians will vaguely acknowledge that all the beauty and mystery, the gaiety and exuberance, which we see in nature and art exist supremely and perfectly in God, but there is little sign of any real appreciation of these qualities in their piety.

The effort of appreciation involved is great not only because God is great and mystical vision is rare, but also because the dead weight of the present aesthetic conception is hard to overcome. This is partly due to the fact that those who mould the Church's life and live most deeply within it are largely unaware of the defect. They do not realize that many, many souls prefer impersonal ideas of God, not because they are more satisfying intellectually, but because they do not offend the aesthetic sense, even though they may not stimulate it so much. They prefer the impersonal God, not because they believe that God is a blind and mechanical principle, but because the personal God or Christianity has been presented to them as an uninspiring or even offensive kind of person. Nor has this picture of God been helped by certain prevalent conceptions of the personality of Jesus.

I I

Despite the fact that while God is living he is not a man, and that while he is called "he" (for "it" would indicate something lifeless), God has no sex, the image of God which determines so great a part of our relations with him is that of an immeasurably great man and of a male. This is true not only of popular notions of God, but also of that important type of Catholic mysticism in which the soul plays the female role of the Beloved, while God the Lover is the male who "ravishes" the soul. For the history of the Christian idea of God begins in the patriarchal culture of the Hebrews where the supremacy of the male was unquestioned.[5] Yahweh was the King of kings and Lord of lords, titles of those Oriental tyrants of whom he became the heightened image.

Philosophically, we do not think of God as having the

[5]One of the cults which the prophets denounced most harshly was the worship of Ishtar or Ashtoreth, the Queen of Heaven *(melekheth hash-shamayim)*. Cf. esp. Jeremiah 44:17–19, 25. Her cult was especially popular with the women of Jerusalem.

peculiar personal characteristics of a tribal patriarch, nor yet of an Oriental despot of uncertain temper and undoubted power, whose every whim is law and before whom all must grovel in the dust. Even when this awesome creature is endowed with a sense of perfect justice and mercy, he does not fit our philosophic conception, because he is still very much of a man—ridiculous in that he takes himself too seriously. Nearer to our intellectual idea of God is the type of emperor envisaged by Lao-tzu, who advised the would-be ruler to be like the Tao, governing his subjects without letting them know that they were being governed.

The great Tao pervades everywhere, both on the left and on the right.
By it all things come into being, and it does not reject them.
Merits accomplished, it does not possess them (or, lay claim to them).
It loves and nourishes all things but does not dominate over them. . . .
Because it never assumes greatness, therefore it can accomplish greatness.
Therefore the Sage (as ruler), in order to be above the people, must in words keep below them;
In order to be ahead of the people, he must in person keep behind them.
Thus when he is above, the people do not feel his burden;
When he is ahead, the people do not feel his hindrance.
Therefore all the world is pleased to hold him in high esteem and never get tired of him.
Because he does not compete, no one competes with him.[6]

In our spiritual tradition this sublime idea of the greatness of God consisting in his humility appears first in Deutero-Isaiah's conception of the "suffering Servant," and finds its highest expression in the humility of

---

[6] *Tao Te Ching*, xxxiv and lxvi. Trs. Ch'u Ta-kao. London, 1937.

Christ, for "whosoever will be chief among you, let him be your servant."

But in our working image of God the masculine element of the Oriental tyrant and the "feminine" element of the mysterious and self-effacing servant of the universe have not been quite happily combined. However incomplete and crude it may be, there is something gloriously robust and splendid in the figure of the wise and all-merciful King of kings, enthroned on high in infinite majesty, whose gaze is so terrible that none may look upon it and live. This conception lives on in the Mohammedan picture of Allah, and, for all its limitations, is aesthetically sound.

The problem is to synthesize the feminine qualities of cherishing love, self-effacement, compassion and graciousness with a figure so positively and aggressively male, and to achieve a result which is not mere effeminate masculinity, a "wishy-washy" compromise. With this symbolically feminine element go also the qualities of beauty and playfulness, which have, as we have seen, to be included in an image of God almost exclusively righteous and purposeful. Lacking the feminine element this righteousness is stiff and solemn, and incompatible with all forms of beauty excepting the sculptural and architectural. Purely masculine righteousness is rigidity and tension, unbending self-control and fixity of principle. Here, projected upon God, is all that fear and distrust of suppleness and charm which man on the defensive associates with "woman's wiles." A woman may yield easily to tears while, for shame of being thought a woman, a man will grit his teeth and remain as unmoved as a rock. Yet a rock is more damaged by a hard blow than yielding water, which may be struck and cut a thousand times without leaving any

163

wound. And rock, for all its hardness, is easily worn away or cracked by the softness of water and plants.

> Man when living is soft and tender; when dead he is hard and tough. All animals and plants when living are tender and fragile; when dead they become withered and dry. Therefore it is said: the hard and tough are parts of death; the soft and tender are parts of life.[7]

A purely male God is therefore dead.

The root of the matter is this: that an image of God in which the rigid qualities predominate, which excludes the beautiful, the fluid, the playful and the feminine, simply mirrors that fear of life and Reality which we saw as the chief obstacle to our realization of union with God. The rigid, male God embodies the ideal of the possessive will—to grasp and hold the mystery of life, to freeze the desired form of the living moment into an eternal and immobile possession. And so frozen, the thing is quite dead. The moment, the movement, the life has passed on and gone free. The feminine element is lacking in our image of God because we fear it in life as the beauty which burns our fingers when we try to hold it—the supple, flowing, changing aspect of things which so exasperates us because we desire to possess it and cannot, since it is the created reflection of the life and the mystery of God. Here is the origin of all the Manichaean and Gnostic horror of the earth and of woman which has so infected the Christian Church.

This fear, too, was responsible for involving our theology so deeply with Neo-Platonic and Aristotelian conceptions of the divine nature as the impassive and unmoving One, as if the suppleness of movement im-

---

[7] *Ibid.*, lxxvi.

plied some imperfection, perfection being identified with the finished, the complete and the symmetrical, which is again the dead. Bound up with this particular idea of perfection, theology has never been able to explain how or why this inert Unity should have produced such an active multiplicity as the created universe. But in God conceived as non-duality rather than unity, or oneness, there is room for movement and life.

With all his robust masculinity, the God of the Hebrews is a long way from this frozen rigidity. He is the embodiment of *true* manliness, however crudely conceived, because his nature contains a subordinate feminine element, for he is above all a creative artist, and the great symbol of his presence is not rock but fire— the burning bush of Horeb. Passage after passage in the Old Testament dwells on his delight in beauty, for there is not a trace of Manichaeism in the Hebrew religion. The woman is subordinate, but not despised. But for those who conceived God as the impassive, primal Unity, the creation was always problematic; the process whereby the One produced the many amounted to a "progressive disintegration" through a hierarchy of intermediary principles or aeons, the number of which was multiplied in proportion to the horror in which the physical world was held. But this device solved and explained nothing. The hierarchy of aeons was the mere postponement of having to admit an impossibility—the causing of the universe by a static and quiescent Principle of pure oneness. With a similar view of the divine Unity, Christian theology has, as we have seen, been unable to bridge the gulf between the Creator and creation. The *ex nihilo* doctrine is simply a confession of ignorance.

But the living God of the Hebrews is an infinity of

inexhaustible life and being—not a mathematical and abstract infinity—and, as the mythos makes plain, he transcends the dualism of activity and rest. The merely one God, in the Greek sense of unity, is *bound* to rest, but the non-dual God is free both to rest and to move, for he worked for six days and rested the seventh. Thus there is nothing in the *truly* Biblical image of God hostile to the feminine principle; it is there in potentiality, and our religious consciousness has never brought it into full actuality. Femininity lies hidden in the artistic nature of the Hebrew God, but when, in Christianity, this God was explained according to Neo-Platonic and Aristotelian principles, the feminine was wholly abstracted and the remaining masculinity became rigid and dead. For man is not truly man without woman.

Nearly all expressions of beauty involve the feminine quality of suppleness, whether in nature as wind, water, clouds, fire, trees and plants, or in art as music, dancing, painting and poetry.[8] But that aspect of the Hebrew image of God which has impressed itself on the Christian mind is the picture of the Father Almighty sitting in immense dignity upon his throne, propounding a law of righteousness as rigid as the tables of stone upon which it is engraved. And yet, "He shall come down like rain upon the mown grass: as showers that water the earth."[9] If we may be permitted to say, in imagery, that

---

[8] Occidental painting and design tends to be architectural and symmetrical, and lacks the living fluidity of Chinese painting where beauty is always associated with lack of symmetry. The Chinese idea of God as Tao has an essentially fluid quality, and is likened by Lao-tzu to water. "The highest goodness is like water. Water is beneficent to all things but does not contend. It stays in places which others despise. Therefore it is near Tao." *Tao Te Ching*, viii.

[9] Psalm 72:6. But his fluidity is in no way incompatible with his righteousness—"Let judgement run down as waters, and righteousness as a mighty stream." Amos 5:24.

God sits upon a throne, there is no reason why he should not play the flute like Krishna or dance like Shiva.

> St. Francis tried to bring that music into our religion; but we think him quaint, odd, even a little mad. There was a time when the dance began to steal into our worship; but it has been expelled, and now we only bow and kneel as if we were at Court.[10]

But Western, and especially Anglo-Saxon, man's inhibited feeling nature does not want to let this gracefulness enter into his image of God. He has the adolescent's fear of emotion and of the dangerous allurements of life into which he is being thrust, and as he has neither courage nor wisdom in the exercise of feeling, it emerges, under pressure, as mere sentimentality.

What has been said about the absence of beauty and the feminine element from religion applies largely to Protestantism. Popular Catholicism, the religion of the less inhibited Latin peoples, has found a workable though at root unsatisfactory solution—the virtual deification of the Virgin Mary. We Christians know, in theory, that God has these symbolically feminine attributes of love, compassion, mercy and beauty, but it has been hard for us to reconcile them with the image of the King of kings. Thus the demand of the heart for God as Mother as well as Father found an answer, adequate enough for the childlike mediaeval soul, in the gracious figure of the Queen of Heaven, although it meant, in practice, that the Holy Trinity became the Holy Quarternity. She it was rather than the Father

---

[10] A. Clutton-Brock in "Spiritual Experience," a contribution to *The Spirit*. Ed. B. H. Streeter. London and New York, 1919, p. 292. The whole essay is a most suggestive discussion of beauty and the feminine element in religion.

who had given the world the means of redemption, and Adam of St. Victor, her twelfth-century laureate, could hardly find enough divine attributes wherewith to adorn this "Mediatrix of all graces." She was the "Temple of Eternity," the "Ruler of the Angels," the "Empress of the Highest." His Assumption hymn tells even of her birth in eternity:

> *Salve, Mater Salvatoris!*
> *Vas electum! Vas honoris!*
> *Vas coelestis Gratiae!*
> *Ab aeterno Vas provisum!*
> *Vas insigne! Vas excisum*
> *Manu sapientiae!*[11]

Hardly less fervent in their adoration were the official hymns of the Breviary:

> *Ave, Regina coelorum,*
> *Ave, Domina angelorum:*
> *Salve radix, salve porta,*
> *Ex qua mundo lux est orta.*[12]

In the Mass and the Office of several of her feasts she is implicitly identified with the Wisdom of God by the use of the lesson *Dominus possedit me:*

The Lord possessed me in the beginning of his way, before his works of old. I was set up from everlasting, from the beginning, or ever the earth was. When there were no depths, I was brought forth.[13]

---

[11]"Hail, Mother of our Saviour! Chosen vessel! Vessel of honour! Vessel of heavenly Grace! Vessel prepared from eternity! Vessel pre-eminent! Vessel wrought by the hand of wisdom!"

[12]Final Antiphons of the BVM., 2. From the Purification to Wednesday in Holy Week. "Hail, Queen of the heavens! Hail, mistress of the angels! Greeting to thee, O root and portal whence the light of the world is risen."

[13]Proverbs 8:22-24. Used for the Epistle in the Masses of the Conception and the Birthday. The Mass for the Common also uses Ecclesiasticus 24:9, "He created me from the beginning before the world, and I shall never fail." According to the modern Russian sophiological school, she is the incarnation

Whatever they may have meant to theologians, there can be no doubt as to the popular significance of such terms as Mother of God, Queen of Heaven, Mistress of the Angels, or of the hymnody which praised her as the "glorious Lady throned in rest amidst the starry host above," and as "she that riseth up as the morning, fair as the moon, clear as the sun." Mary, rather than Jesus, was the image where mediaeval man (as well as the simple Catholic of today) understood the love and beauty of God, the fertility and creative power of the divine nature. The most sublimely poetic passages of the Western Liturgy are those devoted to the Mother of God.

To her the most depraved sinner could pour out his heart in the certainty that he would be accepted in a loving embrace as infinite and all-inclusive as the sky that was symbolized by her star-decked robe of blue. In the image of the Mother, God was so much more approachable, more loving and forgiving, more tender and careful of her children.

> Mary, we hail thee, Mother and Queen compassionate; Mary, our comfort, life, and hope, we hail thee. . . . To thee we are sighing as mournful and weeping we pass through this vale of sorrow. Turn thou, therefore, O our intercessor, those thine eyes of pity and loving-kindness upon us sinners.[14]

In Mary, the Queen of Heaven, this tenderness is entirely beautiful, but thus far our attempts to mix it in

---

of the Holy Spirit. "She is, in personal form, the human likeness of the Holy Ghost. Through her, with her human form become entirely transparent to the Holy Ghost, we have a manifestation and, as it were, a personal revelation of him." Bulgakov in *The Wisdom of God.* London and New York, 1937, p. 183.

[14]Final Antiphons, 4. Trinity Sunday to Advent.

with the image of the King of kings have been quite disastrous. By a curious perversion of the doctrine that in the Passion Christ suffers for all human sin, there has come about the sad incongruity of a victorious king-God with "tender feelings." Much of the bad emotionalism which often passes for penitence is occasioned by remorse for having "hurt God's feelings," as if, to move men to repentance, he had been reduced to the last resort of the incompetent mother with her naughty children—to sit down and cry. Or when we try to combine righteousness and love in one symbol the result is often that most unedifying type of moral tyrant who enforces his tyranny by constant harping on how much his children's misbehaviour "wounds his love" for them, and administers judgement with the "this hurts me more than it's going to hurt you" line. We allow in God what we deplore in parents and teachers.

Our picture of Jesus has fared no better. With all the love and graciousness of God concentrated in the symbol of the Virgin, the mediaeval Christ was the Christus Victor—robed in glory, stately, austere, hardly human. But this conception was in fact Monophysite; the humanity was lost in the divinity, and after the rise of Humanism both the Catholic and the Protestant conceptions of Jesus attempted to realize his humanity—the former in order to counteract the false man-worship of Humanism, the latter in an effort to discover the Jesus of the Bible and of history. Yet the result was compromise. The humanity of the human and the divinity of the divine became muddled and clouded, as did likewise the two elements of justice and mercy, masculine strength and feminine grace. This compromise is the hermaphroditic Christ of popular Church art-wax images, Bible illustrations—solemn, effeminate, sanctimonious, moralizing, ethereal, neither red-bloodedly human nor majestically divine. And because, having forsaken the image of Mary, we look for the Mother in God's incarnate Word, the result is "gentle Jesus, meek and lowly," the pure *schmalz* of "Abide with me," "Rock of Ages," and such hymnodic abominations as the following from *Hymns Ancient and Modern:*

> *I need Thee, precious Jesu:*
> *I need a friend like Thee,*
> *A friend to soothe and pity,*
> *A friend to care for me.*
> *I need the Heart of Jesus*
> *To feel each anxious care,*
> *To tell my every trouble,*
> *And all my sorrow share.*

All that we have managed to assimilate to our image of God and of his Christ is the tenderness of the feminine, but none of the beauty, the vitality or the allure. That aspect of the feminine we have associated with the devil, because in seeking to possess it we come to grief. But in fact it is the whole mystery and enchantment of God for which we hunger so sorely and which always slips from our fearful grasp. It is Life itself, which we do not trust. It is *la belle dame sans merci*, until we love it enough to let go.

Because to us our Father which is in Heaven means the God whom in our timidity we have emptied of all enchantment, we do not see Christ among the poets and music-makers, his peers, but among the preachers and edifiers. We place him among his own commentators as if he commented on life. He did not: he made music about it, he spoke of it like a poet, but with an audacity beyond theirs. They have seen the fairy angel and desired her, but despaired; he said, Live for her and forget everything else; for she is God. Her beauty is not incompatible with life; to

171

see it is to know eternal life. The universe is not malign, tempting you with siren songs. Its music does not come and go, but sounds for ever if you will hear it.[15]

For more people than we imagine the very names and phrases "God," "Our Heavenly Father," "Jesus Christ," are so contaminated by this bad imagery that, reason as they and we may, the ugliness cannot be driven out. Now we cannot simply sit down and re-touch or redraw the picture. We cannot simply issue an order to our clergy, artists and liturgists, saying, "More beauty and mystery, less sentiment and slush." We cannot institute a systematic program of teaching and worship that is self-consciously designed to propagate a more glorious image of God. The only way to get rid of the bad associations which clutter our religious imagery is to go behind the images and get right at the heart of religion itself. Whoever is troubled by the present images must do this, though he must not force it upon others. He must go to that mystical centre which is beyond all ordinary forms of symbolism, and there touch the Life which will, in due time, express itself in a nobler image of God and enable him to see a more splendid Christ in the pages of the Gospels.

There is no doubt that, in the years to come, many Christians will do this, and as a result the Christian religion will undergo one of its periodic changes of emphasis. From it will emerge an image of God with the principal emphasis laid upon the Holy Spirit, whom until now our imagery, worship and thought have left so much alone. As in the Western Church's infancy the emphasis was upon God as Father-Mother,[16] and in

---

[15]A. Clutton-Brock, *op. cit.*, p. 290.
[16]The Monophysite Christ of mediaeval art is simply a mirror of the Father; the divine humanity of the Son is hidden.

adolescence upon the Son, the suffering Christ, the Jesus of history, so in adulthood the immanent Holy Spirit will occupy the foreground. He, as the One who shall lead us into all truth, will teach us the inner meanings. Above all he will lead us to a fuller understanding of the Incarnation, because he will be Christ's Spirit, and not just his image, in our hearts, and because with the Father he loves the world, he will show us the meaning of the Word made flesh in all the events, objects, actions and encounters of everyday life, and Christ in our brethren. In our hearts he will unveil the heart of God.

III

The symbols of the Holy Spirit are wind and fire—wind which is masculine in its strength and feminine in its softness, and fire which is masculine in its brilliance and feminine in its warmth and volatility. Water, too, is associated with the Spirit as the agent through which it works, for "unless a man is born of water and the Spirit, he cannot enter into the kingdom of heaven." Wind, fire and water—all three are symbols of that Life, that Eternal Moment, which ever eludes the grasp of the possessive will and yet, because it is the love of God, never separates itself from us. The Holy Spirit is the breath of God's life, the flame of his glory, and the stream of his love. In its elusiveness it is God's mystery; in its liveliness it is his playfulness and beauty; in its inescapable presence it is his faithfulness. Through the Holy Spirit we come to know God most intimately, because he is not God above us, the Father "who dwelleth in light unapproachable," nor yet God over yonder, the Jesus of history, but God within us. In the revelation of God as the Father we learned that he is the just Creator; in the Son we learned that he is love; in the Holy Spirit of love we learn that the heart of God is absolute joy. For this is the love which, as Patmore said, raises the soul above the sphere of reverence and worship to the sphere of laughter and dalliance. It teaches us why God made the universe and man within it, and invites us to share in that lofty secret.

Creation springs from the divine joy. It is the celebration and the sharing of God's interior happiness or, as it used to be called, beatitude. There are, of course, the most solid philosophical grounds for asserting that God, who embraces the infinite perfection of Being, possesses an absolute happiness and joy. "Beatitude," says St. Thomas, "belongs to God in a supreme way. For nothing else is understood by the term *beatitude* than the perfect good of an intellectual nature which is capable of knowing that it has a plentitude of the good it possesses."[17] But to understand the divine happiness profoundly, the philosopher has to come down from his desk and play with the children on the floor, for it is written that "except ye be converted and become as little children, ye cannot enter into the kingdom of God."

The natural creation and the spiritual life are on the whole meaningless unless it is understood that in the very heart of God there is that colossal gaiety which is represented in the symbol of the angelic choirs encircling the presence of God in an eternal dance of ecstasy. For it is said that when the foundations of the world were laid, "the morning stars sang together and all the sons of God shouted for joy." The meaning of the

---

[17] *Summa Theol.*, I. Q. 26, a. 1.

creation is not something solemn and terrible as if God wished to have creatures to impress with his dreadful majesty. Viewed as a work of "serious purpose" the creation simply does not make sense. For a great part of the universe seems to have no purpose at all; there is much more of it than is necessary; there is a prodigious waste of space and energy; and it is inhabited by a stupendous variety of weird organisms that apparently have nothing better to do than reproduce themselves in alarming quantities. But the preachers have always talked, rather vaguely perhaps, about God's *purpose*. "God," says the hymn, "is working his purpose out as year succeeds to year." One might think that God is purpose personified, but his universe is on the whole a whimsical contraption filled with much rather glorious nonsense.

Children (and adults who have their wisdom) are usually the most happy when they are doing things that have no particular purpose—making up lunatic stories with friends, walking aimlessly through fields and hitting at old stumps with a stick, whittling hunks of wood just for the sake of whittling, drawing wayward and interminable designs on scraps of paper, and mixing horrible concoctions of all the various types of household liquid from paint-remover to cod-liver oil. There is a timeless and peaceful satisfaction in these actions, a fascination such that it would seem possible to go on with them for all eternity. To sit and watch the changing shapes of clouds, or specks of dust floating in the sunlight, or the patterns of concentric circles made in a pool by the falling rain—the contemplative happiness of these things belongs to that childlike wisdom which must be learned again before one may enter the kingdom of heaven, for the reason, it must be, that the activity of heaven is of a similar kind. Traherne recalls the memory of this vision of the world in trying to explain what it means to become a child again in the kingdom of God:

> The dust and the stones of the street were as precious as gold, the gates were at first the ends of the world. The green trees when I saw them first, through one of the gates, transported and ravished me. . . . Boys and girls tumbling in the street, and playing, were moving jewels. I knew not that they were born or should die. But all things abided eternally as they were in their proper places. Eternity was manifest in the light of day. . . . The streets were mine, the temple was mine, the people were mine. The skies were mine, and so were the sun and moon and stars, and all the world was mine, and I the only spectator and enjoyer of it. I knew no churlish proprieties, nor bounds, nor divisions; but all proprieties and divisions were mine; all treasures and the possessors of them. So that with much ado I was corrupted, and made to learn the dirty devices of this world, which I now unlearn, and become, as it were, a little child again that I may enter into the kingdom of God.[18]

This may be somewhat shocking to modernists in religion who like to think of eternal life as an everlasting progress towards the realization of ever higher ethical ideals, where purpose rises beyond purpose, goal beyond goal, in an infinite series of ascending peaks. Such a conception is weak philosophically because it confounds eternity with unending time, and accords not at all with the traditional symbolism of heaven which speaks of the blessed (*i.e.*, happy) ones as *playing* upon harps, engaged in a timeless celebration of the glory of God. When it is said that their delight is to

---

[18] *Centuries of Meditation*, i, 62.

praise him for ever, it does not mean that they are to surround him as so many flatterers, courtiers and dancing-girls about an Oriental potentate. The point is that the blessed are one with God, and their praise is simply the expression of God's own essential joy which they experience within themselves.

Rightly understood, this old scriptural symbolism will quickly dissipate the dour image of God which so many have formed, as well as the obvious discrepancy between such a martinet for earnestness and the extravagant, fanciful universe which he creates. We shall then understand that God's creative activity is not his labour but his play. It is his "work" only in the sense of something done by him.[19] It proceeds not from the seriousness and earnestness of one who strives and schemes towards a goal, but from the sheer joy of one who is himself the fulness of Being and of all possible perfection. Speaking absolutely, God has no purpose. There is nothing beyond his own infinite glory which he could possibly strive to attain, and because he lives not in time but in eternity, there is for God no future wherein he might possess something which he does not have now.

God has purpose only in relation to the imperfection of man, purposing that man shall attain the divine life of purposelessness. "If one can attain purposelessness through purpose, then the thing has been grasped."[20] For a life without purpose is not necessarily a life without meaning, and it is meaning rather than purpose which gives life its justification. The perfect life has no

---

[19]"The world is the symbol of that which transpires in the spiritual sphere, the reflection of God's 'abandon' as fulfilled in the spirit." Berdyaev in *Freedom and the Spirit*, p. 33.

[20]Jung and Wilhelm, *The Secret of the Golden Flower*, p. 50.

purpose because it is the life of God. God is the end of every purpose, but as purpose ends in God, meaning begins in him.[21] That is to say, in so far as man has not realized union with God he has purpose but no meaning; but in so far as he has realized it he has meaning and no purpose. A purpose is justified by something beyond itself, but a meaning is its own justification. Thus the inner life of God and its created reflection is not purposeful; like the greatest achievements of human art, it is meaningful and playful.

Music at its highest, as in Bach or Mozart, is pure play. The preludes and fugues of Bach are simply a complex arrangement of glorious sounds, entirely sufficient in themselves. They need no programme notes to explain a moral or sociological message, or to call our attention to effects imitating natural noises or conveying emotional qualities. The intricate melodies flow on and on, and there never seems any necessity for them to stop. He composed them in tremendous quantities, with the same Godlike extravagance to be found in the unnecessary vastness of nature. Inferior music, however, needs props and commentaries, since it proceeds from human purpose rather than that playfulness of divine perfection which we find not only in Bach and Mozart, but also in the long Alleluias of Gregorian chant, the arabesques of Persian miniatures, the illuminated margins of mediaeval manuscripts, the wind-swept bamboos of Chinese painting, and the entirely satisfying and purposeless figures of the dance as it may sometimes be seen in Russian ballet. Such playfulness is the very nature of the divine Wisdom.

---

[21] Cf. Romans 10:4, "Christ is the *end* of the law for righteousness to every one that believeth."

The contemplation of wisdom is rightly compared with games for two things to be found in games. The first is that games give pleasure and the contemplation of wisdom gives the very greatest pleasure, according to what Wisdom says of itself in Ecclesiasticus, *My spirit is sweet above honey*. The second is that the movements in games are not contrived to serve another end but are pursued for their own sake. It is the same with the delights of wisdom. . . . Hence divine Wisdom compares its delight to games: *I was with him forming all things and was delighted every day, playing before him at all times: playing in the world.*[22]

Probably there was never such a purposeful, scheming civilization as our own, a people that lived so entirely for the future and with so great a degree of anxiety for the morrow. There was never, for that reason, such a meaningless civilization. It is not surprising, then, that in contemplating the universe we cannot make it consistent with our idea of God, that we cease to believe in God, and worship instead the plan-ridden soul of man. For we have discovered that this vast system of stars is neither the host of angelic choirs, nor a map of human destinies, but only lumps of burning gas and mud. They blaze away so many billion kilowatts of energy to no effect; vacant planets have millions of square miles of unexploited territory going to waste; flowers bloom in their myriads in impenetrable jungles where none may see or pluck them; weeds, insects, fish, birds, micro-organisms swarm in senseless profusion. And since efficiency, plan, economy and parsimony are our bourgeois virtues, we cannot see this

---

[22]St. Thomas, Opusc. lxviii, *in libr. Boetii de Hebdom.*, princ., quoted in Maritain's *Art and Scholasticism*, pp. 34–35. The final scriptural passage is Proverbs 8:29–31. The AV renders "play" as "rejoice" but the former is more exact.

universe as the creation of a virtuous and intelligent God.

We would like to see all the squandered energy of the stars harnessed to drive something at a profit, and the vacant planetary wastes colonized and exploited. We are secretly offended because all those hidden flowers and their surplus seeds cannot be sold on the market. We are baffled because the intricately fashioned jewel of the snowflake lasts but a few moments. We are disgusted at the swarms of mosquitoes and bugs and snakes which protect the jungles from human civilization.

Every attempt to find plan and purpose and respectable rationality in this universe, whether on a supernatural or a merely naturalistic basis, is bound to end in absurdity, and of the two the naturalistic explanations are the more absurd. Perhaps the song of birds is "explainable" simply as a device for sexual attraction; perhaps the radiant wings of insects are no more than protective colouring; perhaps the beauty of the morning-glory is merely to entice the bee, appealing no doubt to his acute aesthetic appreciation of colour and form. Perhaps. But if the aim of so much splendour is merely to stimulate the sexual processes of purely instinctual organisms, the mountain has laboured and brought forth a mouse.

The trouble is that we are too proud to be children and appreciate the playing of God. It is just this pride which has brought tragedy into the universe, marred the happiness which God creates us to share, and made necessary a redemption through the Cross. For sin is precisely the adult, unplayful action of taking oneself seriously. It involves, as is told in Genesis, the curse of labour. And as man likes to conceive God in his own image, it is to be expected that the proud will conceive a serious and unplayful God. Celsus objected to the idea of the Incarnation because he felt it an *undignified* procedure for the Lord of the universe. By sin man kills the child in himself, thinking the playful will of God beneath him and desiring to be God in his own right, working out his own serious and weighty schemes. But if you give yourself weight you fall down to hell.

The way of the Cross is, however, the love and joy of God in contrast to sin, appearing in the so-called "serious" virtues of moral heroism. But the moral heroism of Christ and his saints consists in the very fact that they do *not* take their own lives seriously. As Keyserling pointed out, they *play* with their lives and stake them recklessly, as safe and respectable souls would say, on absurdly lofty visions of the Good. In their attitude to human suffering, which is God's, they are warm, sympathetic and sincere—but never serious. It is not that they feel no suffering; it would not have been suffering that Christ and his saints experienced on the Cross if it was not felt. But even in feeling it to the core they cannot take it seriously, because of the conviction which they burn to share—that Reality itself, to which all temporal suffering must give place, is the eternal joy which sin refuses.

There is no such thing as a saint without joy, without God's own happiness. One may perform all the good works under the sun and be subject to the most rigorous spiritual disciplines, but one cannot have true holiness without joy. St. Francis of Assisi is of course the classic example of this spirit, seeing no inconsistency between the most rigorous asceticism and a spiritual gaiety which expressed itself in the lilting melodies of the troubadours.

> Drunken with the perfect love and compassion of Christ, blessed Francis on a time did such things as these. For the most sweet melody of spirit boiling up within him, frequently broke out in French speech, and the veins of murmuring which he heard secretly with his ears broke forth into French-like rejoicing. And sometimes he picked up a branch from the earth and, laying it on his left arm, he drew in his right hand another stick like a bow over it, as if on a viol or other instrument, and, making fitting gestures, sang with it in French unto the Lord Jesus Christ.[23]

For those "veins of murmuring" were no doubt strains of that angelic music which Dante described as the laughter of the universe[24]—to us a strange phrase to use of a hymn of glory to the Holy Trinity.

Such joy is the gift of the Spirit; to try to manufacture it oneself produces only that superficial effervescence of heartiness which some Christians affect to show that religion may be had without tears. This joy is merely surface joy, like the sugar on a pill, and those who take themselves seriously will of course think of religion as a pill. Yet the joy of the Spirit is available the moment pride is swallowed and the free gift of union with God accepted. Whoever takes himself seriously will never be able to accept this gift because his pride will insistently drive him to try to earn it by his own efforts and merits.

In giving up this pride one becomes again as a child, and, as a child of God, one's virtues, actions and attitudes are no longer proud and purposeful but humble and playful because they express the happiness of God. The saint sees that doing the will of God is joining in the play of God, for he is no longer like the sulky, preco-

---

[23] *Speculum Perfectionis*, cap. 93.
[24] *Paradiso*, xxvii. 4.

cious children in the market place to whom, as Christ said, their playmates call:

We have piped unto you, and you have not danced;
We have mourned unto you, and you have not wept.

The playfulness of the child, the saint, and of God are alike in this: that they are all actions in the mood of eternity rather than the mood of time. In this present world-order eternity is known in its ever-moving focal point—the present moment, and the child in his play and the saint in his holiness both live in the present. Absorbed in twisting string or dropping stones in a pool, the child lives in a timeless realm where a game that goes on and on without goal is like the planets which go round and round to nowhere at God's command. Following the precept of Christ to learn from the birds of the air and the flowers of the field, the saint worries no more about tomorrow and yesterday, and concerns himself simply with doing the will of God as it is presented to him in the circumstances of each moment, sensing his whole life to be, in Patmore's image, the dancing of a gnat in the ray of God.

And in the fulness of eternity the triune God, the Father and the Son in the unity of the Spirit, is ever at the play of love, the divine subsistencies giving themselves one to another in an ageless dance whose finite image is the blaze of aimless splendour that fills the heavens in celebration of the joy of God. This divine activity, the movement of the Spirit, never palls because in eternity there is no yesterday to remember and no tomorrow for which to plan; there is simply Now for ever. There are those who resent such lightness of spirit at the heart of Being, as criminals resent others' virtue; they say that a Godhead at play while the world suffers is like a Nero who fiddles while Rome burns. But this is the sulkiness of pride and envy. For there is so much tragedy on the surface of life that were there not somewhere, right in the centre of things and in the centre of each and every pain, a state of absolute and unconfined joy accessible to all, the whole realm of Being must be damned. The joyous centre is there, and the heart of God is open, in the very midst of every experience that can befall us. To sense and thought it is strait and narrow and impossible to find—smaller than a point, fleeter than light itself. But to love it is wider than space and more enduring than all the ages of time—embracing every creature that was, is or shall be. It is the instant and inescapable presence of the Eternal Moment, the movement of the Spirit of God.

III. THE LIFE OF ACTION

The intellectual revolt of the modern world against what has been understood as Christian morality cannot be dismissed as mere perversity. The picture of the Church as a valiant minority holding grimly to its position against a vast rebellion inspired by the devil is an oversimplification which may appeal to those who love to strike heroic attitudes, but it renders the conventional Christian blind to his own moral failure. While it is true that the "Old Adam" always resents the yoke of Christian love, there are three reasons why this revolt must not be attributed to mere deviltry. The first is that it reflects, in part, the dissatisfaction of mature souls with the morality of infancy and adolescence. The second is that official teaching and popular practice of Christian morality have degenerated largely into legalism or surface imitation of the good life without understanding of its inner meaning—the realization of union with God. The third is that this teaching and practice have not, on the whole, been faithful to the principles of the Incarnation, having adopted an attitude to physical life which is Manichaean rather than Christian. To some extent, therefore, the revolt against so-called Christian morals expresses a perfectly sincere desire for the good life. The widespread and, indeed, growing tendency of Church people to ascribe it to mere perversity is to be deplored, and one may hope that it will subside when the special thrill of congratulating themselves as members of a heroic and reactionary band of stalwarts has worn off.[1]

In the mind of the general public the Christian, and especially the Protestant, religion is essentially a way of morality. Its entire aim is to move men to good actions and to get rid of evil actions. Dogmas, sacraments and forms of worship are of use so long as they assist the growth of morality, but are in general late accretions to the "simple religion of Jesus," which was in essence the new moral law proclaimed in the Sermon on the Mount. Thus when the system of morality attributed to Jesus by members of the Church is called in question, the whole structure of institutional Christianity falls into disrepute.

Thoroughly erroneous as it is to say that Christianity is simply and primarily a system of morality, and that Jesus was primarily a moral teacher, it will take hundreds of years to get rid of this impression. Churchmen have fostered the error by the persistent preaching and teaching of morality to the exclusion of doctrine, worship and the interior life. But because the general public *does* identify Christianity simply and solely with a certain type of morality, the influence of the Church in the world depends largely on the moral attitudes of Christians. And because the Christian moral ideal is in

---

[1]One cannot help detecting something of this attitude in the now widely popular writings of C. S. Lewis. Thoroughly excellent as they are from many standpoints, there is, especially in his *Pilgrim's Regress* and *Screwtape Letters*, a certain ill-concealed glee in adopting an old-fashioned and unpopular position, and in making witty thrusts at characteristically modern positions which are held as not just partially but absolutely off the right track. Able as he is in pointing out the errors in modern paganism and in defending the rationality of the essential Christian doctrines, he has little or no conception of the part which modern criticisms of the Church play in developing a more profound and mature understanding of the Faith. A similar attitude is to be noted in many of the champions of Protestant neo-Orthodoxy, and it is significant that all steer clear of the whole subject of mysticism.

186

itself a thing of tremendous power, perversions of the ideal will have a strong negative influence. Therefore it is absolutely necessary for us to understand Christian morality in the light of the gift of union with God and of the deeper vision of his nature which realization of the gift brings, and spiritual maturity renders possible.

But one thing must be clear from the start: God himself, and not morality, is the end and aim of the Christian religion. Morality is a by-product of union with God, and its purpose is the ever deeper enjoyment, or contemplation, of that union by oneself and others.

> All other human operations seem to be ordered to this as to their end. For perfect contemplation requires that the body should be disencumbered, and to this effect are directed all the products of art that are necessary for life. Moreover, it requires freedom from the disturbance caused by the passions, which is achieved by means of the moral virtues and of prudence; and freedom from external disturbance, to which the whole governance of the civil life is directed. So that, if we consider the matter rightly, we shall see that all human occupations appear to serve those who contemplate the truth. . . . Man's ultimate happiness consists solely in the contemplation of God.[2]

The Christian feeds the hungry, heals the sick, clothes the naked and disciplines himself that all may share and enjoy the very greatest of goods—God himself. Because God is love, to love another soul is to give him God.

I

In Western Christianity the understanding and practice of morality is going through the same course of evolution as the understanding of doctrine—the three

---

[2] St. Thomas, *Contra Gentiles*, III. xxxvii.

stages of infancy, adolescence and maturity. In the stage of infancy, the Church's moral teaching is of necessity authoritarian and legalistic but, save for a chosen few, not too rigorous. Mother can afford to wink at a certain amount of childish naughtiness. In adolescence, where there is not open revolt, morality becomes the individualistic, intensely earnest and self-consciously heroic following of extremely lofty ideals. In maturity we return somewhat to earth, and find the source of morality neither in external authority nor remote ideals, but in the consciousness of God himself in the heart. A morality which proceeds from the inner presence of God is the only morality which is strictly Christian, but prior to maturity the indwelling Holy Spirit operates secretly. To the child he gives holiness as a love of obedience; to the adolescent he gives it as a love of new, tremendous and even impossible ideals. But in the mature soul he arouses holiness by revealing his own inner presence.

Lacking experience and the power of reason, all children need authority, and the beginning of any art, whether music, writing, or living itself, involves the mastery of certain rules. Inspiration and freedom in the use of rules come later. Some of these rules are quite peculiar to childhood, such as an absolute tabu against the use of fire, or against crossing the street without an adult. If the child shows any tendency to disregard the rules the usual, if not always the wisest, way to restore order is to give or threaten punishment, appealing to the sense of fear. Certainly this is the quickest way, if the need for order is immediate and urgent. In general, however, the mother will try to win the child's obedience through love and respect, or, sometimes, through mere bribery. Considering the immense and unruly nature of the mediaeval Church's brood of children, it is not hard to understand why she resorted mostly to threats and bribes—appealing to the fear of eternal damnation, or to the longing for "pie in the sky," or, in the last resort, to the terror of hell here and now in the shape of the Holy Inquisition. In so far as she appealed to the fear of Hell and the Inquisition she was, of course, less than Christian; for punishment, or the fear of it, has no creative result by itself. In default of higher powers of persuasion, punishment is an effective way of protecting children from themselves and from each other until they can learn by love.

Nor is it surprising that Mother Church had to impose certain rigid tabus against things that, while not evil in themselves, are as dangerous for an infant culture as a box of matches for a two-year-old. Chief among these was liberty of religious thought and speech, because a young culture will disintegrate rapidly without intellectual and spiritual unity. A multitude of strong and discordant propagandas would have worked havoc with the credulous and uncritical mind of mediaeval man, to judge from its confusing effect in our own slightly less credulous age. Even when Europe felt the full force of the Reformation, there was a far greater degree of spiritual unanimity than we can dream of today.

Little observed as they were, the mediaeval Church tried to impose the strictest controls upon sexuality. However licentious the modern world may be, mediaeval man's appetite for sex, like his appetite for food, was greater and more easily roused than ours. Modern urban man's erotic desires have to be titillated with sexual suggestions of a subtlety unknown to peasant and primitive, for he has far less physical virility and leads a sexual life which, to a great degree, is purely mental. His enormous mental obsession with sexuality is a clear symptom of the difficulty of physical satisfaction. But when intense physical passion is quickly and easily roused, there is more immediate danger of chaos in family relations and loss of conscious control. Modern man (of the educated, civilized, urban type) is highly conscious and deliberate in his licentiousness; more primitive man is suddenly "swept off his feet" by a violent outburst of passion, which he satisfies without any great degree of subtlety, and thus his psychic integrity must at all costs be protected from complete submersion by physical forces. Modern man's problem is not to guard his soul against the powers of his body, but against those of his mind. "We wrestle not against flesh and blood, but against principalities, against powers, . . . against *spiritual* wickedness in high places."

The danger, common to all cultures in the state of childhood, of losing the sense of ego, of personal identity, under the flood of some natural and physical urge explains much of the failure of the mediaeval Church to teach a truly incarnational morality. We moderns are in no such danger, and we confuse our moral problem disastrously when we speak of guarding against "the sinful desires of the flesh," when we should be speaking of the sinful desires of the mind. As we grow in self-consciousness and psychic awareness, we discover the source of evil, not in the external realms of the material, fleshly elements or of the demons, but ever more and more within ourselves. Herein lies the exasperating moral problem of modern man.

As the morality of the mediaeval Church was simple, definite and rigid in its prohibitions, it was similarly naïve and direct in its positive commandments. There were certain clear duties—actions to be done—by the Christian man, and subtleties of motive were of slight importance. He was to be charitable to the poor, and accordingly those who had wealth, when sufficiently moved, disbursed charity in lordly and reckless style, asking no questions about what would be done with the money, or whether it was immoral to give away money to the needy in order to pay one's own way into heaven. If one had committed sins, one had simply to go and confess them to the priest, which, since they were definite external actions, was easy enough. Few indeed were the souls who asked complicated questions about the sincerity of their contrition, or tried to delve into the elusive ramifications of the spiritual pride which underlay the external transgression. Nothing could be more meritorious than to give or risk one's very life for Christ and his Church, and, therefore, thousands of men (sometimes moved by other considerations than plunder) enlisted year after year in the Crusades, and never bothered their heads with the problems of righteous and unrighteous warfare or Christian pacifism.

The entire attitude of mediaeval morality to sin and temptation knew nothing of the subtle difficulties raised by St. Paul, as a member of a very ancient culture, in his epistles to the Romans and Galatians. Sin and temptation were the operations of highly concrete devils or physical impulses, and the obvious way to deal with them was by sheer violence. Sin must be crushed and temptation resisted by simple force of will, vaguely assisted by divine grace. Even Luther, conscious as he was of the inwardness of sin, assaulted the devil with an inkpot. There was nothing like the degree of psychic awareness to discover the mechanism of repression and unconscious compensation for thwarted desires, which in our own day presents Christian moral thought with a question not to be side-stepped. Nor, as we have seen, was the mediaeval mind troubled by the other side of this psychoanalytic conundrum—the motivation of formally virtuous and religious actions by purely carnal appetites.

From the standpoint of the increased self-awareness that comes with adolescence, the Prostestants saw the shallowness of this kind of morality, and under the stimulus of their criticism Catholic moral theology began to enter far more deeply into the mental background of overt misdeeds. On both sides there emerged a heightened sense of individual responsibility for sin and accordingly a sense of personal guilt perpetually haunting the soul in a degree rarely known in the mediaeval Church. Protestant thought went back to Augustinianism just because it felt so keenly that the origin of sin lay in the ego, and that man was therefore radically depraved. By his own works he could contribute nothing to his salvation; his sole hope lay in faith in Christ's promise of redemption, as in Lutheranism, or in divine predestination to salvation by irresistible grace, as in Calvinism.

Protestantism was a reaction not only against the superficial legalism of popular Catholic morality, but also against the more esoteric aspect of mediaeval Christianity—the quest of the great philosophers and mystics for the life of perfection and contemplation. Obviously the deeper minds of the Middle Ages did not disregard the problems of moral motivation; they realized clearly enough that a mere external fulfilment of the Church's commandments was not to be compared with the pure love of God from the very depths of the soul. Now they held that such a love, such a degree of holiness, was possible. Man's natural self-love could be purified and exalted to the degree where it desired God above all else. With the aid of divine grace, according to St. Thomas, or even *ex puris naturalibus*, according to Duns Scotus and Occam, man was capable of the pure and unalloyed love of God, and by means of it might ascend to the mystical contemplation of the divine essence, and hereafter to the Beatific Vision. A contrition for sin was possible, likewise, in which there was no admixture of fear or wounded self-pride, but which was based on nothing other than the love of God.

This was where Luther in particular rebelled. Like St. Paul and St. Augustine, he had a high degree of self-awareness, and, looking deeply into his own heart, he found himself quite incapable of a wholly unselfish action, and that the more spiritually and inwardly the law of love was interpreted, the more impossible it was to fulfil.

> But this understanding of the law spiritually is far more deadly, since it makes the law impossible to fulfil and thereby brings man to despair of his own strength and abases him, for no one is without anger, no one without lust: such are we from birth. But what will a man do, when oppressed by such an impossible law?[3]

To Luther's mind the mediaeval concept of sanctity was an attempt to meet God on his own level of holiness, and he could see in this nothing other than a colossal spiritual pride since the whole essence of Christianity was that in Christ God had come down to man —not that man had ascended to God.

---

[3] Luther, WA i, p. 105, 14ff., quoted by Nygren in *Agape and Eros*, Part II, vol. ii. London, 1939, p. 476 *n*.

Beware of ever aspiring to such great purity that thou refusest to appear to thyself, nay to be, a sinner. For Christ dwells only in sinners. For to this end he descended from heaven, where he dwelt in the righteous, that he might even dwell in sinners.[4]

It was therefore necessary to disconnect personal holiness entirely from salvation. We are saved simply and solely by faith in Christ, because in Christ we see that God loves us as we are now, as sinners, and as sinners we are justified by the pure generosity of the divine love. Salvation is a free gift, and personal holiness can have no other cause or motive than gratitude for it.

Well now! my God has given to me, unworthy and lost man, without any merit, absolutely for nothing and out of pure mercy, through and in Christ, the full riches of all godliness and blessedness, so that I henceforth need nothing more than to believe it is so. Well then, for such a Father, who has so prodigally lavished upon me his blessings, I will in return freely, joyously and for nothing do what is well-pleasing to him, and also be a Christian towards my neighbour, as Christ has been to me.[5]

Man's love for God can only be pure when divorced from the motive of gaining heaven, and this can happen as soon as he understands that salvation is a free gift quite independent of his own holiness. He then becomes a channel for God's own love, spontaneous, motiveless, seeking not its own.

Luther's unfortunate role as the great disrupter of the Church's unity has perhaps led Christians in general to forget how right he was in this respect—as far as he went. For Luther grasped what the mediaeval

---

[4]Enders, *Dr. Martin Luthers Briefwechsel*, i, p. 29, in Nygren, *op. cit.*, p 468.
[5]Luther, WA vii, p. 35, 25ff., in Nygren, *op. cit.*, p. 509n.

Church failed to see all along—the essential principle of the Incarnation as God's *descent* and gift of himself to man in the state of sin. But the subsequent history of Protestantism shows us wherein Luther's answer was incomplete.

The Calvinist view of man's fallen nature was even more thoroughgoing than the Lutheran. Not only was man incapable of deserving salvation by works of holiness; his fallen soul was also incapable of faith, so that salvation had to depend on divine predestination alone. But since the New Testament made it clear that some were to be saved and some damned, this led to the terrible conclusion that while God saved some he damned others, so that human freedom disappeared absolutely.

We see, then, that the two principal forms of Protestantism, stressing the fallen and helpless state of man, were the result of a higher degree of self-consciousness and introspection. The mediaeval assumption that man was, of course, capable of pure love was naïve rather than proud, and it was with a similar childlike innocence that heaven was thought attainable by simple and literal obedience to a moral law. But Protestant self-awareness was adolescent rather than mature, because it was complicated by an acute sense of guilt. This feeling of guilt was caused not only by the perception of man's natural depravity, but also by a vague uncertainty as to the new theories of salvation. Luther's idea of salvation by faith alone always seemed too good and too easy to be true, and one could never be sure, in Calvinism, whether one was among the predestined elect. To suppress this sense of guilt Protestantism became violently and rigorously moralistic. The same sense of guilt obsessed souls of a high degree of self-consciousness who remained in the Catholic fold. Under the influence of an analytic and searching moral theology, the Sacrament of Penance became, for pious souls, far more than a perfunctory confession of formal misdeeds. It became a habitual act of self-analysis, a constant reminder that salvation was uncertain, and that God would be merciful only if one were sufficiently penitent. Instead of liberating man from the sense of guilt, the great sacrament of forgiveness was in practice used to foster the sense, because one knew that the more deeply the soul was explored, the more surely one would find that pride had eaten into its very core. Thus frequent confession became part of every devout Catholic's rule of life, because he knew he would never be free of guilt; he saw that he could never be penitent enough to deserve God's mercy. The easy gaiety associated with Catholicism is only possible for those still childlike Catholics (of whom there are immense numbers) who do not look into themselves too deeply. This accounts for the contrast between the happy, light-hearted Catholicism of peasants, and the dour, puritanical Catholicism of the more civilized (as distinct from cultured) and self-conscious religious and laymen.[6]

In our own day, Calvinism has become simple moralism. The modern Calvinist cannot admit the full doctrine of predestination, and strives to buy his way into

---

[6]This is especially true of Catholicism in "Protestant" countries such as England and the United States, *i.e.*, in the great industrial and urban centres of modern civilization where people in general have a high degree of self-consciousness. Writing in *Dieu Vivant*, vol. i, no. 3, pp. 105–115, Rudolph Morris says that this kind of Catholicism lacks "the typically Catholic serenity towards all things human, that generosity towards all things real, that broad wisdom, that ravishing charm of the true mystics. . . . There is no smile, no superiority of heart, no inner freedom, but clenched teeth, and a pretense of purity resulting from a forced zeal of purism and a complete lack of artistic sense—which lack is to be considered a moral virtue."

heaven by merit as much, and more, than any mediaeval Catholic. Lutheranism, too, has fallen to the general
secularism of modern Protestantism, for the very reason that, in this day and age, it has been found hard—
for purely intellectual reasons—to have faith in Christ
as the redeeming Son of God. Modern man therefore
leaves the Christian religion altogether, subscribes to
the doctrine of the Fall as promulgated by Freud and
Watson, and has no hope that human nature will remain anything but fallen.

It is apparent, then, that none of these answers to the
moral problem will work for modern man. He is too
self-conscious to profit from the old Catholic answer; he
cannot simply regress to the naïve state, and self-conscious Catholicism is, without doubt, Catholicism at its
worst—guilt-ridden, bigoted, puritanical and morbid.
The Calvinist answer involves a conception of God so
immoral that it inspires no more love and devotion than
an impersonal Fate. The Lutheran answer involves a
faith in Christ which modern man finds difficult for
intellectual reasons, or, if the intellectual obstacles are
surmounted, difficult for the reason that he would *like*
to have faith but does not know *how*. And the answer
of modern liberal Protestantism, the religion of "ethics
tinged with emotion," does not impress him as religion
at all and supplies no spiritual power by means of which
such ethics may be practised.

All the Christian moralists—Catholic, Calvinist, Lutheran and liberal Protestant—seem, furthermore, to
be agreed that sin must be fought and pride eradicated.
But the modern psychoanalyst echoes the ancient Chinese proverb, "When the wrong man uses the right
means, the right means work in the wrong way." Your
motive for fighting sin is itself sinful; the idea that you

are, and must continue to be, a sinner hurts your pride. What is more, you may drive sinful desires out of your conscious mind, but they will merely assume some other form. Your suppressed lust will emerge as a cantankerous disposition; your suppressed bad temper will emerge as nervousness and anxiety. Why not accept yourself as you are? You can't change yourself; you're an animal, and it's no good trying to be an angel. This sounds tremendously convincing to modern man, unless he happens to have met and known saints. Looking into himself, he sees that it will be harder for him to become a saint than for a camel to go through the eye of a needle. But there is still the ultimate answer of Christ: "With men it is not possible, but with God all things are possible."

I I

We have seen that Luther grasped the point of the Incarnation which the mediaeval Catholic mythos contained but did not realize—or at least part of the point. Salvation is the free gift of God to sinners; in Christ, man is given union with God even though he crucifies it. We are saved through faith in this gift, and through gratitude for it perform good works. But from our present standpoint, Luther's answer involves two difficulties:

(1) We are saved through faith in Christ: but we do not know Christ except through the pages of the Gospels, where he is remote in time and space, through the sacraments, which confuse us with their archaic symbolism and make little more than an aesthetic impression, and through his saints, whom we admire but do not understand because they are other people and we cannot sense their inner experience. We need immedi-

ate and mystical knowledge of Christ, but Luther firmly rejected mysticism because he only knew mysticism in the mediaeval Catholic form, which was, at least superficially, the soul's effort to *ascend* to divine knowledge through renunciation of the flesh. Rightly, he saw that this was opposed to the idea of the Incarnation. But for Luther the Incarnation stopped with the historical Jesus; it was still bottled up in its historical symbol.

(2) Having no sense, therefore, of an incarnational mysticism, Luther's theology was at root world-despising. It had none of that "generosity towards all things real" which characterized naïve Catholicism because of that thoroughgoing sacramentalism with which the mediaeval *mystics* were never quite happy. Luther regarded the creation as depraved, but redeemed *in spite* of its depravity. He did not see that the Incarnation, flowing out beyond the historical Jesus, had already in principle transfigured the creation. His theology stopped with the Crucifixion; it did not go on to the Resurrection and Ascension, and the coming of the Holy Spirit. That is to say, he saw God descending to earth with love, and that love ever being rejected and denied on Calvary, ever being spattered with the filth of the flesh, and yet never withdrawing himself. But he had no adequate vision of earth ascending with Christ into heaven and becoming the tabernacle of the Holy Spirit. For Christ not only died for man on Calvary; he ascended for man on Olivet. He has not only come *down* to the world; he has also taken the world *up*. For lack of this vision, both in Lutheranism and Calvinism, Protestantism eventually fell back into moral legalism, into the attempt to earn one's way into heaven.

Considered in itself, the world is indeed evil, fallen, depraved, for evil and the Fall consist precisely in considering the world as an end in itself apart from God. But this is a false, illusory and subjective view of the world. Considered objectively and in reality, the world is the creation of the God who is incarnate in it. God became incarnate historically in a local symbol to draw our attention to the truth about the world: that in reality the flesh is good enough to be his own garment, good enough to be loved into conformity with the divine will. Thus St. Paul could say that everything is good when received with thanksgiving, for thanksgiving is the acknowledgement, the realization, that everything has God as its source and its incarnate principle.

Here, then, is the groundwork to a solution of the moral problem created by Western man's adolescence and growth of self-consciousness. The Protestants, the Humanists, the modern psychoanalysts have turned their eyes upon man and considered him in and by himself. The Protestants saw nothing but inherent depravity. The Humanists saw at first the wonderful endowments of reason and power, but their vision ended at last in the disillusionment of psychoanalysis, and the disillusionment of the collapse of Humanist culture. For the psychoanalysts also considered man by himself, and saw only animal libido and mechanical process. In every instance the conclusion was simply the result of the method of observation. Look into yourself and you will become conscious of nothing but a vicious circle, for the very reason that the act of introspection is viciously circular: you cannot see what you are looking for, because what you are looking for is the thing that looks. Every self-conscious attempt to know oneself, to improve oneself, to save oneself, to unite oneself with God, must come to this exasperating and impossible conclusion.

This bad self-consciousness is in fact the root of evil, and is nothing other than what we have formerly referred to as the attempt to possess one's own life through fear and pride. Somehow, therefore, man must be persuaded to let go of himself, to stop running around in circles and making himself miserable. This is the intended effect of the great mystical and incarnational revelation that we have been given union with God, here and now, just as we are. The point is to give us an inner contentment, security and confidence so that, for the first time in our lives, we shall cease worrying about ourselves and whirring around in circles, walk straight ahead and achieve some creative result. In the naïve child state man can get this confidence through symbols. He receives absolution from the priest and takes the Holy Communion, and somehow or other God is in him and with him, and all is well. He goes about his business and stops worrying about the fate of his soul. That is why the Zen master, when asked what the Tao is, answers, "Walk on!" But modern man, who cannot at once or in the same way as mediaeval man accept the Catholic symbols of union with God, has to find his confidence through mystical realization.

Thus we direct him to look at the Eternal Now which lovingly carries him all the time, or, if this will not do, we speak to him in purely psychological language and tell him to accept himself as he is, now at this moment, completely and entirely, with all his faults, sins, bad moods, perplexities and ignorances. Translated into religious language, this is the same thing as telling him that he is loved and accepted by God, that he must love himself with God's own love, or that he is saved as he is, a sinner, by simple faith in Jesus. Until this act of acceptance has occurred by one means or another, creative morality in any Christian sense is quite impossible. People who look upon the process from outside, who have never realized God's love, never accepted themselves, never dared to receive union with God, naturally have misgivings. They say that those who presume so cocksurely that God accepts them and that they are united with him will abandon themselves without qualm to a life of vice.

Their misgivings might be well-founded if those who so presumed were still in the child or adolescent stage, for whom this is indeed a dangerous doctrine. But for those who have been through the hell of acute self-consciousness the results are otherwise. Both St. Paul and St. Augustine were utterly certain of their union with God, and spoke of it with a confidence from which the guilt-ridden piety of our own day would shrink. And whatever the faults of these two saints, they certainly did anything but abandon themselves to a life of vice! Yet it must be remembered that both of them had been through the impasse of self-consciousness, and had realized thoroughly and profoundly the impossibility of self-improvement. But when a similar attitude was adopted by certain cults of the Middle Ages, such as the Brothers of the Free Spirit, the results were sometimes disastrous because of the lack of self-conscious experience.[7] Speaking, from his standpoint as a psychologist, of the therapeutic value of accepting oneself as it is, C. G. Jung says:

> This attitude would be poison for a person who has already been overwhelmed by things that just happen (in the psyche), but it is of the highest value for one who, with an exclusively conscious critique, chooses from the things

---

[7]Cf. D'Aygalliers, *Ruysbroeck the Admirable*. London, 1925, pp. 43–47.

that happen only those appropriate to his consciousness, and thus gets gradually drawn away from the stream of life into a stagnant backwater. . . . Only on the basis of such an attitude, which renounces none of the values won in the course of Christian development, but which, on the contrary, tries with Christian charity and forbearance to accept the humblest things in oneself, will a higher level of consciousness and culture be possible.[8]

As we have seen, man in the child state can readily be overwhelmed by "things that just happen" in himself, such as violent outbursts of anger or of the physical passion of sex, and this was why mediaeval man needed an authoritarian and legalistic morality. The adolescent and "Protestant" stage of acute self-consciousness was, however, absolutely necessary for his further development, but now that this is coming to an end our concept of Christian morality will change accordingly, realizing the full implications of the moral teaching of Jesus and St. Paul. This mature morality will be grounded on three principles:

(1) The *given* union of the soul with God. Because God is love and forgiveness he has accepted man as he is and taken him into his heart with all his sins and imperfections.

(2) Love instead of hatred and violence will be the principle of "combat" with evil, for the flesh and the devil will be brought into conformity with the divine will by love rather than force.

(3) The motivating power of morality will be gratitude for the gift of union and the indwelling Spirit, rather than the sense of guilt and obedience to law and authority. The moral law will remain in a secondary function, as an elastic technique for expressing love. It

---

[8] *Secret of the Golden Flower*, pp. 91–92 and 126.

will no longer be the dominant principle whereby moral actions are judged and directed. Thus we shall realize the fulness of St. Augustine's saying that Christian morality is, "Love, and do what you like."

The first principle has already had sufficient discussion, and the third is so clearly set forward by St. Paul that it is, or should be, an accepted postulate of Christianity. But the second is contrary to the spirit of practical Christian morality as we have thus far known it—as a technique of war upon evil symbolized by the conflict of St. Michael and the Dragon. Without doubt this technique has its use as a temporary measure during the child and adolescent stages, but it will never do anything more than suppress or change the external symptoms of evil, and alleviate an urgent danger for a brief period. It is like taking aspirin for a toothache or bicarbonate of soda for stomach ulcers—and sometimes like curing a headache by cutting off the head.

In practice this violent treatment of evil achieves only superficial results, even when applied with all the help of sacramental grace. The most devout Christians who apply this technique are rarely free from its "viciously circular" results, crushing down lust or anger only to promote such compensatory evils as sourness of disposition or subtle cruelty towards others. To a great extent they are unaware of these compensations, since attention is diverted from them either by the intensity of the struggle against other evils, or by unconscious mental mechanisms which conveniently hide them from observation. Such compensations, both individual and social, are familiar among all forms of Christian rigorism and puritanism. We see them in fanaticism, morbid and sensational psychic phenomena sometimes called "mystical," meanness, or that peculiar gloominess of soul so characteristic of self-conscious Protestántism and Catholicism. Or again, we see them expressed socially in such manifestations as the Inquisition, Puritan witch-hunting, and the various forms of Satanism which appear regularly in communities with a highly ascetic religion.

Traditionally, these compensations are explained on the principle that w.1enever the devil sees that he is about to be defeated, he increases his resistance and multiplies temptation to the utmost, as in the famous case of the visions of St. Anthony. But the extra temptation of which the soul is aware is a blind against the .devil's real victory in other directions, of which the soul is *not* aware. According to Catholic moral theology, sins of which we are unaware are not sins because they are not deliberate acts of the will. Nevertheless, they are evils harmful to oneself and to others, and in fact the will has created them indirectly by having devilish feelings towards the devil.

> Our attitude towards evil must be free from hatred, and has itself need to be enlightened in character. . . . Satan rejoices when he succeeds in inspiring us with diabolical feelings to himself. It is he who wins when his own methods are turned against himself. . . . A continual denunciation of evil and its agents merely encourages its growth in the world—a truth sufficiently revealed in the Gospels, but to which we remain persistently blind.[9]

Fought sins only appear to be conquered; in fact they are simply pushed out of consciousness to assume other forms where they are the more dangerous for not being noticed, and moral theology cannot overcome them by the method of the ostrich.

---

[9]Berdyaev, *Freedom and the Spirit*, p. 182.

The natural world, expressing as it does the nature and methods of the divine mind, offers many analogies of the futility of this moral technique. Nothing, for example, makes a hedge grow so fast as clipping it back. The man who swims against a strong current will usually be drowned. To try to smooth troubled water with a flatiron is only to trouble it the more. An unpleasant noise is not mitigated by the vociferous singing of hymns; the result is only a louder and more discordant uproar. To attempt to get rid of wandering thoughts by efforts to destroy them only centers attention on their wanderings; conversely, to try to eliminate them by *strenuous* concentration on the task in hand centers attention not on the task but on oneself trying to perform it. For evil is overcome neither by direct opposition nor by concentration on its contrary virtue. Perfume is no antidote to a bad smell, especially when the smell is increased in response to the perfume.

Thus far we have been afraid of applying the Gospel principle of "Resist not evil." The most that our morality has grasped of the principle of overcoming evil by love is the idea of loving the sinner but hating the sin, whereby it was possible to justify the burning of heretics on the grounds that such torture would save them from eternal damnation. We have not had the courage to admit either that we have been given union with God or that one who is in union with God need neither fear evil nor hate it in any violent sense. God, as we have seen, is in principle greater than evil, and as it would be *lèse-majesté* for him to fight it, it would likewise be so for the soul in union with God. If such an idea fills us with fear, it is only because we do not really believe in the gift of union with God.

The love and acceptance of evil is not, however, the

condonement of evil. We are not saying, *"Peccate fortiter! Let us sin that grace may abound."* The point is that all evil actions come from pride and fear, which cannot be rooted out by violence but only by the conviction and the realization of inescapable union with God. The more vivid this truth becomes, the less point, the less satisfaction, the less interest there is in evil. But the more a hostile attitude to evil develops the sense of guilt and separation from God, the less vivid this truth will be; pride and fear will increase and plunge the soul into black despair. If the soul is afraid that evil conduct will separate it from God, it will cling to God through fear, and thus not realize union with God at all, because, as we have seen, realization cannot possibly come through fearful and possessive clinging. The soul must understand that while God does not condone evil, he does not cast out the evildoer or his deeds in any active sense. To try to affect God with evil is like trying to cut water with a knife.

There is, of course, the risk that the soul will be moved to evil before it has realized union with God vividly enough to lose interest in evil. But we must take this risk, for the Christian religion is not a "safe and sure" way to heaven for moral cowards. Even if, having only a partial realization of union, a soul does commit evil without the deterrent of guilt and fear, this will do far less damage in the long run than a reversion to the guilt-ridden state. At this stage repentance will consist, not in guilty sorrow for the sin, but in turning again to the truth of union with God, which, during the act of sin, will almost invariably have been put out of mind. If the soul has a spiritual guide or confessor, he must stress neither the guilt nor the future avoidance of the sin; he must do everything possible to increase the conviction of union with a God who in himself is absolute love. There are risks and falls in the process, but they are temporary and must be taken if there is to be any real progress.

It is questionable whether at the present time this can become part of the general and public teaching of the Church, for there are so many people still in the child and adolescent state who will attain a great holiness according to the rules of their state. They are to be provided for in every possible way, and on no account to be regarded as an inferior kind of Christians. To some extent they will be protected from the harmful possibilities of this truth by inability to understand it. On the whole, it would seem safer to make such teaching a part of that personal spiritual counsel which the Catholic priest may give in the confessional and the Protestant minister in his study.

In this connection it is obvious that in many cases there is need for a revision of normal practice in the use of the Sacrament of Penance. All wise clergy and psychologists recognize, for a variety of reasons, the value of this sacrament. It is clear that for a soul in the child state the act of confession and the gift of forgiveness, pronounced authoritatively and sacramentally by the priest, involve an immediate and glorious relief from guilt. But in the awkward adolescent stage this does not happen, and nothing much can be done about it. Whatever counsel the priest may give, self-examination and confession will only increase the penitent's self-consciousness and sense of guilt. The gift of absolution will be temporary indeed in its effect, because the penitent knows perfectly well that he is going to sin again, try as he may to avoid it. The child, in his naïveté, has no particular thoughts about the future, or imagines that

he will not sin again. But Protestants refrain from confession because the practice aggravates their self-consciousness and leads them to despair. Catholics in the
adolescent state who continue with it lose their spiritual
joy, and go through an inner hell of guilt. All that the
priest can do is to try to help them through this stage
as quickly as may be, even intensifying the struggle and
conflict, until he feels that they are ready to take the
risk of maturity, of knowing that God accepts them
absolutely and unconditionally. This naturally requires
profound spiritual and psychological insight on the
priest's part, and although mistakes will, as in medicine,
occur from time to time, we should have enough trust
in the independent action and love of God not to shirk
the task. Where we fail, he may heal, for we are not
indispensable. In general, however, souls in this state
should be entrusted to a wiser confessor by priests who
do not really feel able to advise them.

The soul which is in or entering the mature state is
a new problem in this respect. It would seem probable
that in their case we should revert to the practice of the
early Church, and advise or require confession only
when they feel in need of it or commit some sin of
public scandal.[10] For in this stage the sacrament will
have three main uses. It will assist the soul over relapses
into the guilt-ridden state. It will give opportunity for
counsel directed to increasing the realization of union
with God. It will provide a useful *voluntary* discipline
for those who are using law simply as a technique of
love and are shaping their characters for no other motive than the glory of God. Under these circumstances
the use of the sacrament must be governed in freedom,

---

[10]During the first four centuries the Church required use of the sacrament
only for murder, adultery and idolatry.

and shame or guilt must not be attached to its disuse, for it will cease to be free and loving. Emphasis must be laid upon repentance as returning to the thought of union with God, and not as promising to try not to sin again, which is a negative thought full of all the dangers of challenging the devil to a fight. God permits us to be tempted, and when we say the prayer, "Lead us not into temptation," we are asking him not to let us descend to fighting evil on its own ground and in its own way.

The point which modern Church religion seems so far from understanding is that a full and mature Christian morality can never be based on the sense of guilt; to far too great an extent organized Christianity thrives on the exploitation of this sense, appealing simply to man's pride and fear. Of course the arousing of a sense of guilt is the easiest and quickest way of giving evil a temporary check, and creating a rudimentary kind of repentance. Real repentance, however, is not a self-regarding action; it is turning away from self and towards God, but it has been assumed that the horror of oneself experienced in guilt is the most effective way of getting a soul to turn from itself. For guilt in the sense of which we are speaking is not simply the consciousness that one has done wrong, but the self-recrimination and self-loathing which generally follow from it. Obviously it is essential to know that one has done wrong, but consequent self-loathing does not effectively turn attention upon God. The horror or hatred of a thing is a form of strong attachment to it, since an object of hatred fascinates and holds the attention despite all efforts to turn away. This accounts for the bad self-consciousness which so often mars Christian piety, particularly in its penitential mood. But it has been said that he prays best who does not know that he is praying, for prayer is self-forgetful absorption in God. The fascination of self-loathing therefore inhibits prayer, and because communion with God is the only possible means of overcoming evil, the sense of guilt will, in the long run, only increase the degree of sin.

In short, therefore, self-loathing must give place to self-acceptance, which is permitting oneself to be loved by God.

> The acceptance of oneself is the essence of the moral problem and the epitome of a whole outlook upon life. That I feed the hungry, that I forgive an insult, that I love my enemy in the name of Christ—all these are undoubtedly great virtues. What I do unto the least of my brethren, that I do unto Christ. But what if I should discover that the least among them all, the poorest of all the beggars, the most impudent of all offenders, the very enemy himself—that these are within me, and that I myself stand in need of the alms of my own kindness—that I myself am the enemy who must be loved—what then?[11]

The trouble is that many Christians do not perceive in God the very virtues which they expect in the saints. Jesus told us to forgive our brethren even if they sin against us "seventy times seven." He said nothing about withholding forgiveness until we had extracted an apology and been assured that the offender would do his best not to let it happen again. But apparently such charity cannot be expected from God himself, "to whom it belongeth justly to punish sinners," and who dangles the soul over hell until there has been contrition, confession and satisfaction. We forget that retribution is a dispensation of the divine love, wholly curative

---

[11]Jung, *Modern Man in Search of a Soul.* London and New York, 1933, pp. 271–272.

in its aim like the surgeon's knife. God has no need to punish in the vengeful sense because he has no need to protect himself. He is not weak and vulnerable like human society, and the teaching of Jesus has to be separated from some of the Bronze Age elements in its Old Testament background. [12]

III

As the ever-deepening realization of union with God is the only way of final victory over evil, so it is the only source of creative virtue. Delivered from the vicious circle of bad self-consciousness, the infinite regression of chasing oneself around and around, it is possible for man to move forward. But in moving forward his principle of action will no more be a moral code; it will be the indwelling Holy Spirit, the ever-present fact of our union with God. The corporate nature of the Church as "the fellowship of the Holy Spirit" consists in this fact and not, as is so often assumed, in obedience to a common rule or external authority, whether the formal discipline of the Catholic Church or the "moral precepts" of the Sermon on the Mount.

St. Paul made it clear that Christian morality is an art and not a science; it proceeds from a new Life and not from a new law. One may master all the rules of gram-

---

[12]It has long been the custom of theologians to interpret certain of the Biblical attributes of God—his walking, sitting, sleeping, etc.—in a symbolic sense, and, as we have seen, his "wrath," considered as retribution for sin, is in reality a "surgical" measure prompted by his love. His withholding of forgiveness is to be understood in a similar way. Thus the saying, "If ye forgive not men their trespasses, neither will your Father forgive your trespasses" would indicate that a person who does not forgive does not appreciate God's forgiveness, and thus neither understands nor enjoys it. If you are one with God, you will share in his forgiving nature and manifest it to others. If you do not, you are not sufficiently awake to your union with God and need to realize it more vividly.

mar but fail to be a good writer for lack of anything to say. One may master all the rules of conduct but fail to be a Christian for lack of love. Mere obedience to a law will never of itself produce love, because love is the very life of God and there is no system or set of rules whereby one can become its possessor. Thus the mission of Christ was not to teach a new moral law. There was nothing particularly original in his moral principles, all of which may be found in earlier Jewish literature or in the precepts of other and older religions. The mission of Christ was to bring into human consciousness a new life and a new power which will make it possible not only to carry out the old precepts but also to reform them.

Bach did not write his music by looking up the rules of harmony and counterpoint and following them slavishly in sundry combinations. He studied the keyboard until he could identify the sounds which he heard interiorly, reproduced them in writing and *gave* us the rules of harmony. What we call rules are simply our analysis and classification of the forms of expression created by the great masters. We can teach others the forms, but we cannot teach them the genius because genius is life itself which ever evades capture. The astonishing thing about Christianity, however, is that we are invited not simply to emulate the Master, but to share his genius or Spirit. For the Spirit of God, unlike the spirit of music, is given to the whole world. This is where Christianity is different in principle from Judaism and other legalistic religions, and this is why "monkey religion" is of necessity sub-Christian.

It is rare indeed, however, that a man of genius, whether artist or saint, breaks entirely with tradition. If his message is to have any value at all for his contemporaries, its forms of expression must grow out of existing traditions. A writer, to make himself understood, must use the language of the people, and must state new ideas in terms of old ideas. Thus the new life of Christianity expressed itself to the world in terms of existing Jewish, Greek and Roman traditions, giving them at the same time a fresh significance. In the same way, the new Christianity of maturity will express itself in terms of the old Christianity of childhood and adolescence both in doctrine and morals, for development through tradition is the *modus operandi* of the Spirit.

Matter for whole volumes could be found in discussing the detailed application of these principles to specific moral problems in politics, economics and culture, and in family and sexual relations. Here we can do no more than suggest some of the general directions which a mature Christian morality will be likely to take, and of these three seem to be of special importance:

(1) It will be an incarnational morality seeking to transform the world and the flesh rather than to deny it. But it will not seek to transform them beyond their proper limits. It will transform man into some approximation of perfect manhood—not into superman, angel or demigod. This trend is indicated in the concern of most Christian groups for the improvement of man's material condition, and for the application of Christian principles in politics and economics.

(2) It will lose, however, the adolescent's itch to change the world over night, which has long characterized Western Christianity in its schemes for spiritual and material reform. We shall learn from the terrible chaos of modern civilization the folly of giving that which is holy unto dogs, and casting our pearls before swine. We shall also lose much of that spiritual conceit

which blinds us to the work of the Holy Spirit in cultures and religions other than our own. Zealous interference with other people's lives will be tempered by faith in God, and the knowledge that spiritual growth cannot be forced.

(3) Our morality will again become conscious of its true end, and will thus be more intelligently applied. Since the Reformation we have largely regarded morality as an end in itself, and have clung to certain principles without understanding their object or asking whether, in this or that application, they really achieve the object. A morality which proceeds from the realization of union with God will see that its end is the perfection of this realization for all human beings.

The function of the Incarnation is to unite man as man with God as God, without "confusion of natures." Human nature does not become divine in the process, but perfectly human, for when Spirit is in union with created nature it does not overwhelm it but perfects it. The vast difference between the Four Gospels and the later Apocryphal Gospels is that in the former Jesus is always human; in the latter his humanity is lost in divinity. For Jesus was God in terms of man, not superman, and as man he had the finite limitations proper to humanity. He experienced fear and sorrow, hunger and thirst and pain; he had to eat and drink; when tired he had to sleep. His human knowledge was not divine omniscience, and thus while its quality was illumined its quantity and extent was limited.[13] He did not marry because his blood was to flow through the whole human race, and no occasion could be given for a line of physical descendants to claim a special union with him. He

---

[13] It was thus impossible for him to know that Moses did not write the Pentateuch!

taught in terms of the Hebrew tradition into which he was born (being the best for the purpose), and thus accepted some of the limitations of that tradition.[14] Unlike St. John the Baptist and the Nazarites and Essenes, he was not an ascetic, for "the Son of Man cometh eating and drinking, and they say, Behold a gluttonous man and a wine-bibber."

For man, a perfect realization of union with God consists in a realization that extends to all his human functions, for no human function is incompatible with God. Man is a totality of body, mind and spirit. As body he eats and drinks, has sexual intercourse, feels tired after work, and is subject to pain, death and decay. As mind and emotion he reasons and speculates, and in response to certain stimuli feels fear, anger or love as rightly and naturally as the body feels heat when close to fire. As spirit he comes into conscious touch with the life of God, which, through spirit, flows down to his "lower" nature. But it does not deliver that "lower" nature from its proper limitations on the plane of time and space. It does not make the emotions incapable of fear and desire, or the body incapable of fatigue and decay. On the contrary, those who expect religion to effect a complete spiritualization of body, mind and emotion on the space-time level are indulging an absurd spiritual pride. True spirituality involves the acceptance of our limitations just as true poetry involves

---

[14]Limitations of knowledge and understanding are not positive errors. If a man perceives the moon as a disk and not a sphere, his perception is not so much wrong as incomplete. It would be wrong if he perceived it as a square. Looked at from a distance, hills are blue. If, upon closer inspection, we find that the hills are covered with green grass we have not shown that the former perception was wrong. On the contrary, it was quite right *from a distance*. The artist who paints distant hills green because he knows they are covered with grass gives his picture a false colouring if "realistic" representation is intended.

accepting the limitations of a metric or other prosodic form.[15]

Union with God implies, therefore, the control and beautification of man's natural functions, but thus far we have not clearly understood the meaning of control. We have confused control with partial or total abstinence. But a controlled dancer is not one who dances rather seldom; he is one who dances often and well. His control comes into play *in the act* of dancing. Of course, if he dances too much he will get tired and stale, and to this extent control does involve relative abstinence. The same is true of man's natural functions and appetites, but the distinctive Christian and incarnational method of control is lost altogether if identified with simple moderation or abstinence. For example, a person is not sexually controlled in any real sense by mere limitation of the frequency of intercourse or the number of his partners. To realize union with God in terms of sexual life, he must exercise control within the act of sex, and as this will require practice the act cannot be too infrequent. It may well require limiting the act to one partner, for human beings are so complex and diverse that mutual adaptation in sex can take many years to perfect. As yet our moral theology has little conception of this kind of control. So far as these natural functions and appetites are concerned it is largely prohibitive, and has thus left the incarnational principle quite unapplied.[16]

---

[15]The ultimate resurrection and incorruption of the body would seem to occur in eternity rather than space-time, as indicated above, pp. 80–81. The Resurrection of Christ, being a special case, occurred also in time and space in order to be accessible to man's space-time consciousness.

[16] *Monastic* chastity and celibacy is a separate question. There is no reason why certain people should not be free to renounce sexual life if this will enable them to serve God in a special and intensive way. But the monastic life is a specialized vocation, one of many varied ways of serving God, and

As applied to eating and drinking, to sexual relations and all other natural functions and enjoyments, Christian morality involves much more than wise moderation and restraint in the frequency of use. It requires that the love and beauty of God be realized and expressed to the fullest possible degree in the actions themselves. To some extent we have already grasped this truth in relation to politics and social intercourse, but if we hesitate to apply it to our so-called lower functions we imply that in some way these are incompatible with God. But material things and processes become occasions of evil when not related to God. If, as is usually the case, the devout Christian puts God out of mind when engaged in sexual relations, he is simply inviting them to be a source of temptation. Failure to relate the world and the flesh to God accounts for much of the ugliness and sourness of traditional Christian morality.

The adolescence of Western man has been marked by an attempt to dominate the world with his religion and his morals which has brought much more disaster than good. His extreme political and economic imperialism has been the shadow of spiritual and moral imperialism, for the trader, and then the soldier, have always followed the missionary. However superior the Christian religion and Christian morality may be, to try to force truth upon others is always a sign of immaturity. Although Christian principles must be applied in our political, economic and social life, this simply will not come to pass in a hurry. No amount of

---

is altogether legitimate so long as it does not lay claim to a greater perfection or nearness to God than any other way of life. To regard virginity as spiritually superior to the married state is certainly a Manichaean and un-Christian point of view.

218

shouting, preaching, denunciation and propaganda will do anything but drive political and social abuses underground, for there is no such thing as an abiding public morality without a very general realization of union with God, and this, as we have seen, does not come in response to pressure or force of any kind.

The primary work of the Church is to realize and share the gift of union with God, and if its attention is diverted to the imitation and sharing of the fruits of that union as its main object, and if, furthermore, such imitation is demanded of others, only disaster can follow. It is a fruit of union that men should desire to heal the sick and to prolong life and health. It is a fruit of union that they should study the secrets of nature and develop sciences and skills to this end. But when these goals are pursued for their own sake, when their original impulse and their final end are forgotten and untaught, the power of healing becomes a power of destruction. It is a fruit of union that men should study agriculture and engineering to feed the hungry and clothe the naked, but when the object of production becomes profit alone, and the object of food and clothing becomes "living for back and belly," the moral impulse has failed in its object and become positively immoral. Worse still, when all this wholesale dispersion of wealth, gadgets and skills becomes identified with Christian civilization, when peoples who have not developed this kind of life are thought backward and heathenish, and are forced into conformity and compelled to ape our institutions, our morals, our dress, our beliefs, our sciences, our industries and our armies—so-called Christian culture becomes a curse upon the face of the earth.

Thanks to our zealous and self-righteous interference, the ancient and splendid cultures of India, China and, more particularly, of Japan have been largely ruined. Although the peoples of India and China may not starve and die of plague in quite such vast numbers as heretofore, they are busy with excitement for our more fatuous political theories, with building armies on Western models, using our sciences to equip them with the necessary weapons, and with opening schools and universities to impart the scraps of information we call wisdom and to teach peasants to read so that they can understand and believe the propaganda and dope-literature in the newspapers. Perhaps no one can really be blamed for this, since it was done to a great degree with sincere intentions. But it should no longer be necessary to send missionaries to the peoples of Asia with vastly misunderstood versions of their religions and ours. As St. Francis Xavier and Robert de Nobili proved long ago, it is not impossible to teach Christianity to Orientals in the framework of their own cultural forms and traditions, without giving them the desire to ape our merely external and sensational accomplishments.

Western man has an amazingly naïve belief in the moral excellence of his high standard of living and information, which he confuses with culture and education, thinking that the mere dissemination of wealth, health, cleanliness and knowledge is a virtue of the highest order. But when all this is separated from the inner essence of the Christian religion it becomes an effrontery to people of real culture and a danger to people of none. It is not charitable to the poor to try all at once to abolish poverty, with the exception, indeed, of really abject poverty. As Christians we must feed the hungry and go hungry ourselves for their sake. But most of the wholesale and impersonal charity we practise today is mere patronization of the poor, motivated by pity and fear of their estate and not by respect and honour. We assume that poverty is an evil and in the name of Christian love try to give all a high standard of living, only to enslave millions of souls to cravings which they never had before. Instead of giving the poor love and dignity, we give them money in exchange for their souls. Christian poverty is honourable, and has been embraced by the saints, not because it delivers the soul from the chains of "evil" matter, but because in poverty material goods are more profoundly loved and appreciated, for the senses are cleansed from surfeit and excessive titillation and realize to their full capacity the beauty of the world. To the extent that the poor man is a real materialist he is a real Christian, because he reverences matter.

Almost more evil than the thoughtless dissemination of wealth is the indiscriminate spreading of knowledge, which we mistake for wisdom and truth. Truth is knowledge in the service of God; anything else is mere fact, and the knowledge of facts is an amoral power which, of itself, gives no goodness at all to the recipient. Universal education, as we practise it, has no relation to the spreading of truth, and for the most part its effect is to put vast forces and skills at the disposal of stupidity and evil. This naïve confusion of knowledge with truth reaches insanity itself when sincere men of science, for example, think it honest and moral to inform the general public or notoriously immoral governments about discoveries such as that of atomic energy, which, in the present state of public morality, is a menace pure and simple. The bacilli of virulent diseases are "truths" in the debased current sense of the word, but we do not spread them deliberately in the atmosphere. General

221

knowledge of these discoveries may be inevitable, but it certainly is not good.

So much of this absurdity has come to pass because Christians have been moral monkeys, confusing the externals of charitable behaviour with religion itself. Moral "monkey business" may be harmless enough in certain circumstances, but when the whole world is adjured in the name of God to join in with it, the externals of charity are hopelessly perverted through loss of the original motive. The function of the Church is not to be the world's moral policeman, insisting on the observance of various modes of conduct by those who do not understand their inner meaning. The work of the Church is to share a sense of union with God by all the means at its disposal, symbolic or otherwise. The *Christian* morality of love, as distinct from the secular morality of justice, has meaning and value only in relation to this background. Apart from it, it disrupts the *natural* order of society, which, based as it is on fear and collective self-interest, is to be preferred to Christian and supernatural virtues running amok in separation from their source. To arrogate supernatural virtues to oneself apart from union with God is not only the sin of hypocrisy, but also the *hubris*, the supreme and damnable audacity, of thieving the powers of the only real Possessor of goodness and love.

Christian morality becomes perverted and destructive not only when unmotivated by sacramental or mystical union with God as its initial impulse, but also when it is not seen clearly that God is its end. A Christian gives material benefits to those in need for the reason that, lacking things necessary for the body, they are distracted from their true aim as human persons, which is God himself. It is hard to love God in abject poverty, and hard to love him when mind and emotions are obsessed with sensations and passions. Thus the gift of material and intellectual goods is an act of Christian charity only when it is the outward form of the gift of God—that is, the gift of real love.

This becomes obvious as soon as we ask what human life is for, but most modern world-reformers do not ask this question. The morality of giving material and intellectual goods to others consists for them solely in the fact that it makes possible what they term "fully developed personality" for the underprivileged. A fully developed personality is presumably one who passes the time and helps others to pass the time as painlessly as possible in gratifying biological urges and intellectual curiosities, which, in so far as it is a form of play, has a deceptive resemblance to the activity of heaven. But just because it has no conscious relation to the eternal play of God, it is meaningless play, for it takes place, not against the background of eternal Reality, but against that of eternal Nothingness, which will shortly swallow it up. This causes a sense of anxiety and futility which mars the character of human play with lust and greed, for fear that we shall "miss something" before all is dissolved in death.[17]

The active life of morality has no significance unless directed to the contemplative life. Now, however, that it is possible to think in terms of an incarnational mysticism, it is no longer necessary for us to make such a

[17]Evil is closely connected with the anticipation of death, when death is feared as the ultimate end of life. Apparently animals do not anticipate death to any great degree, taking, as Jesus said, no thought for the morrow. When the Genesis mythos states that death comes into the world as a consequence of sin, this may well refer to the anticipation of death rather than death itself, which is no more than one temporal boundary of a finite being, birth constituting the other. This is the more likely for the reason that saints return to that primitive innocence which lives in the Eternal Now.

sharp *formal* difference between the active and contemplative lives as was usual in the Middle Ages. The form of the contemplative life need not be so exclusively religious that it requires the cloister for its fulfilment, for in an incarnational mysticism contemplation and action are united as they were united in Christ's own life.

Contemplation and action are united not only in actions that are formally moral, such as deeds of kindness to others, but—ideally—in all actions whatsoever. It will therefore be recognized that the sphere of Christian action goes far beyond charity, social service and the like, and this will relieve the teaching of Christian action from that overemphasis on formal morality which has given it such a "preachy" atmosphere. This will help to free our idea of the Christian life from the false heroics of adolescence, that running around in search of great moral deeds to do, which is so often no more than hypocritical interference with the lives of others. In the realization of union with God it is no longer necessary for men to prove to themselves that they are saved, and thus it is easier for them to love one another genuinely and sincerely without self-consciousness. They will show mercy, love and consideration for others not because this is "good," not because such conduct assures them that they are leading the Christian life, but because the contemplative life will make them aware of God in all human persons, and, knowing him in themselves, they will burn to let others know him also. For union with God demands absolutely to be shared. Not to share it is not to enjoy it; like the blood, it is a living thing and must be circulated.

This sharing of union is not, however, to be done in a spirit of pride and condescension, for a person who has genuinely realized union with God is humble just because he sees no difference between himself and others. Before realization it seems that there is a difference between those who are awake to God and those who are not. A gateway stands on the spiritual highroad, with the sheep on one side and the goats on the other, and the gate puzzles us because it seems that God has foreordained some to salvation and some to damnation, or else that the sheep have been clever and good and wise enough to pay their way through. This is a theological conundrum which the best minds of Christendom have pondered for centuries without arriving at any logical explanation or solution. In logical and intellectual terms there is no solution. For to those who have passed through the gate there is no gate, and everyone is inside the kingdom of heaven. But to try to draw logical conclusions from this experience is fatal; lacking the experience itself, it leads to moral blindness and confusion of good and evil. Apart from the experience, the idea that all are in the kingdom of heaven suggests laziness and indiscrimination; but with the experience it suggests action and love.[18] The experience itself fills the soul with the inscrutable life of God so that the vision of his universal love is without evil consequence. The only difference between souls that seems to remain is between those that are greatest and those that are least *in* the kingdom. But all are within, and everywhere the will of God reigns supreme.

---

[18]Cf. William Temple in *Nature, Man and God.* London, 1940, p. 381. "The doctrine of the universal Sovereignty of the divine will is paralysing so long as it is doctrine only; but when it is matter of personal experience, it becomes impulse and energy and inspiration."

IV. THE LIFE OF CONTEMPLATION

As vision, contemplation is the beginning of action; as enjoyment, it is its end. But the enjoyment of God and of union with him is not only something to which we may look forward when our work is done; it is the constant condition and accompaniment of meaningful work. It is obvious that the life of action will be shallow indeed if it does not go hand in hand with an interior spiritual life wherefrom the strength and vision needed for action are drawn. To be effective, this spiritual life must be the enjoyment of union with God, and Christian action is now so largely ineffective not only because there is no consciousness of union but also because Church religion almost completely ignores the interior life. It is rare indeed to find even the simplest teaching about prayer and meditation save in religious groups of the "cult" type. In general, Protestantism ignores it for action and Catholicism is still apt to relegate it to the cloister and retreat house. Furthermore, much of the teaching about the spiritual life which does manage to "trickle through" has two serious limitations: it savours too much of "monkey business," of trying to get union with God by imitation, and it is so separated from ordinary everyday life that it tends to be artificial and self-conscious.

We have seen that there is no method for *getting* union with God, because all such methods will, in the end, make us blind to its actual presence. Therefore the life of worship and meditation is not the getting but the enjoyment of union, and for that reason consists of praise, thanksgiving and adoration. Formally and sacramentally this is expressed in the liturgy, the corporate worship of the Church. Informally, yet still in a deeper sense sacramentally, it is expressed in the living of everyday life. By this means both liturgical (*i.e.*, formally religious) actions and everyday actions are turned into contemplation—into that enjoyment and perfection of union with God which is man's true end.

I

Because, in the growth of man's spiritual life, symbolic religion comes before mystical religion, worship through liturgy is the first kind of worship. Christian liturgy has three characteristics. Firstly, it is corporate because Christ, the gift of union, has not been given to one but to many, and the many have thereby been made one Body. Secondly, it employs formal words, that is, a ritual, both because they express formally religious thoughts and because liturgical worship is not something which we on the one hand do towards God on the other, but something which God does through us. Thus liturgy uses, not our own words, but the words of scripture understood as the words of God.[1] Thirdly, it involves formal actions because worship is not some-

---

[1] While this is obviously true of the Divine Office it is perhaps less obviously true of the Mass. However, where the Ordinary of the Mass is not a compilation of scriptural phrases, it is none the less the official and traditional prayer of the Church. But because the Church is the fellowship of the Holy Spirit, its official prayer is regarded as the voice of the Spirit just as much as scripture. The Mass, however, is primarily an action—that is, the action of Christ hallowing, breaking and distributing the Bread of Life. The principle, therefore, is the same: it is not an action which we do towards God, but an action which God does through us.

thing done with the mind alone but with the whole man; like the love between man and woman, it includes both mind and body.

The Christian liturgy is therefore the formal and corporate celebration of union with God in mind and body. It is symbolic worship because both the spiritual reality of God and the physical reality of human life are present in it under symbolic form, which is, significantly enough, one and the same symbol—the bread and the wine, which is at once our own concrete life and the Body and Blood of Christ.[2] Properly carried out, the liturgy is an act of symbolic contemplation, for its purpose is not to edify the people nor to unite them by mere presence in one place and performance of one action. Its purpose is to concentrate thought and action upon God so that the group realizes unity through corporate self-forgetfulness in God. Christian liturgy is essentially theocentric, for which reason forms of worship, or rather, of Church service, having as their main emphasis the edification of the people and the promotion of fellowship on the human plane are sub-Christian and fall short of true contemplation. In preaching services and meetings for informal vocal prayer the people are, as a rule, much too conscious of themselves (or of the preacher) to find unity in God.

If the service of the Church is for edification, the motive for attending it is to "get something," which is quite alien to the contemplative spirit and, indeed, to the whole genius of Christianity. For if it be true that the Christian is one who has accepted the gift of union with God, he has no other purpose in going to church than to celebrate the gift. Lacking consciousness of the

[2] It must be repeated that the word "symbol" is here used in its strict sense, as a sign conveying what it signifies.

gift, the ordinary modern Church service is an insufferably stodgy and joyless affair, where people go to acquire merit for the penance of boredom. It must be admitted, as more and more thoughtful Protestants are beginning to see, that Catholic liturgies embody the spirit of worship far more effectively than informal Protestant services of edification, and that their pattern must be followed if the Church's corporate worship is to have any real value. Protestantism has lost the art of worship for the very reason that it is itself the symptom of Western man's self-consciousness, and there can be no real worship or contemplation until self-consciousness is transcended.

The problem of an appropriate way of the interior life for modern man will not, however, be solved merely by a return to liturgy. In so far as liturgy is symbolic worship it is not immediately comprehensible to modern man, and he cannot use it effectively unless it is thoroughly related to his ordinary life. One of the most encouraging trends in modern religion is the effort of Catholic liturgical reformers to do this very thing by explaining the history and meaning of the liturgy, by encouraging the people to take a full and intelligent part in its celebration, and by pointing out its implications for personal and social life, which begins to deal with the real problem. Yet it is one thing to know, intellectually, what symbols mean; it is quite another to realize that meaning in life. It is one thing to say and think, "Glory be to the Father, and to the Son, and to the Holy Ghost"; it is quite another to *live* it. Until one has lived it, he does not really know what it means. The liturgy, as has always been obvious, must be carried over into life, and not merely into one's personal moral life, but, as the foundation for this as well as for its fulfilment, into one's personal spiritual life. The Church's formal and corporate life of prayer and contemplation must be extended into the prayer life of the individual, or rather, interpreted in terms of his spiritual life as it goes on from day to day. But so far as modern man is concerned, this simply does not happen. Even if he is a practising Christian it happens but rarely, because, for the modern mind, the traditional ways of the personal spiritual life are for the most part unacceptable.

It is easy to dismiss the problem by saying that this absence of the interior life is due either to laziness or lack of instruction; that the traditional ways of this life are tried and true, and that if the modern mind can't accept them it's too bad for the modern mind. But the situation here is the same as in other aspects of religion. The old ways of the spiritual life are right and marvellous for those who can use them; they have produced lives of the highest beauty and sanctity, and will continue to do so. At the same time, they do not satisfy the needs of the mature religious consciousness and should not be forced upon it. They fail to satisfy this type of mind because they are symbolic rather than mystical, and consist largely of mixing the liturgy into life instead of living the liturgy in terms of life.

In the old type of spirituality mystical prayer was regarded as exceptional, and the personal prayer life consisted of certain formal religious actions performed in private. The Church's corporate liturgy was simply personalized, usually to its detriment, and the "saying of one's prayers" involved using scraps of the liturgy and other material for talking to God. In principle and in proper circumstances there is nothing wrong with this, provided that the splendour of the liturgy is kept as much intact as possible.[3] But the method of formal religious acts in private, whether these be taken from the liturgy or made up out of one's own head, is neither the only nor the necessary way of the spiritual life. On the contrary, for the mature type of consciousness it is usually more of a hindrance than a help, even when the individual is a mere beginner in the interior life.

For one thing, modern man finds, as a general rule, that formal religious acts in private do nothing but make him absurdly self-conscious. This is not because he is not used to them or because his friends do not "say their prayers." The reason is that his mind is ready to go beyond a certain type of symbolism, and that therefore devotions and gestures and other practices of a formally religious nature are a total distraction from God. He finds that talking to God in so many words, or deliberately sitting or kneeling down to think about God, only puts God at a distance. He thinks much more about himself trying to pray or to meditate than he thinks of God. That this is true even in the best Church circles is obvious from some of the current jargon of the spiritual life, for apparently one does not simply pray and meditate; one "*says* one's prayers" and "*makes* a meditation." Devout souls struggle along with this kind of thing for years and years; many of them never happen to discover mystical prayer, or, if they do, a myopic spiritual director discourages it; and although they become more and more deeply involved in the vicious

[3]"Just as the hymns in the hymn-book seem keyed for high sopranos, so the prayers in the usual prayer-books are apparently composed for school-girls of the giggly age or for the more gushy sort of women. For this reason, if for no other, the use of the missal and the breviary should be urged upon the people. Those prayers are simple, austere, restrained, dignified, virile, quite in contrast with the prettified, sissified 'Oh' and 'Ah' stuff that turns the stomach or softens the brain." J. M. Gillis, quoted by Gerald Ellard, S.J., in *Men at Work at Worship.* New York, 1940, p. 264.

circle of self-consciousness, they are persuaded that forging blindly ahead on this path is "holy patience." By the same reasoning it is "holy patience" to polish a brick for the glory of God in the hope that some day it will shine.[4]

When a man "communes with himself" he does not, unless he has a rather primitive mind, talk to himself in so many words. If God is nearer to us than we are to ourselves, there is no reason why we should have to talk to God when we commune with him. Talking suggests that God is not altogether here and now, within the very centre of the heart and mind. It is absurd to imagine that interiorly silent prayer requires a high degree of spirituality, or to say that formal religious acts will keep the mind from wandering. For many people they do nothing of the kind, but, on the contrary, divert attention from God to the words and actions and symbols used, or to the attempt to think thoughts about him. In some cases even the deliberate setting apart of a certain period of the day for spiritual exercises fails entirely in establishing conscious communion with God, and becomes nothing more than an exasperating interval in which one is self-consciously "spiritual" for ten or fifteen minutes. In other words, the same problem arises whether one is practising Christian prayer or Yoga, for both are forms of symbolic religion.

There would be no serious difficulty in these spiritual exercises if, in every case, practice and persistence

---

[4]The principles of Catholic spirituality emerge for the most part from monasteries, where the situation is very different. There the so-called *personal* life of devotion is actually corporate, and thus wonderfully protected from excessive self-consciousness. But very many religious live their *real* interior lives in an entirely mystical way, for when not engaged in corporate devotions and meditations they simply "practise the presence of God" in their ordinary work, without formally religious thoughts about him.

would make perfect and at last eliminate self-consciousness. But with the type of mind in question this does not happen for the reason that souls of this order are charged with a different task—the incarnational task of so uniting religion with ordinary life that ordinary life becomes religious in itself. This presents no insuperable difficulty once there is some realization of union with God, and a degree of this realization is in fact quite simple. The presence of God as the Eternal Now is a truth which, at least in part, should be able to penetrate our consciousness with ease. God has made it that way out of love. When this is understood it is obvious that walking, eating, sitting, washing and working are done in God, may therefore be done in a contemplative way, to the glory of God, and thus done constitute the real translation of liturgy into life.

Nevertheless, it must be repeated that there is a definite need and place for formal religion even in the life of the most accomplished mystic. Our human weakness is ever confronted with the danger that when everything is religious, nothing is religious, that formless religion will degenerate into mere worldliness. That is the very reason why we have the liturgy, and, having it, there is no objection to confining formal religion to the liturgy, for in corporate worship, properly conducted, there is less danger of falling into the vicious circle of self-consciousness. If religious symbolism is kept pure and apart, and not muddled with daily life, it will be easier to relate it to life. To unite you must first divide; you must keep your thinking and your terms straight. Colours are not harmonized by mixing them, nor forms by blending them; harmony is the right juxtaposition of pure colours and pure forms.

While there is less danger of self-consciousness in the

liturgy for the reason that it is a group action, we have noted that in many cases the modern mind finds even corporate worship awkward and unreal, both with and without ceremonial refinements. On the whole, however, it is probably safe to say that it impresses him as less awkward when the form of worship is very frankly archaic and symbolic. It may still seem unreal and remote from life, but this will only be true so long as the Church fails to complement symbolic religion with mystical religion. Given an understanding of mystical religion, we shall not need or desire to mix formal religion with everyday life or make any compromise between secular forms and religious forms. On the contrary, we shall keep our forms separate and realize complete harmony of inner meaning. It is highly probable, therefore, that as the mystical understanding of Christianity increases, as union with God is realized more and more in everyday life, our forms of worship will become unashamedly archaic and symbolic.[5] We shall keep the ancient symbols of the Christian religion in all their original purity, for our spiritual progress will not consist in a development and adaptation of symbolism, but in an increased understanding of its meaning.

By and large, a prayer meeting in a modern living-room leaves one with nothing but a bad taste in the mouth. The characteristic mentality of our time finds this kind of thing totally awkward and absurd, not because it "brings religion home" or too close for comfort, but because it smacks of exhibitionism.[6] Yet at Christ-

---

[5]In this connection it is significant that the Catholic liturgical movement is revolting against the late symbolic developments of the Counter-Reformation and adopting the simpler forms of earlier times.

[6]The following Zen story may illustrate the point. A monk had been pestering his master for some comment on his spiritual progress. At last the master turned to him and said, "You are all right, but you have a trivial

mas intelligent pagans go by thousands to Midnight Mass in the local Roman or Anglican church and enjoy themselves immensely. That they do not go more often is chiefly due to the fact that they have no real understanding of the relation of the Mass to life, or because they are afraid of becoming involved in the trivial and obscurantist aspects of modern Church religion. Of course, they go in part to "see the show" and to hear fine music, but there is also the attraction of the numinous, the infectious fascination of the holy which delivers the soul from its own futility.

The danger of returning to archaic forms of worship is the temptation to religious aestheticism. It will be observed, however, that the true religious aesthete has no particular interest in mystical religion, and that he mixes liturgy and life abominably, cluttering his home and his person and his spiritual life with every variety of liturgical contraption. He is wholly under the domination of the symbol and does not actually understand its meaning at all.

The last hundred years have seen a very considerable recrudescence of archaic forms in churches of all kinds and denominations, and the process is likely to continue. It will, however, be of little value unless, as already suggested, the Church gives a great deal of strictly informal teaching on the mystical life in terms of digging potatoes, washing dishes and working in an office. For very many people, this inner aspect of religion is and will be the only one of interest; symbolic and liturgical religion leaves them absolutely cold. The

fault." "What is that?" "You have altogether too much religion." "Well," protested the monk, "if one is studying religion, don't you think it the most natural thing to be talking about it?" "When it is like an ordinary everyday conversation, it is somewhat better." "But why do you so specially hate talking about religion?" "Because it turns one's stomach!"

catholicity, the completeness, of the Church, however, necessarily includes sacramental worship, and another century or more will see it widely adopted by Protestants, who have already been building themselves great Gothic churches with altars and stained glass windows.[7]

Liturgy at its best is contemplative in spirit—a corporate forgetting of human personalities in the adoration of God. Its mood is therefore impersonal, quiet and simple; it is completely ruined by self-conscious dramatics and by the intrusion of ministerial individualisms. Liturgy is thus the concrete witness and symbol of everyday life lived as the contemplation of God, and of union with God given to us in the midst of everyday life. As the mystical life must be free from self-consciousness, so must the liturgy. The liturgy is corporate because everyday life is corporate; we do not live, we cannot exist, as separate and isolated individuals, and the liturgy symbolizes the truth that union with God is given to man both as individual and as society, and has consequences both for personal and for communal life. The liturgy is the concrete bond of union between Christians of every stage of psychological growth—the naïve, the adolescent and the mature, for when this principle of growth is understood there is no reason why Christians at different stages of growth should separate themselves from the common Body. All can find common ground at the symbolic level, provided that the mature are not expected to understand it in the same way as the naïve, and, on their part, do not give themselves airs of superiority over the naïve.

---

[7]The use of archaic forms of worship need not and, it is to be hoped, will not mean the slavish imitation of antique art styles. The purity of symbolic forms is fully preserved in much of the liturgical art of modern schools, some of which is of the highest excellence.

The mature, however, will be able to distinguish a clear difference of function between contemplation in its liturgical form and contemplation in its secular form, and will not attempt to sanctify their daily lives by cluttering them with truncated odds and ends of liturgical practice.[8] Quite naturally a mature soul, genuinely religious, will seek periods of quiet and retirement from the buzz of life, and then make his sitting still, his silence of mind, his quiet walking to and fro, an act of contemplation. But he cannot wisely be expected to do this kind of thing self-consciously and by rule. The Spirit of God will drive him to it as naturally as the body is compelled to sleep when tired. He will simply retreat; he will not "*make* a retreat" armed with a small library of devotional manuals and "spiritual" literature.[9] He will have discovered the secret, discussed somewhat darkly by mystics of the past, of union with God "without means"—that is, without formal contrivances of mind and feeling.

---

[8]This must be distinguished clearly, of course, from the daily attendance of genuine liturgical worship, whether it be the Mass in the local church, or the formal recitation of the Divine Office *en famille,* as well as from the definite rites of the Church for the sick, for the blessing of homes and crops, etc. All this belongs in the realm of corporate and formal rather than personal and informal spirituality. Personal prayer, it must be repeated, is at this stage the translation of the liturgy into one's everyday, secular actions, rather than the simple addition of liturgy to life and the use of bits and pieces thereof for private devotions.

[9]In dealing with souls of this type, spiritual counsellors and directors must be most judicious in regard to their advice about "aids to devotion." The normal and popular manuals currently used in Church circles have "cured" plenty of people of the Christian religion, especially the little books of private prayers and much of the excessively self-conscious spiritual literature produced in the seventeenth century, with the outstanding exception of De Caussade's *Abandonment* and *Spiritual Letters.* The fact that a large number of Christians use this kind of literature today is no necessary guarantee of its current value. Many use it because they think they "ought" to, and know of nothing else, with the result that they are leading very artificial spiritual lives.

Because the contemplative life has, in the past, been so largely liturgical in form, it has generally required some degree of separation from the world. It could not be maintained at all fully without the cloister. The reason for this was not only that it was aided by the *opus Dei*, the Divine Office, but that contemplation itself was to a considerable degree identified with prolonged periods of gazing into the "divine darkness." That is to say, the contemplative spent long hours in the chapel or in his cell practising a sort of Yoga and acquiring a state of mind which he tried to preserve while working in the kitchen or the fields. The state of mind consisted in a prolonged act of loving attention to the invisibility of God. Ordinary thoughts were banished; by the gentle rhythm of vocal prayers the mind was set at peace, until leaving aside all particular considerations it was confronted by a seeming blank. To this voidness the will reached out in love, knowing by faith that God himself dwelt invisibly in the void. This practice was continued for years until it became a natural habit and could be carried on without effort, and such habitual and effortless contemplation was termed union with God "without means." Such a spiritual exercise necessarily required the highest degree of external quiet and freedom from distraction. The cloister was its ideal place.

It is clear, however, that a mysticism of this kind is not fully incarnational. The realization of union is still something attained by effort, and as a mental state is only able to exist together with other mental states by sheer force of habit. Until perfection in the exercise is attained, which requires years of practice, the mystical life is largely incompatible with life in the world. Modern devotees of mystical religion, such as Aldous Huxley and Gerald Heard, are trying to restore this kind of life and commend it to non-Christians as the true essence of religion.[10] But for the religion of the Incarnation there can be no such gulf between the active and the contemplative lives. There is little evidence that Jesus practised such a mysticism, and none that he taught it or considered it important. But we are not to conclude from this that his religion was not mystical. On the contrary, Christ was the mystical truth himself, and imparted that truth not by spiritual exercises but by free grace. Nor are we to conclude that cloistered contemplation was in any sense erroneous. In an epoch of *symbolic* religion it was the sole means of keeping the mystical element of Christianity alive until the time was ripe for a full integration of contemplation and action.

The monastic type of contemplation has, however, a definite value so long as it is not confused with a means for acquiring union with God, or even of realizing union. Huxley, Heard and many others have made this confusion. Monastic contemplation is a way of loving God, and is one of several ways of *deepening* the realization of union. We have seen throughout that union with God does not depend on our love for him, but on his love for us. There is nothing in it to be attained; it is here and now in all its fulness. Therefore contemplation is for the appreciation and not the acquisition of union with God. The initial realization does not come

---

[10]See especially Huxley's *Perennial Philosophy* (New York, 1945) and Heard's *Preface to Prayer* (New York, 1944). Despite certain excellent features of these works their basic attitude is Gnostic rather than Christian, for which reason the sense that union with God is a gift as distinct from an attainment is altogether dim. Significantly, Huxley confuses the creation with the Fall.

through contemplation or any other method; it comes through the abandonment of methods and through *faith* in the given truth. Contemplation is a *work* resulting from faith. But for all its simplicity of form, monastic contemplation, the spiritual exercise of gazing into the "divine darkness," still belongs to the liturgical or formally religious type of spirituality. It is the love of God and the enjoyment of union in the form of a specifically religious action.

It is possible and, indeed, necessary to love God and enjoy union with him in the forms of secular actions, and this type of contemplation is obviously the more incarnational. In this type of contemplation the focal point of adoration is not the "divine darkness" perceived by the emptying of the mind; it is the Eternal Now in which all the events and experiences of daily life occur. The two are really the same thing approached from different points of view. Furthermore, the method of adoration is not to be still and gaze into the Eternal Now with love; it is to give oneself wholeheartedly to the work which the present moment brings; it is to go straight ahead with the Eternal Now, accepting its changing forms with one's entire being but not grasping hold of them. This contemplation does not need to involve any formally religious thought of God because he presents himself to the soul beyond religious forms, in and as the Eternal Now.[11]

This contemplation differs from *mere* living in the present in two respects. The awareness of given union with God as the Eternal Now is its constant undertone,

---

[11]The contemplation of the "divine darkness" also dispenses with the formal thought of God, but it remains a formally religious way of contemplation because of its setting. It is a specific act of prayer distinct from other actions.

and the forms, experiences and events of the moment are not just passively received but actively willed. In the former respect it would seem to differ from the other type of contemplation which is still strongly characterized by *eros,* the longing of the soul for God, the striving after him as if he were not present. According to Dom John Chapman, "the *principal* stage consists of this: 'O God, I want Thee, and I do not want anything else.'—This is *the essence of pure contemplative prayer,* until the presence of God becomes vivid."[12] It would appear, however, that this prayer does not sufficiently grasp the truth of the Incarnation, which has already fulfilled the yearning of the Psalmist—"Like as the hart desireth the water brook, so longeth my soul after thee, O God."

> O Love! will men never see that thou meetest them at every step, while they seek thee hither and thither, where thou art not? When in the open country, what folly not to breathe its pure air; to pause and study my steps when the path is smooth before me; to thirst when the flood encompasses me; to hunger for God when I may find him, relish him, and receive his will through all things![13]

Or as Dom John himself says elsewhere:

> We are living in touch with God. Everything we come in contact with, the whole of our daily circumstances, and all our interior responses, whether pleasure or pains, are God's working. We are living in God—in God's action, as a fish in the water. There is no question of trying to *feel* that God is here, or to complain of God being far, once he has taught us that we are bathed in him, in his action, in his will.[14]

[12] *Spiritual Letters.* London, 1944, p. 289.
[13] De Caussade, *Abandonment,* xi, p. 110.
[14] *Ibid.,* p. 143.

In the latter respect we see that this way of contemplation is quite different from quietism, since the events of the moment, expressing as they do the will of God, are not passively received but actively willed. To quote De Caussade again:

> If we knew how to greet each moment as the manifestation of the divine will, we would find in it all the heart could desire. . . . The present moment is always filled with infinite treasures: it contains more than you are capable of receiving. . . . The divine will is an abyss, of which the present moment is the entrance; plunge fearlessly therein and you will find it more boundless than your desire.[15]

Perceiving, then, that the circumstances of this moment are the adorable will of God, and that to desire God's will is a higher thing than to desire even the Beatific Vision, the soul says "Yes!" with all its might to the whole of experience. This is the full realization, in concrete action, of the liturgy's praise of God, for praise as participation in the divine joy is the essence of contemplation. This is the meaning of doing all things for the glory of God. *Tout ce qui arrive est adorable.*

Especially is this true in regard to suffering, for suffering is transformed and its meaning realized only when the sufferer affirms it as the divine will. To struggle against inevitable pain is only to intensify grief, and when the moment brings pain the praise of God consists in entering into its very heart, cooperating with it, and telling it to be as painful as it likes. At first thought this seems madness itself to the sufferer, but the total acceptance and affirmation of pain is the essence of the way of the Cross whereby suffering is overcome and its purpose understood. No words can convey the under-

---

[15] *Ibid.*, ii. 3, pp. 79–81.

standing which comes through this acceptance of pain because it belongs to the innermost mystery of God. But the universal testimony of the saints is that suffering affirmed as the will of God was suffering which they would not have missed for the world, and such understanding enables them to reconcile the agonies of human life with the existence of an omnipotent God of love.

Such acceptance is naturally most difficult, for there are times when our whole physical and moral being revolts and shrinks uncontrollably from pain, when we are quite certain that we *cannot* face it. In these circumstances what we are to accept is not so much the pain itself as our own reaction to it, our own fear and horror, our own desire to protest, to fight and to flee. When this is done we discover invariably that God permits us to suffer in order to "debunk" our egoism, and that this is mercy itself because it opens our eyes to his splendour and love, giving us an infinite joy in return for a finite pain. There is no proof of this truth but experiment.

We should, however, note in passing that it illumines one of the greatest problems of Christian theology—the reconciliation of the divine love with the possibility of eternal damnation. It is almost impossible to weed the doctrine of damnation out of Christianity without discarding whole sections of the New Testament and the clear words of Christ himself. Leaving other considerations aside, there is a higher point of view which renders this unnecessary if not unwise and erroneous. It is actually possible to reconcile the doctrine of *eternal* damnation with the idea of universal restoration or *apocatastasis* taught by Origen and St. Gregory of Nyssa in an incomplete form which the Church found

243

unacceptable. The mind of the Church has always taken the view that in eternal life souls *will* their own state and cannot do otherwise. Thus it is conceivable that if a soul were to will its own damnation, to affirm it utterly as the adorable justice of God, which is simply an aspect of his love, the inner character of hell would be changed and its eternal fire transformed into the vision of God. This would render the suffering of hell an act of praise, so that hell itself would join in the chorus of the holy saints and angels. Eternal suffering would therefore be apprehended as identical in essence with eternal joy. To will one's own damnation in this sense is, of course, different in principle from willing sin. It is an affirmation of God's justice made possible by a grace analogous to the *lumen gloriae,* whereby the blessed are enabled to see the divine essence in heaven. For souls are unable by their own power either to see God directly or to admit and affirm the justice of their own damnation. It would seem probable, however, that God will make himself "all in all" by giving these powers to the redeemed and the damned respectively.[16]

It is worthwhile looking at the doctrine of hell in this way because, even if it is nothing more than a theological nightmare, it is the extreme instance of the problem of reconciling suffering with the love of God. Taken literally as a doctrine of everlasting torture without any kind of mitigation or solution, it amounts to blasphemy itself, for if it were in the power of human freedom to produce a consequence of this kind there must be something radically diabolical in the order created by God, and in God himself. Such an interpretation of the doctrine may vindicate human freedom, but at the cost

---

[16]It is interesting to note that in the *Divina Commedia* Dante and Virgil seem to find their way out of hell through its very centre. Cf. *Inferno,* xxxiv.

of demonizing God. Furthermore, when understood in this way the doctrine does not even guarantee the freedom of the human will to resist God eternally, because if the damned continue inevitably to resist God they do *not* do so freely; if they did, they would be able to repent. But if eternal suffering may be transmuted by the same principle as temporal suffering, and brought to that mysterious point where pain turns into joy, it is possible to believe that hell is consistent with the divine love. For it would seem that the transmutation of suffering into a joy purer than could ever be known apart from suffering is the central action of the divine economy.[17]

The affirmation of one's own suffering is the supreme act of worship because it is the most intimate participation in the Crucifixion. But it is vitiated by self-consciousness, as when one deliberately seeks out suffering to accept for the glory of God. This is an act of presumption analogous, though by no means the same in degree, to incurring deliberately the pains of hell. For we have no other concern than to affirm the will of God as it is presented to us in this moment and to offer him the suffering which he sends in this moment. It will certainly be sent when needed. To seek out suffering is to give the lie to the prayer, "Lead us not into temptation," and to indulge oneself in those false moral heroics which have so disfigured the Christian life. Naturally, it is another matter when it is known that suffering will be the consequence of an act of mercy, but to be merciful *in order* to suffer is a perversion of charity.

Thus a contemplative life fully in accord with the principle of the Incarnation consists in adoring the will

---

[17]We should note again that some of the sublimest passages in music involve the resolution of dissonances.

of God as it comes to us in the given union of the Eternal Now.

> The present moment is like an ambassador which declares the will of God. The heart must ever answer *fiat*, and the soul will go steadily on by means of all things to her centre and her term—never pausing in her course, spreading her sails to all winds; all ways, all methods equally further her progress towards the great, the infinite. All things afford her equal means of sanctification. The one only essential the soul finds in the present moment. It is no longer either prayer or silence, retirement or conversation, reading or writing, reflections or cessation of thought, avoidance or seeking of spiritualities, abundance or privation, illness or health, life or death, but simply what comes to her each moment by the order of God.[18]

This is the true union with God "without means," for on the one hand union is the gift of God and not the product of one's own action, and on the other the contemplation of the union involves no special technique other than that which the divine will supplies here and now. Retirement from the world and adoring God in the "divine darkness" of a mind emptied of particular thoughts are special, "liturgical" means to the contemplative life which are necessary in certain periods and for certain people. There will always be the special vocation of the monastic life because there will always be a need for specialists in formal religion, for liturgists in the widest sense of that word. There will always, too, be the need for places of retreat from the nervous irritation of the world for all spiritually minded people. But in mature Christianity the grand way of contemplation will be identical with the life of action, for this

---

[18]De Caussade, *Abandonment*, ii. 10, pp. 101–102.

ordinary everyday life will be understood as participation in the divine playing of God and in the worship of heaven, for in the Eternal Now we shall find that strait and narrow gate, that needle's eye, through which we are taken into the infinite life of God.

I I I

By this full union of contemplation with the actions of everyday life we shall overcome the strange and unhappy paradox that in practice the religion of the Incarnation has not realized its own essential meaning—the wedding of the flesh to the spirit. Instead of effecting the union of God and the world, which is its central purpose, Christian sacramentalism has kept the two apart. God became man and imparted his life to us in forms and sacraments with the very object of indicating that the union of his Spirit with all flesh is his supreme will for the world. But in practice Christians have frustrated the divine will by confining the life of the spirit to the forms from which it was intended to spread and flow for the sanctification of all created things. The process of the Incarnation has been made to stop with the historic Jesus, the process of transubstantiation with the bread and wine of the altar, the life of contemplation with the walls of the cloister, and the life of holiness and Christian action with formal morality. We have never actually allowed God to enter into our entire life. He came down to earth and entered our earthly forms, but we swiftly got rid of him by raising the first, indicative forms which he touched to heaven. Whether as Catholic sacramentalism or Protestant moralism, Christianity is the most formal of religions, and thus leaves the greater part of human life untouched.

For in ordinary everyday life the average human be
ing is necessarily occupied for the greater part of hi
time with actions where there is opportunity neithe
for great moral deeds nor formal prayers, and Chris
tianity, as generally explained to him, has no particula
relation to this side of his life. At best he may have been
informed that the relation of religion to, say, being a
banker's clerk, consists in being an honest and hard-
working banker's clerk, in doing the job well. But this
only relates his work to religion's by-product morality,
not to religion itself, to the union of our most trivial
actions with God. Because the only aspect of Christianity which seems to touch everyday life is its moralism,
it is degraded from a religion of "is" to a religion of
"ought." That is to say, attention is diverted from the
contemplation of the present reality of God to ourselves and what we ought to do and be, which is never
a particularly inspiring consideration.

This failure to realize the implications of the Incarnation, to accept the gift of union with God to the flesh in
all its aspects, and the substitution of self-conscious
moralism for the contemplation of God in the here and
now, are the basic reasons for the present weakness of
the Christian religion. Almost all current attempts to
revive the Church are so much whipping of a dead
horse, instead of taking it to him who is the Resurrection and the Life. In general Christians are so self-consciously preoccupied with the things they ought and
ought not to have done, and thus with what they ought
now to do by way of Christian action in a world gone
mad, that they are absorbed in themselves instead of in
God. At this time, therefore, the renewal of Christianity
depends solely on accepting the Incarnation in all its
fulness. For without the realization of God's love for the

world, we can love neither the world nor God.

The vision opened to us by a fuller understanding of the Incarnation affords material for the writing of a new Sum of Theology, applying it to every aspect of Christian doctrine and life in a manner appropriate to the maturing mind of Western man. Here no more has been possible than the barest outline of this vision and its application, for Christian tradition is so rich and modern thought so varied and complex that the fuller task could only be the work of many minds. Such a Sum of Theology may or may not be necessary. It is, however, absolutely necessary for our world that the Church and the Christian religion become the greatest of powers in its life and culture. But there is no true spiritual power apart from union with God, and the Church is not a creative power in the modern world because Christians have, in general, no consciousness of this union.

Therefore it must be said again that the mystical life is *necessary,* not as a special vocation for the few, not as a life practicable only for those who can in some degree detach themselves exteriorly from the world, but as the general and central life of the entire Church. For without the consciousness of God in the soul and of the soul in God, Christianity in this age and for modern man can be no more than a superficial mimicry of spirituality and of the virtues and achievements of the past. Properly understood, the Incarnation shows us that this consciousness is not reserved to the specially holy or the specially favoured; neither does its realization demand a long course of spiritual gymnastics possible only for those who have time and opportunity. In its deepest meaning, the good news of the Gospel is that union with God is a free and universal gift and that the consciousness of it is presented to us in the Eternal Now —in short, that the love of God is generous beyond comprehension. To refuse that love is proud and ungracious in the extreme, even when concealed under such seemingly excellent motives as the fear of presumption.

When we become aware that God's love for the world is literally infinite, the matters with which modern Church religion occupies itself in place of the contemplation and the teaching of this love seem exceedingly small and trivial. It is not surprising that more and more they have become the preoccupation of a relatively small group, consisting for the most part of persons whose vision is both narrow and superficial. Of these, some are sincerely puzzled at their lack of power and are working eagerly but blindly to commend the Christian religion to the modern mind. Others, however, are content to congratulate themselves that they possess a truth which the world must accept or be damned. This kind of religion appeals not at all to the better minds of our age, who believe in all sincerity that institutional Christianity is a dead backwater, and the multitudes simply follow their opinion.

A mature understanding of Christianity may not be immediately possible for immense numbers, but it is by no means beyond the reach of the intellectual and spiritual leaders of the modern world. If it is commended to them, the multitudes will take courage and in due time grasp some of its rudiments. But if the Church wastes all her energy in "going to the masses" with rehashed versions of the religion of our infancy and adolescence, the world's increasingly large number of finer minds will remain unconvinced and therefore the masses too. The Church did not conquer the Roman Empire until, in the terms of those days, she had shown herself intellectually respectable and spiritually mature, and because, underlying and informing that intellectual and spiritual splendour, there was a conviction of union with God that made death and torture seem unimportant.[19]

The problems, the needs and the mentality of the modern world are in some ways similar to but in many ways quite different from those of the Roman Empire in its final phases. We cannot, therefore, contemplate a return *in toto* to the methods and emphases of early Christianity, not only because we are different, but also because Christianity itself, like a living tree, has changed and grown. In the light of a fuller appreciation of the Incarnation we can see, for example, that the early Church's concept of union with God was actually Monophysite in attempting to divinize the flesh beyond its proper limits. But in many respects the principles are the same: there must be the conviction of union, and civilization must be approached at its highest level with an appeal suited to the intellectual and spiritual maturity of its best minds.

But whether the modern world is to be convinced or to remain unconvinced, it is the solemn obligation of the Church not to hide her light under a bushel, not to

---

[19]Cf. Harnack's *Mission and Expansion of Christianity.* London and New York, 1908, vol. i, pp. 238–239. "The supreme message of Christianity was its promise of this divine state to every believer. We know how, in that age of the twilight of the gods, all human hopes concentrated upon this aim, and consequently a religion which not only taught but realized this apotheosis of human nature (especially in a form so complete that it did not exclude even the flesh) was bound to have an enormous success. . . . Even after the great epoch when 'gnosticism' was opposed and assimilated, the church went forward in the full assurance that she understood and preached apotheosis as the distinctive product of the Christian religion." Harnack, as a liberal Protestant regarding the Johannine literature alien to the actual teaching of Christ, was naturally unable to recognize this as the original essence of the Gospel.

conceal the depth and the riches of the divine love under terms and symbols which have become incomprehensible, whose force and meaning have been lost. The central truth of the Gospel and the Incarnation, the gift of divine union, must be stated clearly and without fear. Its implications for theology, for morals and for worship must be thought out, felt out, and made plain. To fail in this is to cloud the splendour of God, which is that without let to his absolute holiness and self-sufficiency he has made himself one in love and one in life with every finite and errant member of his universe—here and now.

BIBLIOGRAPHY

ANONYMOUS. *Orthodox Spirituality*. By A Monk of the Eastern Church. London, 1945.

ATHANASIUS, ST. *The Incarnation of the Word of God*. With an Introduction by C. S. Lewis. London, 1946.

BAKER, AUGUSTINE. *Holy Wisdom*. London, 1876.

BERDYAEV, NICOLAS. *The Destiny of Man*. London and New York, 1937.

— *The End of Our Time*. London, 1933.

— *Freedom and the Spirit*. Trans. O. F. Clarke. London, 1935.

— *The Meaning of History*. Trans. George Reavey. London and New York, 1936.

— *Spirit and Reality*. London and New York, 1939.

BERGSON, HENRI. *Two Sources of Morality and Religion*. Paris, 1932 and New York, 1935.

BETT, HENRY. *Joachim of Flora*. London, 1931.

— *Nicholas of Cusa*. London, 1932.

BINYON, LAURENCE. *The Spirit of Man in Asian Art*. Cambridge, Mass., 1936.

BLAKNEY, RAYMOND. *Meister Eckhart*. New York, 1941.

BREMOND, HENRI. *Histoire Littéraire du Sentiment Religieux en France*. 8 vols. Paris, 1916–1928.

BULGAKOV, SERGIUS. *The Wisdom of God*. London and New York, 1937.

BUTLER, DOM CUTHBERT. *Western Mysticism*. New ed. London, 1946.

CHAPMAN, DOM JOHN. "Roman Catholic Mysticism." Art. in Hastings' *Encyclopaedia of Religion and Ethics*.

— *Spiritual Letters*. London, 1944.

CHAVASSE, CLAUDE. *The Bride of Christ*. London, 1939.

CH'U TA-KAO. *Tao Te Ching*. A Translation. London, 1937.

CLUTTON-BROCK, A. "Spiritual Experience." Art. in *The Spirit*, ed. B. H. Streeter. London and New York, 1919.

Cusanus, Nicholas. *The Vision of God.* Trans. E. G. Salter. London, 1928.

Dawson, Christopher. *Progress and Religion.* London, 1932.

D'Aygalliers, Wautier. *Ruysbroeck the Admirable.* London, 1925.

De Caussade, J. P. *Abandonment to the Divine Providence.* Trans. Ella McMahon. New York, 1887.

De Rougemont, Denis. *Love in the Western World.* New York, 1940.

— *Passion and Society* (English edition of the above). London, 1940.

Dix, Dom Gregory. *The Shape of the Liturgy.* London, 1945.

Ellard, Gerald. *Men at Work at Worship.* New York, 1940.

Faber, F. W. *Creator and Creature.* London, 1928.

Farrell, Walter. *A Companion to the Summa.* 4 vols. New York, 1941.

Field, Claud. *Meister Eckhart's Sermons.* London, n.d.

Frost, Bede. *Priesthood and Prayer.* London, 1943.

Garrigou-Lagrange, R. *Christian Perfection and Contemplation.* London and St. Louis, 1937.

Gilson, Etienne. *The Philosophy of St. Bonaventure.* London and New York, 1940.

— *The Philosophy of St. Thomas Aquinas.* Cambridge and St. Louis, 1941.

— *The Spirit of Mediaeval Philosophy.* London, 1936.

Groddeck, Georg. *The World of Man.* London, 1935.

Harnack, Adolf. *History of Dogma.* 7 vols. Boston, 1896–1900.

— *The Mission and Expansion of Christianity.* 2 vols. London and New York, 1908.

Heard, Gerald. *Preface to Prayer.* New York, 1944.

Hebert, A. G. *Liturgy and Society.* London, 1944.

Hughson, Shirley. *Contemplative Prayer.* London, 1935.

Huxley, Aldous. *Ends and Means.* London, 1937.

— *Grey Eminence.* New York, 1941.

— *The Perennial Philosophy.* New York, 1945.

Inge, W. R. *Christian Mysticism.* London and New York, 1933.

254

JAMES, WILLIAM. *The Varieties of Religious Experience*. London and New York, 1929.

JOHN OF THE CROSS, ST. *The Ascent of Mount Carmel*. Trans. David Lewis. London, 1889.

— *The Dark Night of the Soul*. Trans. G. C. Graham. London, 1922.

JOHN OF DAMASCUS, ST. "The Orthodox Faith" in *Nicene and Post-Nicene Fathers, vol.* IX. Ed. Schaff and Wace. London and New York, 1899.

JUNG, C. G. *The Integration of Personality*. New York, 1939.

— *Modern Man in Search of a Soul*. London and New York, 1933.

— *Psychology and Religion*. New Haven, 1938.

— *The Symbolic Life*. Printed for private circulation only. London, 1939.

JUNG, C. G., and WILHELM, RICHARD. *The Secret of the Golden Flower*. London and New York, 1931.

KEYSERLING, H. *South American Meditations*. London, 1932.

— *The World in the Making*. London, 1927.

KIRK, KENNETH E. *The Vision of God*. London, 1932.

KRISHNAMURTI, J. *Verbatim Reports of Talks* (issued periodically). Hollywood, 1933–1940.

LANDAU, ROM. *God is My Adventure*. London and New York, 1936.

LEWIS, C. S. *Pilgrim's Regress*. London, 1943 and New York, 1945.

— *The Screwtape Letters*. London and New York, 1943.

LINDWORKSY, JOHANNES. *The Psychology of Asceticism*. London, 1936.

MARITAIN, JACQUES. *Art and Scholasticism*. London and New York, 1942.

— *Education at the Crossroads*. New York, 1943.

— *The Degrees of Knowledge*. London, 1937.

— *Ransoming the Time*. New York, 1941.

MARITAIN, JACQUES, and MARITAIN, RAISSA. *Prayer and Intelligence*. London and New York, 1928.

MASCALL, E. L. *He Who Is*. London, 1944.

MCCANN, DOM JUSTIN. *The Cloud of Unknowing and Other Treatises*. By an English Mystic of the Fourteenth Century. With a Commentary on the *Cloud* by Augustine Baker. London, 1943.

MEAD, G. R. S. *Fragments of a Faith Forgotten.* London, 1931.

NIEBUHR, REINHOLD. *The Nature and Destiny of Man.* 2 vols. New York, 1941 and 1944.

NYGREN, ANDERS. *Agape and Eros.* 3 vols. London, 1932, 1938 and 1939.

OUSPENSKY, P. D. *Tertium Organum.* New York, 1923.

PATMORE, COVENTRY. *The Rod, the Root, and the Flower.* London, 1907.

PEERS, C. ALLISON. *Studies in the Spanish Mystics.* 2 vols. London, 1927 and 1928.

PFEIFFER, FRANTZ. *Meister Eckhart.* Trans. C. de B. Evans. 2 vols. London, 1924 and 1931.

POULAIN, A. *The Graces of Interior Prayer.* London, 1910.

ROLT, C. E. *Dionysius the Areopagite.* A translation of the *Divine Names* and the *Mystical Theology.* London, 1940.

SAUDREAU, AUGUSTE. *The Mystical State.* London and New York, 1924.

SENZAKI, NYOGEN, and REPS, SALADIN. *The Gateless Gate.* Los Angeles, 1934.

SOROKIN, PITIRIM. *The Crisis of Our Age.* New York, 1942.

SPENGLER, OSWALD. *The Decline of the West.* 2 vols. New York, 1926 and 1928.

SPIEGELBERG, F. *The Religion of Non-Religion.* London, 1938.

STEERE, DOUGLAS. *On Beginning from Within.* New York, 1943.

STEUART, R. H. J. *In Divers Manners.* London, 1938.

— *The Inward Vision.* London, 1937.

— *Temples of Eternity.* London, 1935.

— *World Intangible.* London, 1934.

STREETER, B. H. *Moral Adventure.* London, 1934.

SUZUKI, D. T. *Essays in Zen Buddhism.* 3 vols. London, 1927, 1933 and 1934.

— *Manual of Zen Buddhism.* Kyoto, 1935.

TEMPLE, WILLIAM. *Nature, Man and God.* London, 1940.

TERESA OF AVILA, ST. *The Way of Perfection.* With an introduction by F. Benedict Zimmerman. London, 1935.

THOMAS AQUINAS, ST. *The Basic Writings of St. Thomas Aquinas.* Ed. Anton C. Pegis. 2 vols. New York, 1945.

— *Selected Writings.* Ed. M. C. d'Arcy. London, 1939.

— *Summa Theologica.* Translated by the Fathers of the English Dominican Province. 12 vols. London, 1912–1917.

TOYNBEE, ARNOLD J. *A Study of History.* 6 vols. London, 1934–1939.

TRAHERNE, THOMAS. *Centuries of Meditation.* London, 1908.

UNDERHILL, EVELYN. *Collected Papers.* London and New York, 1946.

— *The Letters of Evelyn Underhill.* Ed. Charles Williams. London and New York. 1944.

— *Mysticism.* London, 1930.

— *Practical Mysticism.* London, 1931.

— *Worship.* New York, 1937.

VON HUGEL, F. *Eternal Life.* Edinburgh, 1913.

— *Letters to a Niece.* London, 1928.

— *The Mystical Element of Religion.* 2 vols. London, 1927.

WAITE, A. E. *The Holy Kabbalah.* London and New York, 1929.

WATKIN, E. I. *Catholic Art and Culture.* London and New York, 1944.

WATTS, ALAN. *The Legacy of Asia and Western Man.* London, 1937, Chicago, 1938.

— *The Meaning of Happiness.* New York, 1940.

— *The Spirit of Zen.* London and New York, 1936.

— *The Theologia Mystica of St. Dionysius.* West Park, N.Y., 1944.

WHEELER, R. H. *The Laws of Human Nature.* New York and Cambridge, 1932.

WYNSCHENK, DOM P. *John of Ruysbroeck.* London, 1916.

ZUNDEL, MAURICE. *The Splendour of the Liturgy.* New York, 1944.

ABOUT THE AUTHOR

ALAN WATTS, who held both a master's degree in theology and a doctorate of divinity, is best known as an interpreter of Zen Buddhism in particular, and of Indian and Chinese philosophy in general. Standing apart, however, from sectarian membership, he has earned the reputation of being one of the most original and "unrutted" philosophers of the century. He was the author of some twenty books on the philosophy and psychology of religion. He died in 1973.